Lemoyne d'Iberville

Soldier of New France

Pierre Lemoyne d'Iberville

Lemoyne d'Iberville
Soldier of New France

NELLIS M. CROUSE

With a New Introduction by
DANIEL H. USNER, JR.

 Louisiana State University Press BATON ROUGE

Copyright © 1954 by Cornell University Press
Originally published by Cornell University Press
New material copyright © 2001 by Louisiana State University Press
All rights reserved
Manufactured in the United States of America

Louisiana Paperback Edition, 2001
10 09 08 07 06 05 04 03 02 01
5 4 3 2 1

Library of Congress Cataloging-in-Publication Data

Crouse, Nellis Maynard, b. 1884.
    Lemoyne d'Iberville : soldier of New France / Nellis M. Crouse ; with a new
introduction by Daniel H. Usner, Jr. — Louisiana pbk. ed.
        p. cm.
    Originally published: Ithaca, N.Y. : Cornell University Press, 1954.
    Includes bibliographical references (p.) and index.
    ISBN 0-8071-2700-0 (pbk. : alk. paper)
    1. Le Moyne d'Iberville, Pierre, 1661–1706. 2. Explorers—New France—Biography. 3.
Soldiers—New France—Biography. 4. Canada—History—To 1763 (New France) 5.
Louisiana—History—To 1803. 6. New France—History, Military. 7. Soldiers—New
France—Biography. 8. New France—Biography. 9. Louisiana—Discovery and exploration.
10. Mississippi River Valley—Discovery and exploration. I. Title.

F1030.L4683 C76 2001
359.3'31'092—dc21
[B]
                                                                          00-067848

The paper in this book meets the guidelines for permanence and durability of the Committee
on Production Guidelines for Book Longevity of the Council on Library Resources. ∞

To DANIEL MAYNARD CROUSE

this book is affectionately

inscribed by his

Grandfather

Contents

Maps

DANIEL H. USNER, JR.

Introduction to the Paperback Edition

WHEN Nellis Maynard Crouse's *Lemoyne d'Iberville: Soldier of New France* was published by Cornell University Press in 1954, the study of French colonial Louisiana was approaching an important threshold. In the 1950s, readers seeking literature on the origins and early years of the colony still found on the shelves a preponderance of books written by such nineteenth-century authors as François-Xavier Martin, François Barbé-Marbois, Charles Gayarré, Alcée Fortier, and Grace King. During the first half of the twentieth century, important studies by Peter Hamilton, Marc de Villiers du Terrage, Jean Delanglez, Nancy Miller Surrey, and Verner Crane examined archival sources much more closely than those by romantic writers of the previous century, but these scattered and specialized works did little to generate scholarly interest in French Louisiana. Nellis Crouse's biography of Pierre Lemoyne d'Iberville was written, therefore, when Louisiana colonial history still lacked background and direction as a scholarly field.

Crouse's selection of Iberville as a subject derived from his combined interests in European ventures in exploration and French colonial America. His previous books included *In Quest of the Western Ocean* (1928), *The Search for the Northwest Passage*

(1934), *French Pioneers in the West Indies, 1624–1664* (1940), *The French Struggle for the West Indies, 1665–1713* (1943), and *The Search for the North Pole* (1947). His last book, *Le Vérendrye, Fur Trader and Explorer*, was published by Cornell University Press in 1956. Crouse wrote about these subjects with a blend of scholarly distance and lively prose, effectively drawing his readers into the adventure and danger of frontier life. However, he also tended to express sentiments that would become outdated.

Lemoyne d'Iberville opens with Crouse observing how the long struggle between France and England in America "provided posterity with a wealth of romantic events and of no less romantic personalities." A century earlier, Francis Parkman had used similar words to explain his preoccupation with French North America. The notion that New France and Louisiana offered the American reader some fascinating stories about far-reaching adventurers proved a resilient source of curiosity and entertainment. Crouse predictably peopled his story with brave Frenchmen and bloodthirsty Indians, caricatures which will strike today's readers as one-dimensional and offensive. It can be said, however, that very few professional scholars writing about similar events during Crouse's career managed to transcend these common impressions.

Crouse's command of the French language made it possible for him to reveal details of Iberville's life previously inaccessible to native English speakers, few of whom could read Canadian historian Guy Frégault's 1944 biography of Iberville, written in French. Crouse used published sources rather than original manuscripts, but at that time even the printed journals and letters from Iberville's career were available only in French. As Grace Lee Nute of the Minnesota Historical Society noted in a short review for the *American Historical Review*, Crouse conveniently assembled formerly scattered data to produce "a very readable account of Iberville's life." In a *New York Times* review, Mason Wade wrote that Crouse's book lacked the "richness of documentation" and the "grasp of French imperialism" found in Frégault's work, but it "rescues Iberville from the unjustified neglect into which he has fallen in the English-speaking world." William Eccles observed in the *William and Mary Quarterly* that Crouse provided insufficient background on the struggle between England and France in the late seventeenth and early eighteenth centuries. Nevertheless, Eccles concluded that this was the best account of Iberville's activities written in English.

This reprint of *Lemoyne d'Iberville* occurs in a very different era of scholarship on French Louisiana. Over the past fifty years, the study of Louisiana in the eighteenth century—for both the French and Spanish dominions—has advanced steadily. A year before the original appearance of Nellis Crouse's book, French historian Marcel Giraud released the first book in his multi-volume *Histoire de la Louisiane française*. Devoted to the period from 1698 to 1715, this history explores fully the political, social, and economic circumstances surrounding Iberville's voyages to the Gulf Coast. All five of Giraud's volumes reveal the rich detail awaiting future scholars of French Louisiana. Three have been published in translation by Louisiana State University Press. Meanwhile, in the United States, a few other historians produced important specialized studies of early Louisiana. Notable are Charles Edward O'Neill's *Church and State in French Colonial Louisiana* (1966), John G. Clark's *New Orleans, 1718–1812: An Economic History* (1970), and Jay Higginbotham's *Old Mobile* (1977). By the late 1960s, Glenn Conrad at the University of Southwestern Louisiana (now the University of Louisiana at Lafayette) launched a project to microfilm archival materials in France and to assemble a comprehensive collection of colonial records. The Colonial Records Collection eventually expanded to include microfilmed documents from Spanish archives, and USL created the Center for Louisiana Studies in order to publish essential primary sources and to encourage new historical research. At the same time, state and university archives in both Louisiana and

Mississippi purchased their own microfilmed copies of colonial records.

With these records more readily available in the United States, we have witnessed significant growth in the number of historians interested in eighteenth-century Louisiana. Works by Mathé Allain, Morris S. Arnold, Carl A. Brasseaux, Carl J. Ekberg, Patricia K. Galloway, Gwendolyn Midlo Hall, and several others have contributed much to our understanding of the French period of Louisiana's colonial history. We even have translated and edited versions of Iberville's journals, to which readers of Crouse's biography can now turn. The journal of Iberville's first voyage was included in Brasseaux's *A Comparative View of French Louisiana, 1699 and 1762* (1979), and Richebourg Gaillard McWilliams translated all three journals, covering the years 1698 to 1702, in *Iberville's Gulf Journals* (1981). Three centuries after the founding of French Louisiana, we can look forward to the exciting array of works on religion, gender, family life, settlement, slavery, and Indian-colonial relations that are currently underway. The study of colonial Louisiana, including the Spanish era, is finally becoming a prominent area in American history—and is receiving increasing attention from historians who examine the much more familiar English colonies of North America.

But even in the now busier field of French colonial Louisiana, Nellis Crouse's *Lemoyne d'Iberville: Soldier of New France* has plenty to offer. The Canadian origins and military career of Iberville are explored in interesting detail. Military campaigns at Hudson Bay, upper New York, Maine, and Nova Scotia are vividly described, in all the fury and brutality of late-seventeenth-century warfare. Crouse underscores the relationship between private and public service in Iberville's ascent through the ranks of the French navy, tracing how the quest for booty and trade motivated his actions. In addition, the importance of family networks in both the commerce and government of New France is well documented in Crouse's account of Iberville's life.

Lemoyne d'Iberville

Soldier of New France

CHAPTER I

Growing Up with the Frontier

THE long-drawn-out struggle between the French and the English colonists for the possession of New France, a struggle that began with Champlain in the early seventeenth century and did not end until the days of Montcalm in the middle of the eighteenth, has provided posterity with a wealth of romantic events and of no less romantic personalities. As we look upon this period in retrospect we see emerging from the indistinct mass of soldiers, pioneers, and missionaries certain figures that rise above their fellows, thanks to their achievements and force of character. Champlain, Marquette, La Salle, and Frontenac are names familiar to every student of American history; indeed, they form part of the common heritage of the American and Canadian peoples. But there are certain others, not so well known, perhaps, yet worthy to rank with them in the pages of history; and among the more prominent of these is Pierre Lemoyne d'Iberville, one of Canada's greatest soldiers.

Pierre Lemoyne d'Iberville, better known to writers of history simply as Iberville, enjoyed a remarkable career. His military and colonizing activities carried him from Hudson Bay to the West Indies. He captured northerly Port Nelson from the English, assisted in the taking of Schenectady, subdued Newfoundland, drove the men of Boston from Pemaquid, helped found the colony of Louisiana, and ended his adventures by sacking the island of Nevis far down in the Caribbean Sea. A life-long foe of England, he crossed the ocean innumerable times to receive orders from his King and place before him his own plans for driving the English from North America. Though a sea captain by training, he took part in numerous land expeditions and proved himself fully as skillful in leading a detachment through the trackless forests as in leading a fleet across the Atlantic. The expeditions that he headed were small, the armies he commanded and the armies he fought against were miniature armies; but as he was almost invariably successful, one is inclined to regret that his talents were not employed on the more conspicuous stage of European war. At sea his feats were equally impressive; and one feels that, had his untimely death been postponed by a few years, or had he been granted command of a fleet a few years earlier, he might well have equaled the exploits of Jean Bart or Tourville and gained for himself a distinctive place in the annals of the French Navy.

In the year 1646 there came to the little settlement of Ville-Marie de Montreal (known today simply as Montreal) a young Frenchman named Charles Lemoyne, who was destined to play a leading role in the affairs of New France. He was a native of Dieppe, born in the parish of Saint-Rémy in the year 1626,[1] the son of Pierre Lemoyne and his wife, Judith Duschêne. At an early age Charles was taken to the neighboring parish of Saint-Jacques, where his father had recently become an innkeeper. As Dieppe was a rendezvous for merchants and sea captains and a place of departure for settlers going to Canada, young Charles, while he busied himself about the inn, could not fail to hear stirring and no doubt greatly exaggerated tales of far-off lands that roused his love of adventure. Beyond the limitless ocean lay a land of unbounded wealth where an enterprising youth could carve out

[1] E. M. Faillon, *Histoire de la colonie française en Canada* (Montreal, 1865), II, 54.

a fortune. Who can blame him if he chose the life of a pioneer over that of an innkeeper? He talked the matter over with his brother, Jacques, and the two boys decided to try their luck in the newly established French colony. Their parents raised no objections, for Mme Lemoyne's brother, Adrien Duschêne, was then in Canada and had written her suggesting that his nephews be sent over to him; he even offered to advance the money for their passage, with the understanding that they would repay him from their future earnings. The offer was accepted enthusiastically, and in due course the boys landed in Quebec, where they were taken in charge by their uncle. They were followed shortly afterward by their two sisters, Jeanne and Marie-Anne. Charles was sent to the Jesuit outpost on Lake Huron, where he worked for four years at a salary of twenty *écus* [2] until he had become sufficiently proficient in several Indian dialects to act as an interpreter; and it was as interpreter that he came to Montreal.

The settlement of Montreal had been founded by Paul de Chomédy, Chevalier de Maisonneuve, in 1642, four years before Lemoyne's arrival. Its establishment was due primarily to the religious zeal of Maisonneuve and Mlle Jeanne Mance, who were eager to establish a mission which would be a headquarters for work among the Indians. Accompanied by a band of followers numbering some two score, they founded their colony on the island of Montreal; and it is probable that they were encouraged by the traders at Quebec, who saw in the settlement a possible protection against the bands of Iroquois which descended the St. Lawrence to harass the colonists. When Lemoyne arrived there, the town consisted only of a fort, a church, and a few houses; but its advantageous situation at the junction of the Ottawa with the St. Lawrence made it the key to the western trade routes, so that it soon became the second town in Canada. It was just the place

[2] R. G. Thwaites, ed., *The Jesuit Relations and Allied Documents* (Cleveland, 1896–1901), XXVII, 91.

for an energetic young man to begin his career, and the adventurous Frenchman welcomed the opportunity to settle there.

Charles Lemoyne at once plunged into the rough frontier life
of the community, clearing fields, fighting Indians, building, repairing, working. At dawn he would leave the fort carrying his
musket and begin work, ever on the alert for the alarm signal that
warned the colonists of oncoming Iroquois. And eternal vigilance
was necessary, for many a settler was captured and carried off to
the torture fires of these savages. The ever-present dangers and
the natural hardships of this life drew these people together. They
helped each other, fought for each other, and bore each other's
burdens. Devout by nature, they turned to Heaven for aid all the
more readily because of the loneliness of their surroundings, far
out on the western frontier; and the little church inside the fort
became the center of community life. Here they were baptized,
married, and buried; here on Sundays and feast days they gathered
for the celebration of the Mass. Yet despite all this devotion there
came hard times for the colony, and when it was barely ten years
old there was talk of abandoning it. Then came a change for the
better. The Chevalier de Maisonneuve, who had gone to France
to obtain aid, returned in 1653 with over one hundred recruits;
and heartened by this timely addition to their number, the settlers
began to spread out over the countryside.

During his first years in Montreal Charles Lemoyne had risen
to prominence. We find that in January, 1654, he received the
post of *garde-magasin*, with a salary of four hundred *livres*. As he
was now nearly thirty years of age, it was high time for the substantial citizen to think of marriage and the duty of contributing
to the much-needed increase of population. Fortunately for him,
there was in the settlement a young lady barely turned fourteen
who had caught his eye. Catherine Thierry, for such was the
young lady's name, was born in the diocese of Rouen in 1641, the
daughter of Guillaume and Elisabeth Thierry. It happened that
Elisabeth's sister, Martine, and her husband, Antoine Primot,

were eager to settle in Canada, and by dint of pleading they persuaded the Thierrys to confide their one-year-old babe to them for the long journey across the Atlantic. Today we can hardly understand the willingness of parents to part with an infant child whom they could never hope to see again; but perhaps in this case financial considerations were the compelling cause, for the Primots were childless and might be able to make better provision for the girl than her own parents could. At any rate Antoine Primot and his wife brought Catherine with them and in 1650 settled in Montreal, where Charles Lemoyne first saw her. Three years later he decided that the time had come to act, so he agreed with her parents to marry her or pay them six hundred *livres*. But being a man of sound business sense he did not relish the idea of a onesided bargain. An agreement was therefore drawn up in the presence of Mlle Mance, Maisonneuve, and other dignitaries whereby the parents were to pay a like sum if they failed to deliver to the party of the first part the object of his affections. With forfeits thus posted by both sides, there could be but one outcome: on May 28, 1654, the couple were united in marriage.

The prominence of the bridegroom induced the Chevalier de Maisonneuve to make him a handsome wedding gift. He gave him a plot of ground in the vicinity of Montreal, ninety *arpents* [3] in extent, in the quarter known as Pointe Saint-Charles, near the great bay between the St. Lawrence and Jean de Saint-Père Rivers, with the understanding that the Primots should enjoy the use of half of it during their lifetime. To this was added one *arpent* within the town limits which Lemoyne could use for residential purposes. It was situated at the junction of St. Joseph and St. Paul Streets opposite the Hôtel-Dieu and had a frontage of 198 feet on the former thoroughfare and 162 on the latter. [4]

Six years after the marriage a strange situation came to light.

[3] A square *arpent* equals .85 of an acre; a lineal *arpent* 12 rods (i.e., 66 yards).

[4] *Bulletin des recherches historiques*, XXXIV (1928), 234.

By some oversight the Primots had never legally adopted Catherine, having considered her their daughter as a matter of course. Thus Charles Lemoyne, who believed that he had allied himself with the house of Primot, found to his surprise that he had no legal connection with his wife's family, and that, furthermore, his wife's rights as heiress of her adoptive parents might be contested. Once the matter was brought to their attention the Primots were easily persuaded to do the right thing; and to Lemoyne's intense relief Antoine and Martine Primot appeared before Maisonneuve and legally adopted their niece.

The Lemoynes, now settled in their home, began a career of procreative activity that went on unabated for thirty years, giving the colony that remarkable family of sons whose prominence and leadership gained for them the title of the Maccabees of Canada. As his sons grew up, Lemoyne added to their names titles taken from localities near his native Dieppe, and occasionally when a boy died early in life he transferred his title to a younger brother. Chronological lists of the Lemoyne progeny have been compiled which, although they differ in minor details, are fairly uniform. The following one is taken from the most reliable authorities: Charles de Longueuil born in 1656; Jacques de Sainte-Helène, 1659; Pierre d'Iberville,[5] 1661; Paul de Maricourt, 1663; François de Bienville (I), 1666; Joseph de Sérigny, 1668; François-Marie, 1670;[6] unnamed child, 1672; Catherine-Jeanne, 1673;

[5] "Mémoire succinct" (Léon Guérin, *Histoire maritime de France* [Paris, 1851] IV, 469) states that he also bore the title of Ardillers and other places.

[6] Some historians have assumed that an officer named Sauvole who followed Iberville to Louisiana was one of Charles Lemoyne's sons; and since all the sons save François-Marie are given titles in various lists, it is supposed that he must have been the one in Louisiana. The name of Sauvole, however, has been shown to have been that of one Sauvole de la Villantray, who was in no wise related to the Lemoyne family. See Maurice Ries, "The Mississippi Fort called Fort de la Boulaye," *Louisiana Historical Quarterly*, XIX (1936), 851, and the biographical sketch of Sauvole in B. F. French, *Historical Collections of Louisiana* (New York, 1851), pt. III, p. 223*n*. Moreover, François-Marie died at the age of seven-

Louis de Châteauguay (I), 1676; Marie-Anne, 1678; Jean-Baptiste de Bienville (II), 1680; Gabriel d'Assigny, 1681; Antoine de Châteauguay (II), 1683.[7] Thus Charles Lemoyne when he died in 1685 had qualified for the bonus of four hundred *livres* per annum offered by the King to fathers of twelve or more children.[8] The mother got nothing. Such was the division of profits and labor under the old regime.

Pierre Lemoyne d'Iberville, the third son of Charles and Catherine Lemoyne, was born in July, 1661, at Montreal in the little house on St. Joseph Street. The exact day of his birth is not known, as such records were not kept; but we learn from the parish register that the child was baptized by Father Perot on the twentieth day of July in the church of St. Joseph, recently erected near the Hôtel-Dieu. He was named after his paternal grandfather. His sponsors at the font represented the aristocracy of Canada. His godfather, Pierre Boucher (present by proxy), was one of the most distinguished of the early colonists, while his godmother was his Aunt Jeanne, wife of that Jacques Le Ber, Sieur de Senneville, who was soon to become one of the colony's leading merchants.[9] All this was as it should be, for Charles Lemoyne was by now a man of substance, well known in Canada. Four years be-

teen, a fact overlooked by these historians. Louis Le Jeune, in *Le Chevalier Pierre Le Moyne, Sieur d'Iberville* (Ottawa, 1937), p. 16, gives the date of François-Marie's death as 1687, which is correct. Cyprien Tanguay, on the other hand, in his *Dictionnaire généalogique des familles canadiennes* (Montreal, 1871–1890), I, 379, gives no date of death, but assigns the date 1687 to Joseph de Sérigny. This we know to be an error, as Sérigny accompanied his brother to Louisiana in 1701. P. G. Roy, in *Les petites choses de notre histoire* (Levis, Canada, 1919), pp. 86–92, clearly establishes the fact that the Sauvole of Louisiana was not one of the Lemoyne brothers; yet the error persists in some recent historical works.

[7] Tanguay, *op. cit.*, I, 379; V, 336–337; Le Jeune, *op. cit.*, pp. 14–17.

[8] *Edits et ordonnances royaux et arrêts du conseil d'état du Roi concernant le Canada* (Quebec, 1803), I, 57; hereafter *Edits et ordonnances*.

[9] Pierre Margry, ed., *Mémoires et documents pour servir a l'histoire des origines françaises des pays d'outre-mer* (Paris, 1879–1888), IV, xxiin.

fore Pierre's birth he had been given the *seigneurie* of Longueuil, a vast tract of 98,784 *arpents* of land, situated on the St. Lawrence River opposite Montreal (where the present town of Longueuil stands) together with the overlordship of St. Helen's and Ronde Islands.[10] The granting of these *seigneuries* to the more prominent settlers was part of a government plan having for its object the creation of a landed gentry in Canada which would develop the country by encouraging tenants to settle on their domains and cultivate them.

Pierre was, therefore, well connected, and had all the advantages of birth and wealth, such as they were in colonial days. But birth and wealth did not mean a life of ease and luxury. There was no chance for the scion of the distinguished Lemoynes to be pampered. The town in which he spent his boyhood was a frontier town of the roughest sort, where life was a continual struggle. At the time of his birth it contained but 160 men, of whom about a third were married. They lived in some forty houses scattered for the most part on St. Paul Street facing the river, the houses being protected after a fashion by a combination windmill and fort erected on the Côteau Saint-Louis and known as the Moulin du Côteau. Its exact location was on modern Dalhousie Square. As a further precaution, the dwellings were arranged near each other and their walls pierced by loopholes for musketry in such a way that each house was a little fort capable of offering a certain amount of resistance to the assaults of the Iroquois. To provide additional security, Maisonneuve issued a formal order that all persons going outside the settlement to work must be properly armed and must work in groups, and then only in places from which they could make a speedy retreat. All must return home when the signal bell at the fort sounded, and no one should go abroad in the night save for the most urgent reasons. This dangerous life, as we have pointed out, developed among the settlers

[10] W. B. Munro, *Documents Relating to the Seigniorial Tenure in Canada, 1598–1854* (New York, 1907), p. 110*n.*

an *esprit de corps*, a willingness to help one another that would have been lacking in a more civilized community. Each man stood ready to aid his neighbor, and when one of their number was carried off by the Indians, his friends tilled his field for him until he returned, if he returned at all.

It was under such circumstances and amid such surroundings that young Pierre grew to manhood. He was educated in the seminary established by the Sulpitian Fathers, to whom the settlement had been ceded by the defunct Company of Montreal. The head of this institution was Father Gabriel Souart. Needless to say, the religious side of life was stressed in the school, and Pierre early imbibed the feeling of devotion to the Church that was never to leave him. The curriculum comprised Latin, literature, and rhetoric, besides a certain amount of military training, a prime necessity for a boy living in Montreal. That Pierre made the most of his educational opportunities is evidenced by his numerous letters and memoirs (for he was a prolific writer), which are composed in a clear, vigorous style. They are not examples of studied composition and they contain much unorthodox spelling; but they were well suited to their purpose, clear, plain, and distinct in expression.

During his school days Pierre also became imbued with a feeling of loyalty to his King, a feeling that was almost religious in its intensity; and as a corollary to this loyalty came a hatred of the English, with whom his sovereign was almost constantly at war. This hatred also was quite natural, for the struggle between the Kings of England and France was carried on in America with far greater ruthlessness than in Europe, since in the New World the Indians were called in as allies and acted after the manner of their kind. It may well be asked what influence this savage warfare had on the young man's character. That it must have had some influence is obvious. One historian goes so far as to describe Iberville as indifferent to human suffering and as indulging without compunction in "the merciless destruction of his adversaries."

"No one leader," he goes on to say, "can be mentioned as more remorseless in the duties assigned to him; he acted as if he looked upon the slaughter of an enemy as almost a religious duty." [11] The criticism is certainly too harsh; but in justice to the author, it is only fair to say that he wrote at a time when the world believed that savagery in warfare was rapidly becoming a thing of the past, especially in regard to the treatment of noncombatants. But of late years we have witnessed a marked retrogression in this respect. The brutalities of the Germans and the barbarities of the Russians, to say nothing of our own exploits with the atom bomb in exterminating helpless old persons and children, make it somewhat hypocritical for us to criticize a man whose first knowledge of war was strongly colored by the actions of savages. Life on the frontier may have blunted Pierre's finer feelings, yet he never descended to the depths of brutality to which his fellow countrymen were subjected by their savage enemies. On the other hand, when he was warring against white men who were not allies of the Iroquois, as for example on his expeditions to Hudson Bay, he accepted surrender and treated his enemies as prisoners of war were usually treated on such occasions. Even in Newfoundland, where his behavior produced most resentment, his destructive raids were confined chiefly to property; the settlers who did not resist him were spared.

When he was nearly twelve years of age, Pierre made his first communion. Kneeling beside him at the altar rail were his cousin, Jacques Le Ber, Gabriel Testard de la Forest, and several others who played important parts in Canadian history. At this time he is described as big for his age, strong, self-reliant, and distinguished for his piety and cheerful disposition; handsome, with a shock of blond hair, an oval face, clear complexion, and a physique well developed by martial exercises.

Such a youth was always ready for adventure. Living as he did

[11] William Kingsford, *The History of Canada* (Toronto, 1887–1898), III, 50.

in a frontier community where daily life was fraught with excitement and danger, it would have been strange had he wished to settle down to a sedentary existence. And now came the great opportunity. On that morning in June, 1673, when he was received into the Church, there chanced to come to Montreal no less a personage than the new governor of Canada, Louis de Buade, Comte de Frontenac, who was then on his way to a conference with the Indians at Cataracqui (the site of modern Kingston) and had stopped to pick up Charles Lemoyne as interpreter. The situation seemed made to order for Pierre. His older brothers Charles de Longueuil and Jacques de Sainte-Hélène were to go, so why not he? What seems to us his extreme youth could scarcely have been an obstacle, for he had just become a communicant, and this Canadian boys regarded in a sense as the end of childhood. At any rate he succeeded in persuading his father to let him join the expedition. Unfortunately we know nothing of what happened to the boys on this, Pierre's first venture into the wilderness, save that they returned safely, but we do know that the father seized the occasion to obtain from Count Frontenac the position of midshipman in the navy for Pierre. It was a turning point in the young man's life, for now he became a soldier of the sea and embarked on a career that carried him from Hudson Bay to the West Indies, trading, colonizing, and above all fighting the English.

For the next ten years Pierre led a strenuous life studying navigation and naval tactics. He began by sailing the St. Lawrence, making several voyages as far as Isle Percé in a ship belonging to his father, and later made several voyages to France.[12] During this time he may even have seen action under such famous seadogs as Jean Bart, but the records for this period are silent concerning his activities. At the age of twenty-two he was back in Canada, tanned by the weather, strong, healthy, brimming over with self-confidence. It was probably at this time that he met the explorer, Robert Cavelier de La Salle, just returned from his

[12] "Memoire Succinct," in Guérin, *op. cit.*, IV, 470.

famous journey down the Mississippi, and through him became interested in the possibilities of a colony at the mouth of that river. Years later, as we shall see, he devoted considerable time and effort to founding one.

In 1685, two years after Iberville's return, his father died and Charles de Longueuil became head of the family. The elder Lemoyne had indeed secured an enviable place for himself in Canadian history, a place that was recognized by the government long before his death, for in addition to his *seigneurie* of Longueuil he had been granted that of Châteauguay, situated near by and covering an area of 42,336 *arpents*.[13] Previous to this the King in 1663 had rewarded him for his services by ennobling him. Thus Charles Lemoyne became Seigneur de Longueuil, to which title he later added that of Châteauguay. The title of Longueuil as a matter of course devolved on his eldest son, Charles, who in the year 1700 was created Baron de Longueuil, a rank higher than that of *seigneur*. The grant was made in recognition not only of his own services to the Crown but also of those of his brothers. In the course of time the barons of Longueuil added much to their domain, so that at one time it covered an area of 150 square miles, though since then it has been considerably reduced. When the British took over Canada, the then Baron de Longueuil claimed that the change of government did not invalidate his title, and this claim the English government allowed. It is now the only Canadian title of French origin included in the British peerage.[14]

Pierre's apprenticeship was now over and he was qualified to be assigned to a command. Governor Lefebvre de la Barre, who succeeded Frontenac in 1682, presently selected him to carry dispatches to the home government, giving him at the same time a

---

[13] It was granted to Lemoyne in 1673 and was situated on the southern shore of the St. Lawrence between the fiefs of Beauharnois and Sault St. Louis (Munro, *Documents Relating to Seigniorial Tenure*, p. 107).

[14] *Ibid.*, pp. 68–69; W. B. Munro, *The Seigniorial System in Canada* (New York, 1907), pp. 168–169.

letter for the newly-appointed Minister of Marine and Colonies, the Marquis de Seignelay.[15] In speaking of Charles Lemoyne this letter remarked:

I send you his son [Pierre] as bearer of my dispatches; he is a young man very conversant with the sea, admirably well acquainted with this river [the St. Lawrence], has already carried and brought several ships to and from France, and I request you to appoint him an ensign in the marine. He is capable of doing good service, and it is of importance that you have in that line persons who are thoroughly acquainted with this country.[16]

The coveted commission failed to materialize, and Pierre returned to Canada the following year, somewhat crestfallen; but he was young, life was before him, and opportunity soon came to him in the shape of an expedition to Hudson Bay. So the youth, Pierre Lemoyne, now enters upon the scene of future victories as Sieur d'Iberville.

[15] Jean-Baptiste Colbert, Marquis de Seignelay, son of the great Colbert.
[16] *Documents Relative to the Colonial History of the State of New York*, ed. by E. B. O'Callaghan (Albany, 1853–1887), IX, 206; hereafter *Docs. Rel. Col. Hist. N.Y.*

CHAPTER II

Baptism of Fire

FOR some time past, trouble had been brewing in the north. Especially during the last fifteen years, since the founding of the Hudson's Bay Company in 1670, a precarious situation had grown steadily more tense. The new corporation, which had been chartered by Charles II, was (and still is) one of the greatest mercantile organizations of all time; its powers were great, its domain vast.[1] The rights and privileges granted it by its excessively verbose charter made it almost an independent government. The Hudson's Bay Company was entitled to the ownership of all minerals, fisheries, and wealth of whatever nature lying within its boundaries, and had the right, so ran the document, of "sole trade and commerce of all those seas, straits, bays, lakes, creeks, and sounds, in whatsoever latitude they shall be, that lie within the entrance of the seas . . . which are not now actually possessed by any of our subjects, or by the subjects of any other Christian Prince or State." These rights of trade were exclusive, and the company was given power to inflict punishment on any interlopers caught infringing them. In order to carry on trade and exploit the land, the adventurers (as stockholders were then

[1] The original charter remained in effect until 1884; since then four others have supplemented it.

called) were authorized to erect such "castles, forts, fortifications, garrisons, colonies, plantations, towns, or villages" as they
might deem necessary. The company might also pass laws and regulations for the maintenance of order and exact penalties for viola-
tions of the same. The extent of the territory, called Rupert's
Land in the charter, which the King now granted the company
was entirely unknown. In theory the grant extended inland to the
headwaters of all rivers flowing into Hudson Bay. This, as modern
maps disclose, would give the adventurers claim to a territory
covering almost 1,500,000 square miles! In the seventeenth century, however, the inland extent of the domain was ignored. True,
the charter strongly urged that the territory be explored, but the
company's servants were either sailors, whose ideas of exploration
were confined to cruises along the shore, or traders, who saw no
reason for venturing into unknown territory when the Indians
were willing to bring their furs to "factories" (warehouses)
established on the seacoast.

With the establishment of the Hudson's Bay Company there
began a struggle between the British and French traders for the
right to exploit the region watered by the rivers emptying into
the Bay, a region abounding in fur-bearing animals. The merits
of the conflict, in theory at any rate, hinged on priority of discovery; but practically speaking the question was who could
establish fortified posts at strategic points and hold them successfully. The Hudson's Bay Company, by placing factories at the
mouths of the Rupert, Moose, Albany, Severn, and Hayes rivers,
had pre-empted title to the territory, and was able to lure the
northern Indians with their boatloads of furs to these posts. The
result was a heavy loss for the French traders who sought to bring
the Indians southward to the St. Lawrence. To offset the British
factories, the French erected forts of their own, such as the ones
on Lakes Timiskaming and Nemiskau, covering the Moose and
Rupert River routes respectively. Yet despite these protective
measures the English flourished at the expense of the French. The

British fort at Port Nelson, situated as it was on the Hayes River,[2] which flows into Hudson Bay within four miles of the Nelson River, monopolized the northern region; and as the overland route to it had not yet been discovered, there was no way in which the French could deflect the Indian trade going there.

In order to check the encroachments of the powerful Hudson's Bay Company and protect their own interests, the French traders formed in 1682 a corporation of their own, the Company of the North, which professed a desire to extend the Faith among the savages—an object overlooked by the English company—and to enlarge the domains of the King.[3] These excellent objectives the company, no doubt, sincerely desired to promote, though its main purpose was the exploitation of the northern fur trade. The organization soon became the representative of French interests in the north just as the Hudson's Bay Company represented the English. The formal charter was obtained in 1685.

With the English in possession of five forts strategically situated on the five key rivers mentioned above, the situation·took on a serious aspect. In 1683 King Louis XIV wrote to Governor La Barre recommending him to take steps to prevent the English from entrenching themselves more securely, a project he could probably accomplish without too much fear of retaliation, as Colonel Thomas Dongan, then governor of New York, had strict

---

[2] It is necessary to be careful about references to the Nelson and Hayes rivers. The Nelson had been known for some time, and its mouth was generally referred to as Port Nelson, a designation which seventeenth-century documents also used in speaking of the Hayes, probably because the Nelson was the more important of the two. For this reason we read of attacks on Port Nelson when the writer refers to the fortification at the mouth of the Hayes. Fort Bourbon, later Fort York, was at the mouth of the Hayes near the present site of York Factory. The French called the Hayes the Sainte-Thérèse. We shall use the term "Port Nelson" as it was used in the seventeenth century, i.e., referring to the post on the Hayes River.

[3] "Mémoire de la Compagnie du Nord," 1698, Archives des colonies (in the Public Archives at Ottawa), C[11]A, 16, 184.

orders from his sovereign to maintain friendly relations with the French.[4] But by this time a peaceful solution of the problem was out of the question, as the Canadians felt they had suffered too much. Those English establishments on the Bay attracted many Indians who had formerly brought their furs to Montreal, and it took all the influence which the famous *coureur de bois*, Daniel du Lhut, wielded over the savages to prevent a complete rout of the French traders.[5] The members of the French company became panicky. They appealed to La Barre, who in turn wrote the King asking for permission to oppose force with force and attack by land those who many times had attacked His Majesty's subjects by sea. He virtually requested a declaration of war—in Canada only, to be sure—against the British on the Bay.[6]

Louis was now forced to act. James II, his docile ally, had been recently crowned King of England, and perhaps this encouraged His French Majesty to wink at military operations on the part of his subjects in North America which he felt would have no serious repercussions at home. By an order in Council of May 20, 1685, he granted to the Company of the North the district around Port Nelson. The following autumn La Barre was replaced by the Marquis de Denonville,[7] who drew up a memorandum outlining a plan of campaign to reach the Moose and Rupert rivers by marching overland from Montreal, while the fort at Port Nelson was to be attacked by sea. If the King, he said, did not see fit to enforce French claims, then every assistance must be given the company to undertake the land expedition. To this end he urged the people of Canada to back the enterprise.[8] The members of the company were by this time thoroughly aroused, and to add

---

[4] Louis XIV to La Barre, Aug. 5, 1683, *Docs. Rel. Col. Hist. N.Y.,* IX, 200.

[5] La Barre to Seignelay, Nov. 4, 1683, *ibid.,* IX, 205.

[6] La Barre to the King, Nov. 13, 1684, *ibid.,* IX, 251.

[7] Joseph René de Brissay, Marquis de Denonville.

[8] Denonville, "Memorandum on the state of Canada, Nov. 12, 1685," *Docs. Rel. Col. Hist. N.Y.,* IX, 286.

fuel to the flames, news came from Michilimackinac, at the northern end of Lake Huron, telling of the capture by the English of the Sieur Jean Peré and two companions who had gone overland to Hudson Bay. These men had been seized by Governor Henry Sergeant of Fort Albany and were later sent to England.

Nevertheless, the French and British governments continued their efforts to arrive at a peaceful understanding. During the winter of 1686 negotiations were carried on between London and Versailles to arrange some basis of settlement for the conflicting claims in the Western Hemisphere and to arrive at a *modus vivendi* between the two fur companies. It was suggested that commerce on the Nelson and Hayes rivers be enjoyed mutually by the two nations, each without prejudice to the rights of the other. As a result, a sort of agreement was reached, and Governor Denonville was informed that French interests on the Bay must be sustained without attacking the English factories, for the King had just agreed that the two nations should hold Port Nelson independently. [9] But by the time these orders reached Canada, they were too late, for the Chevalier de Troyes was then marching northward on his retaliatory expedition.

While official negotiations were being tortuously carried on in Europe, the Canadians struck. Louis had granted the Hayes River district to the French company, but as they saw no prospect of his furnishing them with soldiers to enforce the grant, they determined to finance the expedition themselves. On applying to Governor Denonville for aid they met with hearty support. He selected as commander of the expedition a man whom he considered the most intelligent of his captains, the Chevalier Pierre de Troyes. This officer had arrived in Quebec at the same time as the governor, in the autumn of 1685, bearing a commission from the King giving him the command of a company in the detachment sent to Canada to suppress the Iroquois. Troyes received

[9] Answer to Denonville, May 20, 1686, Archives des colonies, C¹¹A, 8, 97.

his instructions from the governor on February 12, 1686, and among the officers detailed to accompany him were Pierre d'Iberville and his brothers, Jacques de Sainte-Helène and Paul de Maricourt. In addition to capturing the British posts, Troyes was instructed with special emphasis to arrest those *coureurs de bois* who had deserted to the English, especially that dashing blade, Pierre Esprit Radisson, for whose apprehension a reward of fifty *pistoles* was offered, though, it is interesting to note, he was never caught. Hope was also expressed that Port Nelson would be taken; but in any event Troyes must be back on the St. Lawrence before winter set in, while the brothers Lemoyne were to be left in charge of the captured forts.[10] So we find our hero, now in his twenty-fourth year, starting on his first expedition to that northern gulf where he was to play such an important part during the next ten years.

The attack on Hudson Bay by an overland expedition was not so much of a surprise to the English as one might suppose, though, of course, they had no knowledge of just when the blow would strike. In 1684 the Company of the North, believing Port Nelson to be in French hands, had sent there a trader named Pierre de la Martinière. On reaching his destination, La Martinière found to his chagrin that it had been recently surrendered to representatives of the Hudson's Bay Company. Unable to capture it, he waited until the next summer, seized the English ship *Perpetuana Merchant*, and took her crew back to Quebec as prisoners. Among these men were the captain, Edward Hume, and the mate, Richard Smithsend. Plans for the Troyes expedition were then being openly discussed in the town, and the two officers had no trouble in learning their details. Smithsend managed to get the news through to London, while Hume, who was taken presently to La Rochelle, immediately sent word to the Hudson's Bay Company. The English officials lost no time in appealing to the King for protection and were assured by His Majesty that he would

[10] Instructions to Troyes, Feb. 12, 1686, *ibid.*, pp. 369–384.

give them all the protection he could. That was all, and there the matter rested.[11]

The little town of Montreal was still in the grip of winter when the Chevalier de Troyes began collecting his troops there. For more than a week during the stormy month of March, French soldiers and Canadian woodsmen had been coming to the rendezvous on foot through the forests and over the ice, a gallant body of over one hundred men and officers ready to brave the Canadian winter in the hope of conquest and booty. The expedition consisted of seventy Canadians under the Lemoyne brothers, with thirty soldiers under Gédeon de Catalogne. Troyes, of course, acted as commander-in-chief, and the chaplaincy was assigned to Father Antoine Silvy. The men were well supplied with provisions, sledges, and canoes, and the command was divided into three detachments, each of which was to take the lead in turn. The route selected led up the turbulent Ottawa, then through a chain of lakes and streams to the Moose River, at the mouth of which was the first objective, Fort Hayes. As such a course called for travel by water—that is, when the ice broke up—some thirty-five canoes were taken along. One canoe was allotted to three men, and two canoes were formed into a team to help each other over portages and co-operate in case of accident.[12]

[11] A. S. Morton, "The Early History of Hudson Bay," *Canadian Historical Review*, XII (1931), 412–428. See also affidavits of Hume and Smithsend in J. B. Tyrrell, ed., *Documents Relating to the Early History of Hudson Bay* (Toronto, 1931), pp. 15–17.

[12] There are several accounts of this expedition. The principal one is Pierre de Troyes, *Journal de l'expédition du Chevalier de Troyes à la Baie d'Hudson en 1686*, ed. by Ivanhoe Caron (Beauceville, Canada, 1918). See also Henry Sergeant's report to the Hudson's Bay Company, Nov. 4, 1687, in E. E. Rich, *Copy-Book of Letters Outward, etc.* (Toronto, 1948), pp. 313–316. There are also several pertinent documents in the same work. Bacqueville de la Potherie's letter to the Duke of Orleans is in Tyrrell, *op. cit.*, pp. 238–260. Other accounts are those of John Oldmixon, *The British Empire in America* (London, 1741), II, 561–564; and [Gédeon de Catalogne], *Receuil de ce qui s'est passé en Canada au sujet de la guerre* . . .

On the thirtieth day of March the expedition got under way. It was a gala event for the little community which for over a fortnight had played host to these soldiers and woodsmen, lodging them in their houses, entertaining them at table, and supplying them with whatever attentions they needed. And it was no ordinary journey on which these men were embarking, no military expedition through familiar territory, but a new adventure into northern lands over trails unknown to any save a few *coureurs de bois*. Louis de Callières, governor of Montreal, reviewed the troops as they stood at attention by the riverbank; and as they raised their hands to swear loyalty to the King, he administered the oath of fidelity. Then amid salvos from the fort and the cheers of the inhabitants they picked up the traces of their sledges and started out over the ice. Young Iberville, as commander of the rear detachment, was among the last to leave.

As might be expected, the going was rough, very rough. There was ice, there was melting snow; but the ice was weak, so that after three or four days of trudging over the frozen river, the vanguard turned to the shore. Here camp was pitched at the Long Sault Rapids on the very spot where twenty-five years before Adam Dollard and his gallant band had turned back an army of Iroquois. What a source of inspiration for the young Lemoynes! A day or so was spent in camp, the men patching their canoes as they awaited the arrival of Iberville and his rear guard. While resting here Troyes learned from his guides that the portage around the Long Sault was impassable, so he resolved to plough his way up the rapids, his men dragging their canoes waist deep in the icy waters. This ticklish business was entrusted to Iberville and Sainte-Hélène, and as soon as they arrived the little army

---

depuis l'année 1682 (Publication of Literary and Historical Society of Quebec [Quebec, 1871]).

Differences in dates between English and French accounts are accounted for by the fact that the former used the old-style system while the latter used the new or Gregorian calendar. We shall give the French dates.

started its attack on the rapids. It was a difficult job, this hauling and pushing of frail craft through the foaming waters, and besides the weather was very cold. To make matters worse, an incipient mutiny broke out among the weary men, and strong measures were required to suppress it; but the Lemoynes were equal to the occasion, encouraging, bullying, driving their weary men until the last canoe was landed safely above the cataract.

On Easter Sunday the party halted, for even among the hardships of the campaign this, the greatest festival of the Christian year, must be observed; and Father Silvy, clad in his vestments, celebrated Mass with due ceremony. In the evening after vespers Troyes held a review for the purpose of placing his detachments on a strict military basis. He divided his men into three brigades of three squadrons each, with Sainte-Helène commanding the first, himself the second, and Iberville the last.

On April 15 the march was resumed with Troyes plodding along the shore while the rest followed by water. Led by the indomitable Lemoynes, who alone could undertake such dangerous maneuvers, the woodsmen plunged into the swirling waters up to their necks and by dint of superhuman effort finally brought their little boats to the spot where Troyes awaited them. Exposure was now beginning to take its toll, both physical and moral, on the hardy pioneers; some fell ill and had to be sent back, others became discouraged and mutinied against their officers. Yet the little army pressed forward amid wind, cold, and rain, past the site of modern Ottawa to the upper reaches of the river. Then one day the sun burst forth from the clouds, a favoring breeze sprang up, the little sails were spread to catch the fitful wind, and the men resting on their paddles slipped slowly up the stream. The first day of May, always a holiday in Canada, brought rain; but this in no wise dampened the spirits of the soldiers, who planted maypoles before the tents of their officers, danced, and fired salvos from their muskets. Such indeed was the mercurial spirit of the French Canadians, depressed to the depths one day by adversity, raised to the heights the next by a stroke of good fortune or the promise of a holiday.

Thus the expedition proceeded, sometimes bowling along under a southerly breeze, sometimes struggling against adverse winds and rain, until the pioneers reached a spot not far from the Mattawa River. Here the cold turned rain into snow, keeping them in camp for a day or so. This junction of the Mattawa and Ottawa rivers formed an important milestone in the journey, for up the former stream lay the route to Lake Huron and the post of Michilimackinac, the principal French establishment in the West. Up to this point the Canadians had traveled over familiar ground, but from now on they were to plunge into a little-known wilderness; and to observe the importance of the occasion in a proper manner Father Silvy once more celebrated Mass.

As the expedition was now entering dangerous territory where hostile savages might lurk, guards were stationed around the camps, and the entire detachment was placed under stricter discipline. By the eighteenth they had reached Lake Timiskaming, where they found, situated on an island lying between two rapids in the Montreal (Metabec Chouan) River, an establishment of the Company of the North garrisoned by fourteen men. From this place, according to his instructions, Troyes was to send four men to the region of the Abitibi Indians, where a fort was to be erected as a trading center. The party now halted for three days while Sainte-Helène and Iberville busied themselves with the task of putting the company's affairs in order and the commander secured Indians to handle the canoes. This done, the march was resumed under the command of Sainte-Helène, Troyes giving himself a few days' leave to go with a small detail on a wild-goose chase after a mine said to be somewhere in the neighborhood.

Bad weather still continued to dog the footsteps of the soldiers as they struggled forward. Toward the last of May, however, the temperature rose, the clouds vanished, and the weary travelers got their first taste of spring. But the dangers along the route did not altogether disappear. While they were ascending one of the many rapids that lay across their path, three canoes were wrecked; Sainte-Helène and Maricourt nearly perished in this disaster before they could scramble ashore. Farther on, near Lake Durand, careless workmen lighted a fire at a portage where the men were scurrying back and forth with their canoes and supplies. The fire spread and soon became a raging conflagration that trapped the unfortunate canoemen. They rushed to the riverbank, jumped into canoes filled with kegs of powder, hastily covered them with wet blankets, and pushed off into the stream. Troyes and Father Silvy, who were caught halfway across the portage, barely escaped with their impedimenta, thanks to the timely assistance of a band of friendly Indians.

Thus, paddling their way through the wilderness, dragging their canoes over portages, and overcoming a thousand and one obstacles, they came at last to the divide separating the waters of Hudson Bay from those of the St. Lawrence. The country roundabout was rocky and full of lakes, but there was one important consolation: from now on they would be able to descend rapids instead of struggling against them. On June 2 they encamped on Lake Abitibi, the place where the trading post was to be erected. Here, on a little eminence overlooking the lake, Troyes constructed Fort Abitibi, a structure made of pickets, flanked according to the prevailing custom by four bastions. It was really little more than a stockade of pickets, as no soil could be found suitable for earthworks. This done, the journey was resumed. Dipping their paddles into the turbid waters of Lake Abitibi, the Canadians drove their canoes across its surface to the river of that name, which forms a branch of the Moose, rejoicing that from now on they would travel downstream.

Summer was now approaching. The intense cold and the ice-laden waters, the cause of so much suffering, had disappeared, leaving banks of melting snow to remind the travelers of past experiences. The long span of daylight prolonged the working day, and this, together with the current, enabled the travelers to cover ten, even fifteen, leagues between sunrise and sunset. The river was full of rapids, compelling the men in many instances to carry their canoes over the portages. It was on one of these occasions that Iberville, in a spirit of youthful adventure, scorned the safer route by land and attempted to shoot a particularly dangerous rapid. Accompanied by his canoeman, he threw his boat into the swirling waters, and the little craft, tossed about by the current and buffeted by the eddies, gradually filled, then rising on a towering wave lurched over, throwing both men into the river. Fortunately Troyes happened at this moment to be watching the maneuver. Seeing the peril of his lieutenant, he at once signaled some canoes to go to the rescue. They turned around and hastened to the spot where the empty boat was floating, arriving just in time to drag the exhausted Iberville on board as he was swimming about, looking vainly for his companion, who had disappeared forever in the turbulent waters.

On June 18 the Canadians pitched camp just above the confluence of the Abitibi and the Moose, at a spot but a few miles from Fort Hayes. Here preparations for the coming attack were begun in earnest. Timbers were cut down to be used as covers by the sappers when they were laying their mines, spruce bark was collected for making gabions and fascines, and four scaling ladders were also thrown together as well as a battering-ram. The fort to be assaulted was a substantial affair built on a rise of ground some thirty paces from the riverbank and about eighteen miles from the sea. Its shape was rectangular with four bastions, one at each corner. The bastions were made of a double row of pickets held together by beams which crossed from one row to the other, the intervening space being filled with earth. Connecting the bastions were palisades 130 feet long, made of pickets driven into the ground and rising to a height of eighteen feet. Each bastion was used for a different purpose: one for the storage of furs, another for ammunition, the third for a kitchen, and the fourth as living quarters for a dozen soldiers. In the middle of the enclosure stood the redoubt, a three-story building thirty feet long by twenty wide, its roof forming a terrace surrounded by a parapet with apertures for cannon. For armament three guns were mounted in the two bastions facing the river and two on those facing inland, while on the redoubt were three two-pounders and an eight-pounder made of brass. Entrance to the fort was through an opening in the palisade toward the river, an opening protected by a door half a foot in thickness studded with heavy nails. There was also another door in the rear, opening on a plain some twenty *arpents* in extent. Taken as a sample of wilderness engineering, it was a fortification of considerable strength.

The Chevalier de Troyes got his men under way the following morning and glided down the Abitibi River to the Moose, where he stopped to dispatch Iberville, Guillaume Fabas (called Saint-Germain), and a woodsman to make a reconnaissance of the fort. Toward evening he embarked his detachment and started downstream, arriving, as darkness fell, at an island where he had planned to meet Iberville; and here at dawn Iberville arrived with a report that the garrison were entirely ignorant of the presence of the French. It was now high time to strike, before the English got wind of the enemy, and Troyes transported his troops to a small island half a league from the fort. Here he found Saint-Germain, who told him of an English ship he had discovered anchored four miles from the British post. It was the *Craven* which was conveying Governor John Bridgar and some officers to the Rupert River.[13] Troyes's plan was to bring up the canoes containing the picks, shovels, and the battering-ram and have them follow the men, who would march along the riverbank. He would detail Iberville and Sainte-Hélène to lead eighteen men against the palisade on the side away from the river, leaving six others to make a feint on the right flank, cut through the wall, and fire on the gunners. Meanwhile, the commander himself would lead three

[13] Rich, *op. cit.*, p. 313.

detachments against the side facing the stream, taking with him the ram to batter down the gate. Thus the English would be caught between two simultaneous attacks by a vastly superior force.

As night was falling, Iberville and Sainte-Helène approached the fort with their men. In this latitude and at this time of year dawn followed rapidly on the heels of twilight, so the job had to be done quickly, the maneuver carried out with precision and dispatch. The English, far from expecting the assault, were slumbering peacefully; not even a sentinel was posted. All was quiet as Iberville crept to the palisade and made his way to one of the bastions. Here he managed to put the enemy's artillery out of commission in a rather ingenious manner. He found the guns tied together by two's, and by passing the rope through the embrasure he made it fast to an iron bar in such a way that the recoil of one of the pieces when fired would tear down the wall. He then proceeded to the rear. Here the scaling ladders were planted, and the brothers climbed quickly up and dropped noiselessly into the enclosure. It was then but a moment's time to open the rear door and let in the others. In the meantime Troyes was advancing with his detachment, two of which attacked the flanks while the main body began battering down the front gate with the ram. Iberville's men now opened fire on the redoubt. A gunner who was trying desperately to load his piece with bits of broken glass was cut down by Sainte-Helène. The men outside the palisade thrust their muskets through the loopholes and kept up a galling fire on such of the garrison as ventured to appear, until the ram finally succeeded in breaking down the gate, when all rushed into the enclosure.

The French were now masters of the fort; but there yet remained the redoubt. A tambour of posts stood in front of the door and prevented the ram from being brought into play; but it was quickly removed and the door smashed open. It still hung on one hinge, however, so that those within were able to keep it partly closed. At this moment Iberville, with more valor than discretion, rushed through the opening, only to be pinned between the door and the jamb. So tightly was he wedged in this awkward position that his companions could do nothing to extricate him, though they threw their entire weight against the stout boards. In desperation Iberville managed to bring his pistol into play and hold the English back while his friends completed the work of destruction, finally wrenching the door from its last support. As this gave way, the Canadians rushed in, and led by Iberville, hurled back the besieged with swords and muskets, driving them to the stairway leading to the rooms above from which they had just emerged half-clad. Resistance was no longer possible. So fierce and sudden had been the attack that the rout was complete, and the English commander, dressed only in his nightshirt, bowed in surrender with what dignity he could muster.

The Chevalier de Troyes now paused to take stock of the situation. He had captured fifteen prisoners in two hours' fighting and had made himself master of an important British post. In commemoration of the victory he changed the post's name to St. Louis. From his captives he learned that Fort Charles on the Rupert River was poorly guarded and ill supplied with provisions, while on the contrary Fort Albany was well protected and well stocked. Furthermore, the *Craven* had just sailed, so he was told, to go first to Fort Charles, then to Fort Albany. As Troyes had no boats with which to transport the cannon necessary for attacking a well-fortified place such as Fort Albany, he decided to go to the Rupert River, seize the *Craven* while she was still there, return to Fort St. Louis, drop its guns into the ship's hold, and then, all prepared for a regular siege, sail merrily for Fort Albany. Such a plan, of course, called for immediate action; there could be no delay if he would capture the ship at Fort Charles. He therefore divided his men into two groups: one to remain at Fort St. Louis under Saint-Germain, while the other, consisting of about sixty men, he himself would lead to Fort Charles with his two able lieutenants, Iberville and Sainte-Hélène. For safekeeping he placed the prisoners in an old hulk (a captured French vessel named the *Sainte-Anne*) moored hard by the fort, while the Canadians ensconced themselves in the blockhouse vacated by the erstwhile garrison and made themselves as comfortable as circumstances would permit, deeming their rest a well-earned one after the exertions of the past three months.

Troyes and his command set forth on the twenty-fifth of the month and made rapid progress in their canoes to Hannah Bay, where inclement weather kept them in camp for a day or so. On starting out again, they presently saw the vessel they were looking for, placidly making her way over the waters of James Bay to the Rupert River, and blissfully unaware of the foe lying in wait for her. Keeping themselves well concealed near the shore, the French trailed the ship to the Rupert River, where they saw her drop anchor near the fort. During the night a reconnaissance was made by Sainte-Hélène, who reported the post to be a weak affair, built like all these Hudson Bay outposts, on the same general plan as Fort St. Louis. That is, it was rectangular in shape and flanked by four bastions, which in this case, fortunately for the French, carried no guns. Within the palisade stood a blockhouse with a ladder leading to the roof on which eight cannon were mounted. The post was under the command of Hugh Verner, who was about to put the finishing touches on its fortifications. As the taking of such a place offered no great difficulties, Troyes divided his command into two detachments in order to seize both the fort and the ship at the same time. To Iberville he entrusted the naval part of the program, gave him a boarding party, and left him to his own devices.

Pleased at the confidence shown in him, the young man placed his men in two boats and started under cover of darkness for what was to be another surprise attack. Climbing over the *Craven*'s side, the Canadians found the sentinel sound asleep. They promptly secured this valiant watchdog, then stamping on the deck to rouse the watch below—it was evidently a point of etiquette to waken the enemy before attacking them—they drove the sleepy sailors back with their swords as they swarmed up the companionway. A dose of lead fired into the main saloon nipped an incipient rally in the bud, and the crew of fifteen half-clad men meekly surrendered, together with Governor Bridgar, newly appointed commander of the Hudson Bay posts, and Captain John Outlaw. It was another glorious nightshirt victory.

No sooner had Iberville won this his first naval engagement against the English than he joined Troyes and Sainte-Helène in the operations against the fort. The faithful battering-ram was brought into action and quickly drove in the gate; but the capture of the blockhouse proved quite another matter, for owing to some peculiarity of construction it was impossible to use the ram, and, to make matters worse, the little structure was built of stone, making it possible for the garrison to put up a stout resistance had they been willing to do so. The French opened fire with their muskets, ably seconded by two small cannon they had brought along with them and some hand grenades, which they tossed into the blockhouse through the windows; but the telling blow was delivered when a valiant grenadier climbed up the ladder and dropped a grenade down the chimney "with admirable effect," we are told, as it blew up the cookstove. As the Canadians swarmed into the fort, with Iberville in the lead, cries were heard from one of the upper rooms of the blockhouse. Hastening thither, he broke open a door and found there a lady wounded by one of the grenades. Surprised at seeing a woman in this out-of-the-way post, he inquired how she had come there and learned that she was a member of a party which had sailed for England the previous December in a brig (Captain John Outlaw's *Success*) which had ended her voyage somewhere in Hudson Bay, whence the lady had made her way to the Rupert River and had taken up residence in the fort. She was a Mrs. Maurice, who had originally come over as a companion to Governor Sergeant's wife.[14] Iberville at once summoned the surgeon, who found her injuries no cause for serious alarm. The surgeon gave her what first aid he could at the moment, then left her in charge of a sentinel whom Iberville posted outside the door to prevent the patient from being disturbed.

The Canadians now redoubled their fire with such vigor that the besieged saw the hopelessness of further resistance; but what proved to be the *coup de grâce* was the work of a sapper who had constructed a mine under the building and announced that he was ready to blow it up. Caught in this manner, Captain Verner, like his compatriots at the Moose River, had no choice but to surrender and accept the terms offered him by the victors. He was then severely questioned by Iberville, who attempted to get from him some information about the strength of Fort Albany and what signals were to be given by the English vessels when they arrived. Verner not only parried all these questions but even asked some of his own, for which bit of inquisitiveness he was promptly placed in close confinement and cut off from his companions and the Indians who lived around the place. When he expostulated, asking how the French could thus attack English property when both nations were at peace, Iberville shrugged the matter off by remarking that King James would scarcely quarrel over such a trifle.[15] And in this he was probably right.

When daylight came, the besiegers were in complete control of the post. They brought Governor Bridgar ashore and listened with considerable amusement to his haughty demands for the return of his ship and crew. When he had finished his harangue, they brought him down to earth by offering him a return passage to England in the *Colleton,* a damaged brig that lay alongside the fort; and to show him that they were in earnest, the French de-

[14] *Ibid.*, p. 389; *Acts of the Privy Council of England, Colonial Series, 1680–1720* (Hereford, 1910), p. 107.

[15] Rich, *op. cit.*, pp. 320–321.

tailed shipwrights among the prisoners to make the necessary repairs for the voyage. Later on fifty-one prisoners were placed on board this "weak leaky vessel . . . with scanty provisions to venture to get to Port Nelson or perish at sea whereof above twenty have since miserably died frozen and starved and some fain to be eaten up by the rest of the company." [16] At least so runs a report to the Hudson's Bay Company. Before leaving the fort, the French renamed it St. Jacques.

The next objective was the capture of Fort Albany; this accomplished, a clean sweep of James Bay would be made. Moreover, it was there that the richest supply of furs was stored. Troyes accordingly loaded the *Craven* with his booty, including five guns filched from Fort St. Jacques, and started off with the main body in his canoes, placing Iberville in command of the vessel with orders to destroy as much of the fort as he could before setting sail to join him. The return journey to Fort St. Louis was a harrowing one. The canoes in striking across the bay from Point Mesakonam became separated in a heavy fog. Troyes lost his bearings; a violent wind sprang up, grinding his frail boats between huge cakes of ice. Signal guns were fired, and at last the little vessels arrived safely in the Moose River, where they were presently joined by the *Craven*. It was now the middle of July.

Preparations for the capture of Fort Albany were at once begun. The English prisoners were transported from the hulk (*Sainte-Anne*) where they had been confined to the farther side of the river, given two guns and some fishing tackle, and told to seek their own livelihood. The route to Fort Albany was a difficult one. As the trails through the wilderness were impassable, the French were compelled to go by sea, no easy undertaking for men who had never been in this region before. That part of the coast extending from the Moose to the Albany River, a distance of some ninety miles, is low and uninviting, with shoals and reefs thrusting their muddy fingers out to sea, while the land sloping

[16] *Ibid.*, pp. 306–307.

gently seaward causes the ocean to recede at low tide to a great distance from the shore. To complicate matters, no one knew the exact location of the fort; even the Indians were uncertain. Troyes started out, however, in his canoes, leaving Iberville to bring the *Craven* with the artillery. The commander steered northward along the coast, sometimes running three leagues out to sea in order to double the shallow, sandy points, sometimes hugging the shore line, always on the lookout for the mouth of the Albany River where the fort was situated. As he was groping his way along he suddenly heard a cannon shot; it was the English gunners amusing themselves by firing salutes. By this stroke of luck Troyes was able to locate Fort Albany after a journey of but four days.

Fort Albany, though smaller than Fort St. Louis, was better equipped with artillery. Situated on an island about forty paces from the water's edge, it was protected by a moat, at this time in a state of disrepair. The ground surrounding it was marshy, thus affording some measure of protection against invasion. The curtain or palisade facing the river, as well as that facing the wood in the rear, was fifty feet long, while the side walls were but forty-two. At the corners were the usual bastions built of logs four to eight inches thick, rising to a height of eighteen feet. These bastions were topped by platforms supporting four guns each, while twenty-five more were placed here and there in commanding positions. Inside this enclosure was a large building for the garrison. The commander of the post was Henry Sergeant, who held the position of governor of all the Hudson Bay posts. His commission expired this year, but the ship bringing word that John Bridgar was on his way to replace him had been lost so that he was not aware that his successor had arrived in the Bay.[17]

Proceeding upstream, Troyes came to a platform constructed by the English as a sort of lookout post where they could place a sentinel to watch for the approach of hostile forces by sea. In the best traditions of the Hudson's Bay Company's scheme of de-

[17] *Ibid.*, p. 389.

fense, the post was unoccupied, and Troyes was able to land his men there in perfect safety. His plan was to find the exact location of the fort, then select a good campsite near it and a suitable place where he could erect a battery. Sainte-Hélène, sent on ahead, reported having found such a location on an island within gunshot of the stockade, where they could encamp without being seen by the garrison and bring the guns into position for the bombardment. The following day the commander landed his men there. As his provisions were now running low, he decided to demand the surrender of the fort at once, instead of waiting for the arrival of Iberville with the artillery, in the hope that the British would deem discretion the better part of valor. But Governor Sergeant was not the man to yield without a struggle, and he returned a spirited reply to the urgent request. He was ready to fight, he said; in fact, he was more ready than his garrison, which begged him to surrender as soon as the firing began.

The foundations of the battery were completed on July 23, and it only remained for the guns to be put in place. Iberville's vessel had been held back for several days in the river by contrary winds, during which time Troyes's men had kept up a constant musketry-fire on the redoubt, making their presence felt but doing little actual damage. Scarcity of provisions and the failure of Iberville to put in an appearance began to cause grave apprehension among the officers; but the Canadian woodsmen, true to their religious traditions, invoked the assistance of Saint Anne, vowing to bring her church at Beaupré fifty *sols* of their prize money and a battle flag from one of the enemy's bastions. Scarcely had this vow been registered when a breeze sprang up, the *Craven* sailed in, and Iberville cast anchor near the camp. All now went to work with renewed zest. Eight guns were unloaded and mounted during the night.

The following day the guns were trained on the commander's quarters and a volley fired. The commander was eating supper with his wife and the chaplain at the moment when a cannon ball whizzed through the dining room, causing great damage to the crockery, but fortunately injuring no one. Now the firing became more general, and in the space of an hour the battery had launched 140 shots against the devoted fort, smashing palisade and bastion, and reducing the structure to ruins. With Gallic enthusiasm, the Canadians gave a "Vive le Roi," to which the besieged replied in kind; but, as the narrator tells us, the cheer had a hollow sound, for the garrison had sought refuge in the cellar; in fact, it was no cheer at all; the discouraged defenders were merely trying to voice their willingness to surrender without running the danger of coming out into the open to haul down the flag. To tell the truth, they had no stomach for a fight without pay in advance, for as they told their commander, "if any of us lose a leg the company could not make it good." As Troyes was getting ready for a final salvo, a boat was seen approaching with a flag of truce. On closer inspection it proved to be the chaplain displaying with what dignity he could the maidservant's apron flying gracefully from a stick. With many bows and compliments he informed the Chevalier de Troyes of Governor Sergeant's wish to see him at the fort to discuss terms of peace; but Troyes, having no desire to trust himself in the enemy's camp, replied with equal courtesy that the meeting must take place elsewhere. It was thereupon agreed to hold the conference in midstream, an arrangement entirely satisfactory to the French commander, though he consented with feigned reluctance as he had no desire to have the English discover the destitute condition of his own men.

When these arrangements were concluded, Troyes and Iberville embarked at the appointed time and proceeded to the rendezvous where they were met by Governor Sergeant. Anchored side by side, the rival commanders began the ceremony by opening wine and drinking the healths of the Kings of France and England, a proceeding in which the thirsty Frenchmen joined heartily. Troyes then came down to business by saying that he had not come to drink wine since he had better vintage in his own camp—a pure bluff, as he had scarcely a pint to his name—and by demanding the immediate surrender of the French prisoners, the Sieur Peré and his companions. This demand Sergeant could not satisfy, as Peré [18] had been sent to England and his friends transported to Charlton Island in the southern part of James Bay; but after considerable parleying the following terms were agreed upon for the surrender of Fort Albany: the fort was to be turned over to the French with all the property therein, save that the servants of the company could retain their belongings. These servants were to be sent to Charlton Island, there to await the arrival of an English ship, or if one failed to arrive, they were to be sent back to England in a vessel furnished by the French. The storehouses were to be closed and the keys given to Troyes's lieutenant. Then a formal surrender was to take place, the garrison, save the governor and his son, marching out unarmed.

The terms settled, both parties retired to make ready for the ceremony of surrender, which according to seventeenth-century tradition must be enacted with a certain amount of formality, even though it involved but a blockhouse in the wilderness. The Chevalier de Troyes, accompanied by Sainte-Helène and Iberville, proceeded to the fort with the army, and standing at attention in the full panoply of war with drums beating and flags flying, received the submission of the unfortunate Sergeant as he marched out at the head of his men. The French commander acted chivalrously enough. After removing the garrison to a camp some distance away, he allowed the governor, his wife, and the chaplain to remain in their apartments until such a time as he could arrange for their removal to Charlton Island. Then, in honor of the saint thanks to whose intercession his efforts had been crowned with success, he renamed the fort Ste. Anne.

These *opéra bouffe* sieges we have described, with their complacent surrenders, must not be taken as examples of British military valor in the seventeenth century. The men composing

[18] See above p. 18.

the garrisons were not soldiers of the King but servants of a trading company who had taken service for the purpose of earning a more or less peaceful living. They were not under military discipline; their forts were little more than warehouses protected against the attacks of Indians; and neither they nor their commanders appeared to feel the disgrace of defeat as keenly as they would have had they been members of the British Army.

On leaving Fort Ste. Anne for the Moose River, Troyes ordered Saint-Germain to remain behind and repair the damages sustained during the siege. Arriving at Fort St. Louis, he made preparations for an immediate return to Montreal, handing over his command to Sainte-Helène and Iberville. These two were to remain during the winter with forty men to guard the fort. To Iberville were given particular instructions to destroy the *garde logis,* as the establishment on Charlton Island was designated, lest the English should fortify it later. This done, Troyes left for Montreal in August, arriving there two months afterward. The loot at Fort Ste. Anne amounted to 50,000 skins.

Of Iberville's activities at Moose River during the winter we know very little. Presumably he had nothing much to do save while away the time as best he could. The short span of day in these latitudes gave him no opportunity to accomplish more than to maintain discipline among his men, not an easy task when there was not enough to do to keep idle hands busy. We have, however, one incident which shows how he kept his eyes on the activities of the English. He had received word, probably from some neighboring Indians, that an English bark named the *Hayes* coming from Port Nelson had been caught in the ice at Charlton Island. This island, which had been used for some time as a depot by the Hudson's Bay Company, was situated some fifty miles northeast of Moose River, and therefore commanded the approach to the three forts on James Bay. Since it was not fortified, it was looked upon as a rather vulnerable spot by the directors of the company, and they had urged Bridgar to abandon it and move its contents to the Moose River post where they could be more easily guarded in case war broke out.[19] This Bridgar had not had time to do before the French captured Fort St. Louis.

Iberville now seized the occasion to send out four men to investigate the situation. One of these fell by the wayside, but the other three, pressing forward over the ice, soon reached the vessel, only to be ignominiously captured and promptly clapped into the hold. Later, one of the trio escaped and brought the news to Iberville. Nothing could be done at the time, as winter was fast approaching, but preparations were made for a rescue as soon as the ice broke up. When spring came, however, the prisoners proved capable of taking matters into their own hands. One of them had been set to work with the crew bending on a sail and helping put the ship in condition for the coming season. One day when most of the sailors were aloft, this fellow seized an ax, struck down the two men working on deck, and ran to release his comrade. Grabbing muskets that were lying against the bulwarks, the two now made themselves masters of the ship, and ordering the crew at point of gun to weigh anchor, they set sail and brought their prize to the Moose River just as Iberville was starting out to rescue them.[20]

When the English prisoners captured by the Chevalier de Troyes eventually reached England, great was the outcry of the Hudson's Bay Company. A treaty of neutrality had just been signed by France and England (November 16, 1686),[21] which, while it contained nothing specific about the Hudson Bay question, pledged the colonists of both nations not to make war on each other by land or by sea; and now came news of the loss of James Bay. John Churchill, governor of the company in London, drew up a petition to his sovereign demanding redress from the

---

[19] Rich, *op. cit.*, p. 182.   [20] *Docs. Rel. Col. Hist. N.Y.*, IX, 344.
[21] *Collection de manuscrits contenant lettres, mémoires, et documents historiques relatifs à la Nouvelle-France* (Quebec, 1884), I, 372–381; hereafter *Collection de manuscrits.*

King of France for the seizure of the three forts and 50,000 skins. He also embodied in his complaint a gentle reminder of the previous losses he and his partners had suffered at the hands of these French freebooters. This placed King James in a difficult position; his allegiance to Louis was hampered by his duty to his petitioners. He could not declare a general war for such a trifling cause, yet Louis would pay no damages, as the members of the Company of the North were equally loud in their complaints of the harm inflicted on them in the past by British interlopers. In fact, the French traders had written their government that the money subscribed for the Troyes expedition had all been spent, while the profits of pillage had been dissipated by the *coureurs;* hence they requested that the trade at Port Nelson be taken from the English and given to them.

The upshot was, as might be expected, the appointment of a commission to study the subject. After considerable wrangling the French representatives offered to exchange the forts Troyes had captured for Port Nelson, claiming the English had taken that post from them three years before. But the English commissioners reminded James of the Hudson's Bay Company's rightful title to the entire Bay, warning him at the same time that unless he backed up the company and helped them recover the lost posts, the fur trade in this great region would eventually fall completely into French hands. James, after thinking the matter over, decided to stand by the company's territorial rights, and his commissioners so advised the French; but as an immediate aquiescence could not be obtained from the French representatives, an agreement was finally reached in December, 1687, by which everything was to be left *in statu quo* until January 1, 1689. Doubtless it was hoped that something would happen before then. It did. In November, 1688, King James was driven from the throne, and William of Orange, Louis' implacable enemy, was called to wear the British crown.

CHAPTER III

Schenectady and Port Nelson

LATE in October, 1687, Iberville arrived in Quebec with his brother, Sainte-Helène, having left Maricourt in charge of the forts on James Bay. On stepping ashore he found himself the center of an affair that had supplied the back-fence gossips of Montreal with enough scandal to last them several months. It appears that two months after he had left Montreal, on that memorable day in March, one Mlle Jeanne-Geneviève Picoté de Belestre appeared before the local bailiff accusing him of having seduced her under promise of marriage and naming him as the father of her expected child.[1] Mlle de Belestre was a young woman nineteen years of age, and being a minor, was a charge of her brother-in-law, Jacques Moleray de la Mollerie, who had been appointed her guardian. She does not appear to have been a very admirable sort of person, for she informed the bailiff that she would not take care of her child when it arrived, a decision which left that unfortunate official with no alternative but to order her sister to take charge of it. Charles de Longueuil at this point got wind of the trouble and secured a ruling from the authorities setting the matter aside until his brother returned from

[1] For details of this affair see *Jugements et délibérations du conseil souverain de la Nouvelle-France* (Quebec, 1885), III, 194–264, *passim*.

his expedition and could defend himself. The Sieur de la Mollerie, however, was not one to allow such a blow to the family honor to go unchallenged. He appeared before the Council at Quebec on November 6 and requested the arrest of Iberville, offering at the same time to pay any damages the latter might claim if the accusation could not be proved. The Council does not seem to have been willing to go to such lengths, but satisfied La Mollerie by forbidding Iberville to leave the country under pain of being convicted *in absentia*.

Fortunately for Iberville, Governor Denonville saw fit to intervene at this stage of the proceedings. The governor had been highly impressed by the reports that the Chevalier de Troyes had given him of the young officer's conduct in the field, so when Iberville landed in Quebec he decided to send him at once to France to make a report to the home government on the current state of affairs at Hudson Bay. Since Iberville was to go on His Majesty's service, the honor of the Belestre family had to wait. Denonville accordingly issued an order overriding that of the Council, and Iberville was permitted to sail for France with the understanding that he should be back in Canada the following spring to answer the charges against him. Thus balked in his first attempt, La Mollerie did not give up hope but quietly bided his time until Iberville's return.

When Iberville reached France he found that the Company of the North had already made plans to send out an expedition to collect the furs which the traders on James Bay were getting from the Indians and storing in the recently captured posts. For this purpose the company had written the Minister of Marine, requesting the loan of a two-hundred-ton vessel. This was granted them, and Iberville was placed in command of the *Soliel d'Afrique*, a fast-sailing craft, with orders to take her to Canada. The position of skipper of this vessel appears to have been entrusted to Pierre de Lorme, a valiant young man whose courage had gained for him the sobriquet of Sans-Crainte. We can imagine the feelings of Pierre d'Iberville, not yet thirty years of age, when he stepped on the quarterdeck of this splendid ship, his first independent command, and set sail across the Atlantic. On reaching Quebec (June 3, 1688), he found other honors awaiting him. Denonville had appointed him commander-in-chief of all the posts on Hudson Bay, and now proceeded to issue a commission, dated June 8, ordering him to proceed to the Bay at once. Now we find our hero no longer a subordinate subject to the orders of a superior, but a commander in his own right, the leader of an expedition, the supreme authority on the Bay. He had indeed come far in the last two years.

But there was another surprise in store for him, a surprise of a very different character. Just before Iberville's arrival the Sieur de la Mollerie had again appeared before the Council to demand his arrest, fearing that the commission Denonville was about to issue might enable his man to escape. A few days later Iberville was hailed into court to answer the charges against him. He entered the defense usual in such cases, offering as an excuse for his action—which apparently he did not deny—that Mlle de Belestre was not a lady of irreproachable reputation. The case was barely under way when Governor Denonville once more saw fit to intervene, informing the Council that the King's service demanded Iberville's immediate presence in Hudson Bay. The Council, obliged to bow before such an order, permitted the young man to depart, with the understanding, however, that he appoint a representative to look after the case in his absence, for a settlement of the affair could no longer be delayed. Iberville named Denis Riverin to act for him, then sailed for the Bay, glad to be rid of the unsavory business. M. Riverin appeared before the Council in behalf of his client, and stressing the unfavorable reputation of Mlle de Belestre, succeeded in convincing them that the case was a civil not a criminal one. In the end the Council handed down a decision the following October, ordering Iberville to take charge of his inamorata's daughter, unless she was otherwise provided for, and bring her up in the fear of God until her fifteenth year. What Iberville did in the way of providing for the child we do not know, but five years later her uncles, brothers-in-law of her mother, made up a purse of 3,000 *livres* to pay for her board and lodging at the Hôtel-Dieu, where she remained for the rest of her short life.[2] When Iberville returned from the Bay, the matter was settled and he probably gave it little thought. At any rate he did not have to marry the girl.

Pierre d'Iberville left Quebec late in June or early in July with the *Soleil d'Afrique* and the *Saint-François-Xavier*, the latter a slow-moving craft that was soon left behind to make her way to her destination as best she could. He had with him as a lieutenant his cousin Jean-Baptiste Lemoyne de Martigny. On September 9, the *Soleil d'Afrique* reached Charlton Island, where the commander learned from his brother Maricourt that some 22,000 skins had been collected at Forts Ste. Anne and St. Louis during his absence. A bark with a consignment aboard had been awaiting him at Charlton Island, but a few hours before he dropped anchor there it had left for Fort St. Louis, as the season was now so far advanced that no one believed the skins would be called for that year. Iberville and Maricourt decided to waste no time in getting their furs. Commandeering a boat, they at once sailed to the Moose River, where they found the bark and brought her back to Charlton Island. She had a cargo of 35,000 furs. The *Soleil d'Afrique* was now loaded with the valuable skins and put in De Lorme's charge. He was ordered to sail for La Rochelle in eight days if he did not hear from Iberville, who was going to Fort Ste. Anne to get a large supply of furs collected there during the winter.

Iberville arrived at Ste. Anne without mishap, quickly tossed the furs into his boats, and started back for Charlton, but on reaching the river's mouth he saw in the offing two ships flying the British flag. They were the Hudson's Bay Company's *Churchill*

[2] *Bulletin des recherches historiques*, XXI (1915), 224.

(Captain William Bond), eighteen guns, four *pedereros* (cannon used for throwing loose missiles), and the *Young* (Captain John Simpson), ten guns, four *pedereros*, with crews aggregating eighty-three men, come down from Port Nelson to reclaim the fort. When the British sighted Iberville's craft, they lowered their boats and sent them scurrying after the French, who were desperately trying to cut away the buoys that marked the entrance to the channel. For two days the occupants of these boats sniped at each other without much effect, but the damage done the channel markers was enough to cause the *Churchill* and the *Young* to run aground as they breezed into the river. After considerable effort the smaller of the two ships got off, and preceded by two boats armed with sounding leads, made her way up the stream and anchored at a spot where her crew landed and pitched camp. Under cover of darkness Maricourt attempted a surprise attack, only to be repulsed. Later the second ship joined the first, and the two, escorted by their boats, ascended the river to an island a quarter of a league below the fort, exchanging shots with the French as they sailed along the shore.

Thus far honors were fairly even. Iberville with seventeen men was able to prevent the British from seizing the fort; but he feared to drive them off entirely lest they make for Charlton Island, where a large supply of furs had been left, guarded by only six men. He therefore decided to leave them in peace for the time being, as the ice was beginning to form and would presently freeze the ships in for the winter. On October 10, he sent Martigny back to Quebec by the overland route with a letter for the company's directors expressing his confidence in a favorable outcome of the campaign. This done, the young commander, by a series of clever maneuvers, began to capture the enemy piecemeal—despite the fact that he was outnumbered five to one—until he forced the last remnant into an ignominious surrender. As cold weather began to settle down on the two forces, the English soon perceived the wisdom of suspending hostilities, at least until the following spring. One day as Iberville and his lieutenant, La Motte, were surveying the British camp from a point of vantage, the English called out to them suggesting the two forces remain at peace and requesting that they be allowed to hunt partridges in the neighborhood. Alarmed lest they should discover the weakness of the French force, Iberville returned a peremptory refusal. Yet despite this prohibition two officers started out from their encampment next day to replenish their larder. The French, as it happened, were out on a similar errand, and seeing the Englishmen's tracks, they followed them up and had no difficulty in taking the two men prisoners. The next day the Canadians met with the same success, picking up a party from the camp who had ventured forth to seek their missing comrades.

The good fortune of the French so far caused the English to take stock of the situation, and after two or three days they advanced to the middle of the river bearing a flag of truce to open negotiations, promising to live in peace with their neighbors if they could obtain permission to trade with them. They even offered a hostage. An agreement was hastily drawn up and signed by both parties, Iberville exacting a promise from the enemy not to venture south of the island where they were then standing. Goods were now exchanged, the officers were feasted by the French commander, and good will appeared to be established.

Unfortunately, on reading over the treaty Iberville, whose knowledge of English was no better than the English commander's knowledge of French, experienced some misgivings. There had evidently been some linguistic difficulties at the conference which he had been unable to overcome. He had, however, noticed among the English an Irishman who spoke French fluently and who told the Canadians he would like to come over to their fort. Maricourt was dispatched with a guard to secure this man and managed to bring him back the same day by promising to indemnify him for the property he had been obliged to lose by his desertion. On arriving at the fort the deserter warned his new friends against putting any trust in the treaty they had signed or in Captain Bond's promises to live at peace with them and engage in trade; for the sole purpose of the expedition was to drive the French from the Albany River and seize the post for the Hudson's Bay Company. The treaty that had been signed was merely a ruse to gain time until Bond found a favorable opportunity to attack.

Enraged at this alleged double dealing, Iberville stormed into the camp accusing Bond of treachery. All efforts to placate the angry Frenchman failed, as indeed might be expected, and to make matters worse he was led to believe—probably by the Irishman—that the hostage now offered him as evidence of sincerity, one Captain John Abraham, was merely a captured pirate for whose fate the English cared nothing. As a matter of fact, there was no truth in this, for Captain Abraham had been prominent in Hudson Bay affairs for many years and had at one time been in command of Port Nelson.[3] As it turned out Captain Abraham proved communicative, for the French were able to learn from him that the English were only waiting for the ice to break up to launch an attack on the fort.

It was now necessary for Iberville to assume the offensive for his own protection. In order to weaken the foe, he lured, by various stratagems, as many Englishmen as possible from the camp until he had some twenty prisoners. A cannon was then placed on the island and a bombardment begun. It appears to have had a chastening effect on the British commander, though it did but little material damage, for he promptly surrendered, probably in the belief that the French forces were greater than his own. An agreement was now signed by the two leaders whereby the captured Englishmen were to return home in the *Young*, leaving the *Churchill* behind, while the French were to pay the officers' wages amounting to 2,100 *livres*. Fort Ste. Anne

[3] Rich, *op. cit.*, pp. 370–373.

was thus saved, and Iberville was now at liberty to turn his attention to the other posts.

Toward the beginning of summer (1689), just as Iberville was commencing to assure himself that he had the situation well in hand, unpleasant news was brought to Ste. Anne by some friendly Indians who had come across James Bay to trade their furs for trinkets. They told of an English boat they had seen lurking in the vicinity of Fort St. Louis, which contained a winter's accumulation of beaver and was guarded by only four men. This boat, it turned out, belonged to a Hudson's Bay Company's ship, the *Huband,* commanded by Captain Richard Smithsend (the same Richard Smithsend who had been a prisoner in Quebec in 1685), then anchored in the Rupert River, and the captain had seized the occasion to reconnoiter the Moose River fort. He was now returning to his ship, so the Indians said, to notify those on board of the conditions at St. Louis, and in all probability there would be an attack.

Iberville at once turned over the command of Fort Ste. Anne to Maricourt. Embarking on the captured *Churchill,* he started for the threatened post, taking with him his younger brother, Louis de Châteauguay, then but a boy thirteen years of age, who had been brought along on this expedition to gain his first experience in the field. On arriving at the Moose River the commander found nothing to alarm him: Captain Smithsend was nowhere in sight. Of the four men left there to guard the fort one had died and two others were incapacitated by severe burns, but this does not seem to have caused Iberville any anxiety; he merely made a few changes in the fort and left that very night for the Rupert River. The wind was against him, and it was four days before he reached the site of his first naval exploit of three years before, where he now found the *Huband* at anchor near the fort. The following day, as he was hurrying toward her, he could discern in the distance through a light haze the boat that had been reconnoitering the Moose River and was now striving desperately to reach the *Huband*. Putting on all speed, he quickly overtook the little craft and captured it, finding, much to his delight, Captain Smithsend among her passengers. It was a simple matter now to take the ship. No resistance was offered; the pilot, ably seconded by the crew, expressed his willingness to surrender on payment of the wages promised them by the company, terms which Iberville readily granted, since he had no desire to push the large *Churchill* into the river and was anxious to get to Charlton Island, where he was to pick up some provisions for Fort St. Louis.

This little matter of surrender being thus amicably adjusted to everybody's satisfaction, Iberville returned to Fort Ste. Anne, arriving there August 15. Here he found Sainte-Helène, who had just arrived from Montreal with thirty-eight *coureurs* at his back. The directors of the company were well informed as to the situation on the Bay, as in April Iberville had sent down the Sieur de Bellefeuille with a complete account of all that had transpired since Martigny had reported six months before. It was the directors who had raised the contingent of *coureurs* and sent it overland to Fort Ste. Anne. To Iberville's intense joy Sainte-Helène brought letters from the governor, who ordered him to return at once to Quebec with his largest ship and a cargo of furs. Preparations for the return journey were at once begun, and the *Churchill* was chosen for the voyage. On September 12, after bidding goodbye to Maricourt, whom he left with the *Saint-François* in charge of Ste. Anne, garrisoned by thirty-six men, and to Sainte-Helène, who was to return overland, he weighed anchor and set sail. The success of this brief campaign may be judged by the value placed on the three vessels and their cargoes captured by the French which the Hudson's Bay Company estimated at £15,000.[4]

Iberville's course lay northward through Hudson Bay. On nearing Southampton Island at the western end of Hudson Strait,

[4] *Calendar of State Papers, Colonial Series, America & West Indies, 1699*, No. 1358, hereafter *C.S.P. Am. & W.I.*

he sighted an English ship homeward bound from Port Nelson. She was under the command of young Médard Chouart, nephew of the famous Pierre Radisson. Here, indeed, was a worthy prize that would be a fitting climax to the year's work if only he could bring her to Quebec. But encumbered as he was by the number of English prisoners on board, he realized the danger of giving battle, so he determined to seize the ship by a ruse. After hoisting the English flag he approached within hailing distance and invited the commander to visit him on board at the first opportunity. Chouart was not unwilling and signaled acceptance of the kind invitation. Then, fortunately for him, a storm sprang up, the vessels parted, and when the weather cleared they had lost sight of each other. On October 25, Iberville rounded Diamond Head and unloaded his precious cargo on the docks of Quebec.[5]

On his return to Canada Iberville found a drastic change in the relations between France and England: King William III was on the British throne and war had been declared. It is interesting to note that one of the principal causes of the war listed in William's declaration was the seizure of the three forts on James Bay by the Chevalier de Troyes. And now began that long series of wars that caused such suffering along the frontier for the next half-century. Indian raid followed Indian raid, massacre followed massacre, siege followed siege; the hostility between English and French colonists that had lain more or less dormant for many years burst forth in all its fury, until General Wolfe put an end to the conflict by capturing Quebec.

With the formal declaration of war it was now possible for the French to throw away the cloak of pretense and proceed openly with their policy of conquest. The necessity of controlling Port Nelson was from month to month becoming more

[5] For accounts of these events see letter of Iberville, Sept. 21, 1688, Archives des colonies, C[11]A, 10, 237; "Relation of the Events at the Bay, Nov. 14, 1689," *ibid.*, 10, 480–498; Iberville to associates, Nov. 17, 1689, *ibid.*, 10, 499–504; and also various documents in Rich, *op. cit.*

apparent. For one thing, the fort on the Albany River had not yielded as much in the way of furs as had been expected. Then, too, the forts on James Bay were difficult of access, for it was a long sea voyage from Quebec to the bottom of the Bay and a tedious one overland by canoe. Since transportation by sea was the more feasible of the two methods, it was easier to reach Port Nelson than any of the other posts. Besides, the northern skins were far richer than those found to the south. The suggestion previously made by the French government, namely, that the posts on James should be exchanged for Port Nelson, had been renewed; and when it met with the expected refusal Governor Denonville proposed to seize the place by force of arms. He had frequently written the Marquis de Seignelay urging the co-operation of the Company of the North with Iberville in the furtherance of this project, and had also declared the capture of Port Nelson worth any cost.[6] The declaration of war in June, 1689—the War of the League of Augsburg or King William's War (as it is called in America)—greatly simplified matters; it was now possible for the company to apply itself frankly to the business of taking Port Nelson. But before the governor could turn his attention to Hudson Bay, a more pressing situation had arisen that demanded the immediate organization of an undertaking to protect Canada, and Iberville was called upon to play a part in it.

The accession of William III caused a marked change in the policy of Louis toward the British colonies in America. While James II was on the throne, hostilities between Canada and the colonies of New York and New England were held in abeyance; but now anything might happen on the southern border, and, dreadful to contemplate, the Iroquois might be encouraged to raid the St. Lawrence Valley. Governor Denonville at once advocated forestalling such attacks by an invasion of the enemy's territory. He hurriedly dispatched M. de Callières, whom we

[6] Letter of Denonville, Oct. 18, 1688, *Collection de manuscrits*, I, 436.

have met before as governor of Montreal, to Versailles with a plan for attacking New York. Briefly stated, it provided for an army of about 2,000 men to march on Fort Orange under cover of making peace with the Iroquois; then, leaving two hundred men to guard the place after it had been taken, the army would continue down the Hudson River to Manhattan.[7] To assist in the capture of Manhattan the King was to send two men-of-war to intercept any reinforcements the British might send by sea. Callières even suggested that the colonists might surrender peacefully should they remain loyal to King James, as this sovereign might be induced to order such a surrender now that a rebellion had deprived him of his throne. This, it must be admitted, was wishful thinking, as Callières really believed that the colonists would declare for William. But if, on the other hand, as Callières went on to say, the King did not approve of such an attack before war had been officially declared, then preparations should be made at once to act promptly when hostilities began, for a rupture between the two powers was obviously inevitable.[8]

King Louis toyed with the idea of invading New York. It pleased him; and although he did not deem it expedient at the moment, he ordered Denonville to make the necessary preparations and hold himself ready to set the plan in motion when the proper occasion should arise.[9] It was not long before matters came to a head in Europe, for, as we have said, war was officially declared in June. Steps now had to be taken for the protection of Canada; and to insure a more aggressive policy, or rather a more successful policy of aggression, Louis sent back that gallant old soldier Count Frontenac to replace Denonville as governor. Frontenac held the position until his death in 1698.

[7] We are using the term "Manhattan" to distinguish between the town and the colony of New York.

[8] Callières to Seignelay, Jan. 1689, *Docs. Rel. Col. Hist. N.Y.*, IX, 404–408.

[9] Seignelay to Denonville, May 1, 1689, *Collection de manuscrits*, I, 449.

While these plans were maturing, the government had not lost sight of Port Nelson. Iberville, of course, was particularly interested in any venture directed toward the Bay, eager to show his mettle again as an independent commander. He even wrote the members of the company in Paris begging them to purchase a vessel at La Rochelle and have her at Quebec the following May, when he would be prepared to take her northward with two other ships, for he firmly believed that he could take Port Nelson with only sixty Canadians.[10] In principle the idea commended itself to the King, since the English at this time were too busy with the war in Europe to give any attention to the Bay, and he instructed Frontenac to give the company whatever assistance it needed to carry out this worthy project.[11]

By this time Iberville had become a major figure in Canadian military circles. His conduct on his two northern expeditions had marked him, not only as an able leader, but as the one man to command an undertaking to these regions. Governor Denonville had been so pleased with him that he had requested for him the rank of lieutenant in the navy, an unprecedented honor for a Canadian, suggesting at the same time that the granting of such a rank to one so young might serve as an incentive to the youth of Canada. The request was eventually granted, and on March 16, 1691, Iberville received his commission.[12]

When Frontenac landed at Quebec in October, 1689, to carry out the somewhat grandiose scheme of Callières, it was then too late in the year to undertake anything in conjunction with the men-of-war that were to sail to Manhattan. Furthermore, as the imminence of war was keeping the King fully occupied at home, His Majesty felt he could not spare troops for an overseas

[10] Iberville to associates, Nov. 17, 1689, Archives des colonies, C¹¹A, 10, 499.

[11] Instructions to Frontenac, June 4, 1689, *Collection de manuscrits*, I, 452–453.

[12] "Brevets de confirmation," *ibid.*, II, 39.

venture and suggested to Frontenac that he solve the problem, temporarily at least, by making peace with the Iroquois, thus protecting the St. Lawrence from their savage raids. This un-aggressive measure roused the opposition of Callières, who felt that such a policy would be suicidal, and he wrote frantically urging an attack on the British posts. Frontenac, for his part, did his level best to reconcile the Iroquois; but English influence at Fort Orange was too strong for him. Balked in this direction, he turned his attention to an attack on his southern neighbor. Fortunately for his purpose there were at this time over 1,500 soldiers in Canada, and with these as a nucleus he proceeded to organize his expedition.

At this time a chaotic condition existed in the New York colony, a condition engendered by an event known in history as Leisler's Rebellion. The cause of this outbreak was to a certain extent religious. A fanatical German immigrant named Jacob Leisler, who had built up a prosperous wine business in Manhattan, started the trouble. Upon the abdication of James II, whom he detested because of his Roman Catholic faith, Leisler proclaimed that there was no legal government in the colony and proceeded to set up one of his own, terrifying the citizens by spreading a baseless rumor that the governor, Robert Livingston, was about to betray the place to the French. Having gained control of Manhattan, Leisler next turned his attention to Albany and sent a force under one Jacob Milborne to seize Fort Orange. Mayor Peter Schuyler, however, had different ideas about this and bluntly refused to give up the post, thus forcing Milborne to stump the town in a vain attempt to get the burghers to side with him, offering them liberties and privileges which he said had been denied them during the reign of King James. To all this the burghers turned a deaf ear, and after a week's fruitless effort he was obliged to disband his company and return to Manhattan. This was in November, 1689.

Although the authorities at Albany took no stock in Milborne's rantings, they were keenly alive to the danger of an attack from Canada and had taken steps to strengthen their defenses. In midsummer a rumor had gone the rounds hinting that an army of French and Indians had been seen on Lake George, and this rumor was not put to rest until a scouting party sent out to investigate it had reported it to be groundless.[13] Then came letters from Boston warning Mayor Schuyler to be prepared for a coming attack. The mayor needed no urging. He ordered that a stricter guard mount be kept in the town, and to make this effective he ordered a fine to be levied on officers guilty of negligence.[14] But when it came to putting into operation a plan of defense the authorities quickly found that they needed financial help, for it cost money to equip Fort Orange and erect blockhouses at strategic points in the outlying district. In order to obtain the funds a letter was sent to Leisler explaining the situation and requesting aid. Leisler proved unco-operative; he sent four small guns with a supply of ammunition, but he drew the line at money. Nothing daunted by this rebuff, Mayor Schuyler called a meeting of the town fathers at which a tax was levied on the citizens sufficiently heavy to meet current expenses.[15] The convention also passed a resolution forbidding emissaries of Leisler's faction from entering the city before they had given assurance that they came with the intention of assisting, not hindering, in the work of defense; for the fathers had no wish to admit people at this critical hour who might "turn the government of the city upside down, to make themselves masters of the fort and city." [16]

If Milborne met with no success at Albany, he did achieve something at Schenectady. Albany was well established and governed by men of position and means who were able, as we have seen, to take care of demagoguery as well as provide for their

---

[13] Joel Munsell, *The Annals of Albany* (Albany, 1859), II, 108.
[14] *Ibid.*, p. 104.   [15] *Ibid.*, pp. 113–114.
[16] *Ibid.*, p. 132.

own safety. Schenectady, on the other hand, was a small frontier town of four hundred inhabitants mostly of an uneducated class susceptible to the type of blandishment offered by Leisler. Milborne began operations by writing to Adam Vrooman, an influential citizen of the place, suggesting that the inhabitants come to Albany, where they would receive the rights and privileges hitherto denied them by King James. This invitation Vrooman declined in behalf of his fellow townsmen, saying that such an exodus would cause grave disquiet among the neighboring Indians "to the general ruin of the country." [17] Yet Milborne did manage to sow some of his seditious ideas among the people, or at least among enough of them to cause trouble. Robert Livingston in writing to Sir Edmund Andros after the destruction of the settlement lays the blame largely on Leisler's baleful influence. "The people of that town," he says in referring to Schenectady, "were so bigoted to Leisler that they would not obey any of the magistrates neither would they entertain the soldiers sent thither by the Convention [at Albany] of all; nothing but men sent from Leisler would do their turn." They even threatened to harm Captain Joannes Sanders Glenn if he should venture to mount guard. As proof of all this, Livingston asserts that after the massacre copies of Leisler's seditious letters were found "all bloody upon Schenectady streets." [18]

As Frontenac outlined the plan of campaign, the French were to be divided into three detachments, each with a different objective, and each with a different point of departure. The division to which Iberville was appointed was to assemble at Montreal and move against Fort Orange. It consisted of 210 men, one-half French, the other half Indians. The command was given to Sainte-Helène and Nicolas D'Ailleboust de Mantet, while among the officers were La Marque de Montigny and a younger scion of the Lemoyne family, François de Bienville. The second corps was to

[17] *Ibid.*, p. 140.   [18] *Docs. Rel. Col. Hist. N.Y.*, III, 708.

start from Three Rivers, the third from Quebec; these had western and eastern Massachusetts as their respective objectives.[19]

Sainte-Helène's division left Montreal during the bitter cold of early February, 1690. To embark on such an undertaking at this time, when subzero weather held the forests in its tenacious grip, was indeed a bold venture even for these hardy woodsmen; but the very audacity of the scheme insured its success. The orders given Sainte-Helène by Governor Frontenac were of a general nature; even the point of attack was left to the discretion of the commanders, an arrangement which was felt more advisable since those on the spot were the best judges of what should be done. Besides, it was necessary to keep the Indians satisfied, and there was no telling in advance what these fickle savages might do. The wisdom of this measure was justified when the expedition, after a six days' march up the Richelieu River and across the broad expanse of Lake Champlain, halted to discuss the situation. As the leaders paused to decide on their route, the Indians, through their chief the Great Mohawk, clamored to know whither they were being led. Sainte-Helène answered that they planned to attack Fort Orange, though they had the option of changing the objective. The savages for their part considered the forces too weak for such an ambitious undertaking and became vociferous in their objections, one brave inquiring sarcastically, "Since when have the French become so bold?" The dispute waxed hot. Knowing well the vacillating character of these people, the French commander decided to postpone the decision until they arrived at the junction of the roads leading to Fort Orange and to Schenectady. Moreover, as the Indians were better acquainted with the territory, their opinion as to what point ought to be attacked should

[19] Instructions to Frontenac, *ibid.*, IX, 422–426. For an account of the expedition see "Narrative of Occurences," *ibid.*, 466–469. See also M. Van Rensselaer, "Memoir of the French and Indian Expedition against the Province of New York," *Proceedings of New York Historical Society*, 1846, pp. 101–123.

have some weight. For several days more they trudged through ice and snow until they reached the junction, where Sainte-Helène, influenced by the Indians, announced that they would proceed against Schenectady.

One is inclined to wonder at this point whether the French or Indians had any knowledge as to what was going on in Schenectady and Albany. They knew, of course, of the disorders caused by Leisler's Rebellion, and they knew that Albany was by far the larger of the two places, but did they fully understand the weakness of the former caused by Leisler's propaganda? In a letter written by the Convention at Albany shortly after the attack, the writers ascribe the catastrophe

to the factions and divisions which were amongst the people and their great disobedience to their officers; for they would obey no commands or keep any watch, so that the enemy having discovered their negligence and security by their praying Mohawk Indians (who were in the said place two or three days before the attack was made) came in and broke open their very doors before any soul knew of it.[20]

This indicates that Christian Indians—possibly converts of the Jesuit missionaries—had tipped off the French as to the vulnerability of Schenectady. But if this was so it could only have been two or three days before the attack; and there is no reason to believe that the French commanders had any knowledge of the disorganized condition of the settlement when they decided to march against it. They only knew that it was a far weaker place than Albany.

The die being cast, the little army resumed its march, and at the end of nine days, after wading through freezing water, breaking the ice to get a firm foothold on the ground beneath, it arrived at four o'clock on the afternoon of February 19 [21] at a spot within

[20] *The Andros Tracts*, ed. by W. H. Whitmore (Boston, 1868), III, 114–115.

[21] English records say the ninth, which would be the nineteenth according to the Gregorian calendar. The French account, as shown in *Docs.*

two leagues of Schenectady. Here the Great Mohawk harangued the jaded troops. "He urged on all to perform their duty and to forget their past fatigues in the hope of taking ample revenge for the injuries they had received from the Iroquois at the solicitation of the English, and of washing them out in the blood of those traitors." Heartened by this address, the soldiers after a brief rest set out to attack the settlement.

The little town of Schenectady, or Corlear, as it was then called, was built in the form of a rectangle, the palisade being a ten-foot wall of pine logs pierced by two gates, one opening on the road leading to Fort Orange, the other on the opposite side. Its location was slightly west of Ferry Street in modern Schenectady. The population numbered four hundred souls living in eighty houses, practically all of which were within the stockade. At the northerly end of this enclosure was a blockhouse commanded by Lieutenant Enos Talmadge with twenty-four men under him. He had been recently sent there with this detachment to guard against any possible attack. While the French were resting on their arms two leagues from the village, the sturdy Dutch and English settlers were preparing to retire for the night, confident that no danger threatened them at this time of year. The idea of an attack by Canadians would have been ridiculed had anyone been bold enough to suggest it. How could any sane men think of launching a military expedition from Montreal in the depth of winter? So they retired to bed leaving the gates of the palisade wide open, guarded only by two snow men placed there in a spirit of derision.

_____

Rel. Col. Hist. N.Y., IX, 466–469, says that the expedition left Montreal early in February and covered marches of five, eight, and nine days, which would make the date of arrival much later in the month. It is possible, however, judging from the somewhat ambiguous wording, that the eight days' march may be meant to include the first march of five or six days. This, added to the nine days' march, would make it a seventeen days' journey from Montreal to Schenectady, which would jibe with the date in the French account.

When their scouts returned with word that all was clear, the French shouldered their packs and resumed their march. By eleven o'clock they had reached the town. It was now cold, intensely cold; a chill wind blew across the plain compelling the invaders to move about restlessly in vain attempts to keep warm. Immediate action was necessary, if only to keep the men from freezing. The original plan of waiting until well past midnight to insure complete surprise was perforce abandoned, and preparations were made to attack at once. The raiders approached the settlement on its northern side and halted before the open gate. To prevent the inhabitants from escaping by the opposite gate and sending runners to Fort Orange, Iberville led a detachment around the palisade to block this outlet; but in the darkness they missed the opening and made a complete circle of the enclosure only to find themselves back with the main body. At a given signal the entire force burst in upon the settlement. D'Ailleboust de Mantet made for the blockhouse, drove in the door, slaughtered the garrison, and set the building on fire. Then the sack began, the Indians as usual leading in the carnage. The settlers, roused from their sleep, rushed half-clad from their burning dwellings only to be cut down by the attackers as they appeared in the streets. Only in a few cases were the citizens able to offer any resistance, and only in two or three instances were orders given to spare any building. That stout burgher, Adam Vrooman, whose house stood opposite the north gate, was awakened by the uproar and managed to bar his door and arm his family before the attackers reached him. Through windows and loopholes he kept up such a brisk fire that the French at last agreed to spare his life. An effort was also made to spare the home of the Reverend Peter Tassemaker in order to obtain some information from its owner; but as no one knew which it was, the French fired it by mistake, and the minister perished in the flames with all his papers. Better fortune, however, befell a widow with her six children to whose house Montigny was carried when wounded, as orders were given to spare it for his sake. At the end of two hours the village was in ruins, with the exception of five or six houses, while sixty-two men, women, and children lay dead in the streets, many the victims of Indian atrocities.

The details of the massacre do not make for pretty reading. In the French account they are glossed over with the statement that fifty or sixty persons were spared, "they having escaped the first fury of the attack." Of the nature of this first attack we can learn best from the letter of the Convention at Albany referred to above. "The cruelties committed at said place," runs the letter, "no pen can write nor tongue can express; the women big with child ripped up and the children alive thrown into the flames, and their heads dashed in pieces against doors and windows." [22] Such barbarous deeds were merely a repetition of those committed by the Iroquois in their attacks on the French settlements and appear to have been accepted as the usual concomitants of Indian warfare. Between the savage allies of the French and the savage allies of the English there was little choice.

At daybreak Iberville proceeded to the house of Captain Glenn, who resided on the other side of the Mohawk River. He was ready for them, and having armed his servants and Indians, refused to surrender. Earlier Glenn had treated some French prisoners kindly, and this had become known to Governor Frontenac, who had given orders to spare him. Iberville was therefore able to induce him to surrender on promise of protection for himself and his property. The Canadians entered the house, were cheerfully entertained by the captain, and eventually brought him to the settlement where he met the French commanders.

Taking stock of the situation, the French found they had succeeded in completely destroying the town. The amount of damage was estimated at 400,000 *livres*, and the captives when lined up for inspection proved to be some fifty or sixty old men, women, and children, who in some miraculous manner, as we

[22] *The Andros Tracts*, III, 114.

have said, managed to escape "the first fury of the attack." There was also a party of thirty Mohawks whom the French spared, not because of any affection for these savages who for years had been their mortal enemies, but to show the Iroquois nation that the raid was a white man's affair, not in any way directed against them.

So thoroughly had the job been done that nothing more could be gained by remaining, and besides there was always the danger of reinforcements coming up from Fort Orange. Orders were accordingly given for the return march. At noon the troops were lined up for inspection. The officers selected twenty-seven prisoners from the group of wretched beings before them and gave the order to leave Schenectady. The rest of the prisoners were allowed to escape. The journey back to Montreal proved no easy going. Encumbered by the wounded who had to be carried on litters and loaded with whatever plunder they had managed to save from the conflagration, they started off, taking some fifty horses, most of which were killed for food along the way. The return to Canada was not accomplished without some mishaps attributable to bad roads and lack of food. Sixty leagues from Schenectady the French separated from the Indians, as the latter found it necessary to depart on a hunting expedition. At the same time D'Ailleboust detailed Iberville and a companion to proceed with two Indian guides directly to Montreal and advise the authorities of the success of the undertaking. The reception tendered these two Canadians was, we may well imagine, an enthusiastic one; and though the achievement was but the slaughter of defenseless men, women, and children, it was regarded as a triumph for French arms. It was, all things considered, perhaps the best defense that could be offered against the raids on the valley of the St. Lawrence carried out by the Iroquois allies of the English and the Dutch.

The reaction at Albany when news of the massacre reached the town was, as might be expected, immediate and violent. The attack had been made on Saturday night, and at five o'clock Sunday morning one Symon Schermerhorn, who had escaped the first assault, dragged himself into town, bringing news of the disaster. With pardonable exaggeration he announced that the settlement had been attacked by an army of 1,900 men, and the city fathers of Albany jumped to the conclusion that this formidable host would soon march on them. The following day a band of mounted scouts under Captain Jonathan Bull was sent to inspect Schenectady and rouse the Mohawk villages in the neighborhood. The going was hard, as heavy snow had fallen during the night, but they managed to get through. The enthusiasm of the Indians was not great, and it took three days to stir them up to action. They expressed wonder that the Canadians had been able to carry out such a raid when the English had spoken so vaingloriously of the might of their king; but in the end they agreed to accompany the white men on a punitive expedition. The success of this expedition was not impressive. The Indians finally overtook the French on Lake Champlain, where they managed to capture fifteen—the rest escaped over the ice with their plunder—and from them obtained the information that in the spring the French would launch another expedition on a much larger scale with a force of 1,500 men, equipped with all the paraphernalia of war, and march upon Albany.[23]

The expedition against Schenectady was the first of the military expeditions launched by Governor Frontenac on his return to Canada, and it had proved a gratifying success. It might indeed be regarded as an augury of expeditions to come. Accomplished at a loss of only seventeen Frenchmen, of whom one was killed in the assault, it had struck at the very heart of New York, an auspicious beginning for the new governor. The other two undertakings had also met with success. That from Three Rivers had captured Salmon Falls in New Hampshire and had inspired the

[23] Robert Livingston to Edmund Andros, Apr. 14, 1690, *Docs. Rel. Col. Hist. N.Y.*, III, 708.

Indians to take the post of Pemaquid near the mouth of the Kennebec River; while the detachment from Quebec had made a successful raid on Casco Bay, where it had joined the forces which the Baron de Saint-Castin,[24] son-in-law of the Abnaki chieftain Madockawando, sent from his headquarters on the Penobscot River near modern Castine. All New England was now ablaze. A meeting of the representatives of New York and the New England colonies was hurriedly called to decide what plans should be pursued to save the British settlements from the French and Indians. In the face of the triple attack which the Canadians had launched with such marked success, the English realized that they had a formidable foeman in the person of Count Frontenac; and taking a leaf out of his book, they too decided that a powerful offense was the best defense and determined then and there to send out two war parties—one to march against Montreal from Fort Orange, the other to sail for Quebec under Sir William Phips.

Blissfully unaware of the impending danger, Governor Frontenac now determined to attack Port Nelson. The Company of the North had been urging this for some time, while the Court had been won over to the value of such an undertaking, especially since the outbreak of the war. We can easily imagine that Iberville could hardly restrain his impatience to be off to the Bay on an expedition which would be under his sole command. He had already requested the associates of the company residing in France to send over a ship, specifying a twenty-gun craft of 120 or 150 tons, and they had responded nobly by dispatching the *Armes de la Compagnie*. By June he was ready, and on the twenty-second he received his commission from Frontenac. A few days later he sailed with the *Armes* and a ship named the *Sainte-Anne* (not the hulk at the mouth of the Moose River), the latter commanded by Simon Pierre Denys de Bonaventure, who was to be his com-

[24] Jean-Vincent d'Abbadie, Baron de Saint-Castin.

panion in many adventures. He arrived at Port Nelson in the middle of August.[25]

Before Iberville left the governor conferred on him as a mark of his esteem, a fief, giving the rights of high, middle, and low justice to its owner. It consisted of a tract of land on Chaleur Bay twelve leagues front by ten in depth, comprising within its boundaries the Restigouche River. This grant was made on condition of his performing fealty and homage for it at Quebec, and, among other things, of his preserving for the King's use all timber suitable for shipbuilding which might be found thereon.[26] There is no evidence that Iberville ever did anything with this property, as he presently ceded it to Françoise Cailleteau, widow of Richard Denys de Fronsac.[27]

After dropping anchor at the mouth of the Hayes River, Iberville landed with a reconnoitering party of ten men to obtain information on the condition of the post by capturing, if possible, some stragglers in the neighborhood. Unfortunately, as he advanced he came upon a sentinel who had been placed at a spot half a league from the sea to watch for the appearance of enemy vessels. There happened to be in the river at this time three of the Hudson's Bay Company's ships: the *Royal Hudson's Bay*, the frigate *Dering*, and the fireship *Prosperous*, commanded by Captains Leonard Edgecomb, James Young, and Michael Grimmington, respectively. These vessels had been sent out by the British government at the request of the Hudson's Bay Company, which in a petition to the Privy Council pointed out the destitute condition of the posts and the impossibility of defending them against French aggression. The first two ships had crews of fifty men each, the third a complement of fifteen. Against such overwhelm-

[25] Report of Champigny, *Collection de manuscrits*, II, 31.
[26] Frontenac signed the deed on May 26, 1690 (*Titles and Documents Relating to the Seigniorial Tenure* [Quebec, 1852], pp. 118–119).
[27] *Report on Canadian Archives*, 1884, p. 10.

ing odds Iberville felt himself helpless,[28] for his crews numbered but eighty men, and besides he would have to contend with the garrison in the fort. The only sensible thing he could do was to retreat as quickly as possible. But he had been seen, the alarm had been given by the sentinel, and the commander of Port Nelson, Governor George Geyer, hastened to dispatch the *Dering* after the audacious Frenchmen. Seeing the impossibility of resisting such an attack, Iberville hastily piled his men into their boat and rowed desperately to his ship, pursued by two English boats which kept up a running fire. By good fortune, just as he set sail the *Dering* grounded on a rock at low tide too far away to bring her artillery in to play, and the French ships steered out to sea. They headed for Hudson Strait to mislead the English into thinking that they were bound for home, but when night fell the commander veered his course toward the mouth of the Severn River, determined to make the enemy pay for his repulse at Port Nelson.

Here he met his brother Maricourt with the *Saint-François-Xavier*. Together they now proposed to attack a weakly fortified post, dependent largely on Port Nelson, called Fort Churchill. It was probably little more than a warehouse for the storage of furs and the accommodation of a small party of traders. Its capture offered no great difficulty; in fact the defenders soon saw the futility of holding out against the superior French forces. They were unwilling, however, to let so valuable a prize fall into enemy hands, hence they set fire to their buildings and took refuge at Port Nelson. Though unable to extinguish the fire and save the fort, Iberville did manage to rescue a fine supply of beaver skins from the conflagration. These he carried to the Albany River, where he wintered with the *Sainte-Anne*, while he sent the *Armes de la Compagnie* to Charlton Island.

Meanwhile the *Saint-François-Xavier* and a detachment of

[28] Petitions of Hudson's Bay Company, Mar. 27 and Apr. 17, 1690, *Acts of the Privy Council of England, Colonial Series, 1680–1720,* pp. 154–155.

forty men were sent to Fort St. Louis with an assortment of goods to be used in trading with the Indians.²⁹ This done, she collected a supply of furs at Rupert River and, loaded with all those obtained at Fort Churchill, sailed for Quebec in the charge of Maricourt with Bonaventure in command, arriving there in November.³⁰ When she reached the Isle aux Coudres in the St. Lawrence River, Maricourt was met by Charles de Longueuil, who informed him that an English fleet under Sir William Phips was then besieging Quebec. Fearful of losing his valuable cargo to the enemy, Maricourt disembarked with a number of his men and proceeded to the city, at the same time ordering Bonaventure to take the ship to France. Longueuil also brought Maricourt the sad news that Sainte-Helène had been grievously wounded during the siege and was now lying at the Hôtel-Dieu. Sainte-Helène lived on for several weeks; he died on December 4, and his two brothers, Charles and Paul, were with him at the end. He died at the age of thirty-one, the first of the Lemoynes to perish in the defense of his country. One can imagine the grief felt by Iberville when the news reached him later on, for Jacques de Sainte-Helène was the brother who had been closest to him, the one who had shared in the first campaign to Hudson Bay and had accompanied him on the expedition to Schenectady the previous winter.

Of Iberville's adventures at Fort Ste. Anne during the winter we know nothing, save that he did a profitable business with the Indians, and eventually anchored the *Sainte-Anne*, and probably the *Armes*, at Quebec on October 19, 1691,³¹ with a beaver cargo worth 80,000 *livres*, and small furs to the value of 6,600 *livres*. After turning this consignment over to the Company of the North, he sailed at once in the *Sainte-Anne* for France, anxious to interest the Court in a further scheme for capturing Port Nelson.

²⁹ Letters of La Potherie, in Tyrrell, *op. cit.*, pp. 255–256.
³⁰ "Narrative of Occurences, 1689, 1690," *Docs. Rel. Col. Hist. N.Y.*, IX, 491; [Catalogne], *op. cit.*, p. 33.
³¹ *Docs. Rel. Col. Hist. N.Y.*, IX, 526.

CHAPTER IV

Difficulties and Delays

DESPITE his failure before Port Nelson, Iberville was well received at Court; after all, he had struck a serious blow at the Hudson's Bay Company when he carried off the booty from Fort Churchill. This blow may be regarded as the beginning of his career as scourge of the great company, and so heavy were the damages he inflicted upon its trade—damages which were felt long after his death—that for the next twenty-five years the company was unable to pay a dividend.[1]

The King, as Iberville discovered soon after his arrival in France, was still interested in the capture of the British post, very much so; indeed, His Majesty also had plans for the subjugation of New England and New York, for the attack on Quebec by Sir William Phips, even though it had been repulsed, made him realize that the best way to protect his colonies was to launch a bold offensive against those of his rival. For this purpose Count Frontenac had been devising plans that involved, getting control of four distinct territories: the West, Hudson Bay, Newfoundland, and Acadia. The last-named territory had been for years the scene of incessant struggles between the French and the English colonists.

[1] Douglas Mackay, *The Honourable Company* (Indianapolis, 1936), Appendix D.

It was claimed by both, and the boundary line separating the two claims had never been satisfactorily adjusted. The Acadians and the New Englanders were usually in a chronic state of war in which the latter often appeared in the guise of pirates conducting private raids. The English pointed to the St. Croix River, running between modern Maine and New Brunswick, as their eastern terminus, while the French placed the line of demarcation as far down the coast as the Kennebec. Whatever might be the legal aspects of the case, this region was considered by the English as fair game, to be taken over whenever possible.

During Iberville's absence in Hudson Bay important events had taken place on the Acadian frontier. The success of the expeditions sent out from Three Rivers and Quebec had spread such consternation in New England that the inhabitants determined to launch a counterattack as a means of self-preservation. Late in April, 1690, a fleet was dispatched from Boston under Sir William Phips, which captured Port Royal in Nova Scotia and looted the place thoroughly, exacting from the wretched inhabitants an oath of loyalty to William and Mary. Phips's subordinate, Captain John Alden, also seized the Acadian fort of that romantic figure the Baron de Saint-Castin, as well as some minor places. The effect of these successes on the Abnakis, natives of Acadia, was electrical. Long controlled by the French, they began to look upon the victorious Puritans with feelings of respect not unmixed with fear. If these white men were so successful, it might be wise to placate them. Accordingly, a deputation of chiefs signed a treaty of amity with the commissioners of Massachusetts. Decidedly the French were losing Acadia.

To make matters worse, the gallant effort made by the Canadians in repelling the English fleet before Quebec appears to have exhausted them, or rather to have exhausted their supplies. Crops for the past two years had been below normal, and now the warehouses contained but a month's quota of provisions. Prices rose as a consequence, compelling the inhabitants to go on short rations.

The situation was further aggravated by the sudden arrival of 150 refugees, Basque sailors who had been driven from Newfoundland waters by English freebooters and who had to be cared for somehow.[2]

King Louis was not unmindful of the difficulties facing his colonists, and during the winter of 1690-1691, while Iberville was still in the Bay, he evolved plans to remedy the situation both in its economic and in its military aspects. He could not at this time spare soldiers for Canada, but he did appropriate 24,000 *livres* for arms, munitions, and merchandise, in addition to 20,000 *livres* to complete the fortifications of Quebec.[3] On the military side he planned for maneuvers on three fronts: Acadia, Port Nelson, and Newfoundland. At the instigation of the Comte de Frontenac, who had dispatched a trusted aide, the Chevalier Robineau de Villebon, to Versailles to emphasize the necessity of winning back the wavering Abnakis from their alliance with New England—an alliance that endangered all eastern Canada —His Majesty appointed the said Villebon to be governor of Acadia. Villebon was immediately ordered to embark on the *Soleil d'Afrique*, now commanded by Denys de Bonaventure, and proceed to Quebec with a load of presents for the Abnakis. Here he was to consult with Count Frontenac about arrangements for the recapture of Port Royal, and also about selecting a suitable place for a rendezvous with the Abnakis, a place where he could distribute the presents.[4]

At the same time the King placed the Sieur du Tast in command of the *Hazardeux*, loaded her with provisions, and sent her to Quebec with the *Soleil* and a fleet of merchantmen carrying the much-needed munitions and supplies. Here Du Tast was to pick

[2] Henri Lorin, *Le Comte de Frontenac* (Paris, 1895), p. 396.

[3] Minister to Champigny, Apr. 7, 1691, *Report on Canadian Archives, 1899, supplement*, p. 290.

[4] Instructions for Villebon, Apr. 7, 1691, *Collection de manuscrits*, II, 45; instructions for Bonaventure, Apr. 7, 1691, *ibid.*, pp. 48-50.

up the two ships supplied by the Company of the North, join Iberville in the Bay, and serve under him in the proposed attack on Port Nelson. Then he was to proceed to Newfoundland, harass the English settlers there, and return to France—quite an undertaking for one season.[5] The magnitude of the task and the distances to be traversed were not too well understood by the enthusiastic French Court. While issuing these orders, the King, mindful of Iberville's services, seized the occasion to sign a brevet confirming the grant of land on Chaleur Bay which had been previously made him by Count Frontenac,[6] and he also raised him to the rank of frigate captain, or *capitaine de frégatte*, to use the French title. He was then only thirty years of age.

On the first day of July, 1691, the *Soleil d'Afrique* dropped anchor before Quebec, bringing the joyful news that a fleet was on the way with provisions for the needy community; and twelve days later the Sieur du Tast appeared before the city with fourteen sail.[7] Then a hitch occurred in the proceedings, for Du Tast remained in Quebec. The excuse given for failure to carry out the royal orders—that the season was too far advanced for an expedition to start for the Bay—was rather a lame one, since the summer had just begun. Perhaps, if the truth were known, Du Tast resented the idea of sharing his command and the glory of victory, if he succeeded in capturing the post, with a mere colonial officer like Iberville, especially as the profits of the enterprise were to go entirely to the company.

When a board of commissioners was appointed to look into this matter, Du Tast appeared before them saying that the *Hazardeux* was old and unable to resist the ice of the Bay, while his crew was exhausted and without the necessary heavy clothing. The board accepted these excuses and Frontenac concurred in the decision, though his agreement may have been influenced by a reluctance

---

[5] Instructions for Du Tast, Apr. 7, 1691, *ibid.*, p. 44.
[6] *Report on Canadian Archives, 1899, supplement*, p. 289.
[7] *Docs. Rel. Col. Hist. N.Y.*, IX, 519.

to send the commander so far afield when a repetition of the previous year's unpleasantness at the hands of Sir William Phips might take place at any moment. Du Tast was therefore detailed to cruise in the Gulf of St. Lawrence, where some English men-of-war were causing trouble, while Bonaventure was ordered to carry Villebon to his destination and then return to France.[8] Bonaventure reached the St. John River in New Brunswick. It was here that Villebon was to land and take command as governor of Acadia; but instead of establishing himself near the coast he proceeded up the river to modern Fredericton, where near the mouth of the Nashwaak River he built Fort Naxouat, which was to be his headquarters for several years to come. On October 19, after Villebon's departure from Quebec, Iberville arrived there in the *Sainte-Anne* with a cargo of furs from the Bay.[9] After unloading the merchandise, he left at once with this ship for France, where he was presently joined by Bonaventure.

Scarcely had the French Court learned that the attack on Port Nelson had been abandoned when Iberville arrived at Versailles full of enthusiasm for another attempt the following year. While at Quebec he had learned of Du Tast's mission, and he guessed that the King would lend a ready ear to a concrete plan for seizing the northern post. In this he was not mistaken, for by this time the glowing reports of his ability, which Frontenac and his intendant, Jean Bochart de Champigny, had forwarded to the King, pointed to him as the one man to lead such an expedition. Preparations were, therefore, quickly made. Two years before, Louis Phélypeaux, Comte de Pontchartrain, had been appointed Minister of Marine to succeed the Marquis de Seignelay, and it was he who on February 27, 1692, announced the King's intention of sending out the *Poli*, a great Dutch square-stern frigate of 500 tons' burden, carrying thirty-eight guns, under the personal command of Iberville, to be accompanied by the *Envieux*, a frigate of thirty-

[8] *Ibid.*, p. 525.
[9] *Ibid.*, p. 526.

four guns under Denys de Bonaventure.[10] They were to have with them the *Sainte-Anne*, which Iberville had brought from Canada the previous autumn. The two commanders were to sail from La Rochelle and convoy a merchant fleet to Canada, for the war with England made the transatlantic journey dangerous to French shipping. After discharging this duty, Iberville was to pick up two vessels, supplied him by the company, and proceed to Hudson Bay in the *Poli* to effect the capture of Port Nelson. Should he succeed, he was to remain at this post during the winter and send the *Poli* back to France in the charge of Pierre de Lorme.[11]

With this much-desired possibility in prospect, the commander applied himself energetically to perfecting his plans, joyfully announcing that the *Poli* would be ready to sail by the end of April. He hoped, if nothing went wrong, to reach Quebec in about two months, which would give him ample time to refit, collect other ships, and start for Port Nelson in mid-July. Allowing fifty days for the journey, he would be off the Hayes River the first week of September and would have plenty of time to begin military operations. The vessels he now planned to take with him to the Bay were (besides the *Poli*) the *Sainte-Anne*, which was to accompany him from France, and the *Armes de la Compagnie*, then at Quebec, both hardy veterans of the North. On reaching the Bay he proposed to send the *Armes* to the Severn River, there to await a ship coming from James Bay with a cargo that might amount to 80,000 pounds of furs. The *Armes* was to bring these furs to Port Nelson and transfer them to the *Poli*. These two ships were then to return to France, leaving Iberville with the *Sainte-Anne* to winter in the Bay. He hoped to have the vessels ready to leave before September 25, as later on they were likely to run into dangerous weather. Once the *Poli* and the *Armes* had left Port

[10] Minister to Bégon, Feb. 27, 1692, *Report on Canadian Archives, 1899, supplement*, p. 292.

[11] *Rapport de l'archiviste de la Province de Quebec, 1927–1928* (Quebec, 1921–1945), pp. 198–199.

Nelson he proposed to make the *Sainte-Anne* his headquarters for the winter, since there would not be enough time to construct suitable buildings on shore. From this point of vantage the commander would blockade the English post, shutting off the garrison from fishing and hunting, so that they would eventually succumb to scurvy or be obliged to surrender. He also intended to relieve the monotony of these proceedings by occasional bombardments. By these methods he hoped to gain the upper hand before the arrival of spring brought back the Indians—perhaps as many as 1,000— who would seize the occasion to make the English and French traders bid against each other for their furs.

What Iberville was aiming at was, of course, a monopoly. Such a monopoly would, he firmly believed, enable him to gather enough furs to do a very lucrative business; in fact, he urged the King to send out a large well-armed vessel to accompany the *Poli* on her outward voyage, for he expected the English would send out armed help, and he also felt certain that he could fill such a vessel's hold with a valuable cargo. During the winter Iberville would occupy himself with making a thorough geographical survey of the region with special attention to the possibility of finding a passage to the Western Sea, that is, the Pacific Ocean.[12]

Alas for the best-laid plans. Iberville and Bonaventure got off to a fair start on May 14, but the passage was a slow one. It took them three months to reach their destination; the ships were held back by head winds as they buffeted their way across the Atlantic. On entering the St. Lawrence Iberville met a small vessel bound for Hudson Bay with a cargo of supplies. He stopped this ship, and transferring her contents and most of her crew to the *Sainte-Anne* ordered her to follow the fleet. In the St. Lawrence progress was even slower, and it was August 19 before he anchored off Quebec, much too late to think of going to the Bay that year.

Since it was now impossible to carry out Iberville's part of the

[12] Iberville to Minister, Apr. 24, 1692, Archives des colonies, C^{11}A, 12.2, 180.

program, Frontenac turned his attention to the work assigned to Bonaventure. According to his original instructions the commander of the *Envieux* was to continue his voyage by going to Fort Naxouat on the St. John River to bring supplies to Villebon. This was simple enough, but Frontenac, now that he had Iberville and his huge *Poli* at his disposal, determined to turn this peaceful errand into a warlike expedition on a large scale. News had been received that the redoubtable Phips, with one ship of forty-eight guns and two other vessels whose aggregate crews totaled four hundred men, was lying in wait for the Frenchman coming to relieve Villebon. Although the rumor later proved to be untrue, at the time Frontenac thought it unwise to send Bonaventure alone, so he ordered Iberville to accompany him. The two commanders were to reinforce their crews with forty or fifty Canadians who, in addition to the men they already had on board, would give them ample strength to meet any New Englanders they were likely to encounter; and, in order to prevent those in Boston from learning of the expedition, they were advised to capture and destroy any English boats that crossed their path. They were to stop first at Baie Verte in Northumberland Strait, where they were to land Villebon's supplies, as it was safer to have the supplies transported across the narrow isthmus that separates this strait from an arm of the Bay of Fundy, known as Chignecto Bay, than to allow the little fleet to venture into the bay itself. From Chignecto Bay the supplies could be easily carried to the St. John River. After leaving the supplies, the two ships were to proceed to the Penobscot River, where they would meet Saint-Castin and a band of two hundred friendly Indians who had been ordered to assemble there. With these reinforcements they could attack some of the settlements on the New England coast, particularly the fort at Pemaquid. Iberville was also ordered to cruise off the coasts of New England and Manhattan.[13]

[13] Instructions given by Frontenac, Sept. 12, 1692, *ibid.*, C[11]A, 12.2, 187; Frontenac to Minister, Sept. 15, 1692, *Collection de manuscrits*, II,

For some reason there appears to have been considerable delay in getting started; it was September 22 when Iberville in the *Poli* and Bonaventure in the *Envieux* left Quebec, and the Indians were already gathered on the Penobscot. The two ships convoyed three merchantmen to Gaspé. After leaving them there safely they proceeded to Percé. Here they found one M. Jerpos, whom Iberville sent with Bonaventure to pick up some pilots familiar with Acadian waters when the latter went to discharge his cargo of supplies for Villebon. Iberville left Percé on October 5 and nine days later anchored at Sydney, where he was joined by Bonaventure. The two ships then took the route to Mount Desert, arriving there on October 24. Much to the two commanders' surprise they found the place deserted.

In order to understand what now happened it is necessary to describe a curious chain of events that had recently taken place. At this time there was in Quebec an English prisoner named John Nelson who had been captured the year before while on a trading voyage to Nova Scotia. He appears to have been treated in a friendly manner by Governor Frontenac, for he was a gentleman of good family. He was allowed the freedom of the city, so that he was able to learn about a plan for an attack on New England. The plan hinged upon an agreement between Frontenac and a Penobscot chieftain, Madockawando, who had come to Quebec with five English prisoners and had been persuaded by the governor to raise a band of Indians and await the French ships at Mount Desert, or somewhere in the neighborhood. To seal the bargain the governor gave presents to Madockawando and his followers; but they complained loudly of the paucity of the gifts and vented their dissatisfaction by confiding their troubles to Nelson.[14] Anxious to save his countrymen from the impending

---

84–85. The instructions to Bonaventure (*ibid.*, II, 81–82) were superseded, to some extent, when Iberville did not go to the Bay.

[14] Letter of Nelson in Thomas Hutchinson, *The History of the Colony of Massachusetts Bay* (London, 1760), I, 378–379.

disaster, Nelson entrusted a letter telling of the plot to two French soldiers, Arnaud du Vignon and François Albert, and bribed them to carry it to Boston.

At this time Sir William Phips, newly appointed governor of Massachusetts, was attempting to enlist two Canadian prisoners in Boston, Jacques Petitpas and Charles de Loreau, Sieur de Saint-Aubin, in the not-very-creditable plot to kidnap the Baron de Saint-Castin and his family from their headquarters on the Penobscot River as the price of their freedom. When the two deserters from Quebec arrived with Nelson's letter, they too were persuaded to join in the unsavory enterprise. From the outcome it is evident that the Canadians fell in with the governor's scheme in order to escape from captivity, though the soldiers were probably willing to see the business through for the sake of the reward.

Now that he had reached his destination Iberville was eager to get operations under way. He at once sent a boat to Saint-Castin at his place on the Penobscot River, some twenty leagues distant, with a message advising him of the fleet's arrival. Meanwhile a twenty-ton fishing smack, having on board the two Canadians and their two soldier companions, entered the harbor and came to anchor a pistol's shot from the *Poli*. Being a New England vessel, she was at once captured and her crew and passengers brought before Iberville. Surprised at finding Frenchmen in such a company the commander became suspicious and subjected them to a searching interrogation. Unable to give a plausible account of themselves the quartet finally broke down and confessed the whole plot, excusing their conduct by explaining that they had undertaken the business in order to escape from Boston.

From these men Iberville learned much, though some of what he learned was not, as it turned out, exactly correct. He learned that the Boston authorities had ordered a thirty-six-gun ship, stationed at Port Royal, to sail to Pemaquid, where she could join the frigate *Conception* (Captain Robert Fairfax) in protecting Fort William Henry, a new fortification Governor Phips was building there. He also learned of the presence at near-by Piscataqua of a forty-six-gun frigate, the *Nonsuch* (Captain Richard Short) and two flutes (armed cargo ships) of twenty-four guns each. In addition to this the Canadians told him that an army of 3,000 men was being recruited from the country around Boston to attack Quebec the following spring, and that the money for the expedition was being raised by an unpopular levy on the inhabitants. Another force of like number was to march from Fort Orange to Montreal in order to prevent that town from going to the assistance of Quebec. For transportation by sea the Boston authorities had collected a dozen frigates with armaments ranging from twenty-four guns to fifty, while more than forty boats of various sizes were on the ways in the Boston shipyards. Clearly, then, an attack on the fort at Pemaquid with only the *Poli* and the *Envieux* would be a dangerous if not a foolhardy undertaking—and Iberville realized it. There was nothing he could do but abandon the plan and direct his attention elsewhere. In giving his reasons for abandoning his objective he wrote the Minister of Marine:

Seeing, Monseigneur, that it is impossible to succeed at Pemaquid and at Piscataqua, and being unable to lead the savages farther from home because their families stand in the way, I thought it better to cruise along their [the New Englanders'] coasts and go into Boston harbor where they least expect us.

There is, however, another side to the story which completely changes the picture and leads us to believe that Iberville might have captured the fort at Pemaquid had he known the true state of affairs. When Governor Phips landed in Boston during the spring, his first act was to start building a strong fort at Pemaquid in place of the one recently destroyed, and he went there in person to inspect the work. On his return to Boston he received word that French ships had been seen in the neighborhood of Pemaquid. Alarmed at this news, he immediately sent peremptory orders to

Captains Short and Fairfax "to fight the French ships if they met them, and otherwise not to leave the harbor but to stay and secure the fort." Both captains disobeyed the order and returned to Boston, leaving the fort unguarded. This flagrant act of desertion in the face of danger infuriated the governor, for he fully believed that the fort, in its unfinished condition, could be easily taken.[15] All this was unknown to Iberville, who had only the information given him by the two Canadians.

On November 6 and 7 a band of 160 Indians arrived. Yet even these were not enough, in Iberville's opinion, for a successful attack on the fort itself: and he also believed that the English ships were still at Pemaquid. At any rate he turned the savages over to Saint-Castin, who proposed to lead them to the fort, encamp there, and in some manner or other wear down the garrison, so that he could capture the place sometime during the winter. Iberville thought highly of Saint-Castin and believed him capable of accomplishing whatever he undertook. He commended him to the Minister as a man who was wholly devoted to the King and who held the Indians loyal to the French cause despite the vicissitudes of war and the difficulties in getting supplies from Quebec. Saint-Castin did, indeed, have great influence with the savages, for he had married the daughter of the chief, Madockawando.

The two commanders left Mount Desert on November 11, sailing southward until, two days later, they found themselves twenty leagues off Cape Cod. Here Iberville captured an English ketch hailing from the Bahama Islands, took her crew on board, and burned her. He sailed for Boston, hoping that the *Envieux* would join him there. When he came within two leagues of the harbor he found to his astonishment that there was not a single boat to be seen, and this despite reports that a good-size fleet was usually congregated there. Evidently a woman whom he had seen on the shore of Cape Cod had spread the news of his presence

[15] Phips to Nottingham, Feb. 15, 1693, *C.S.P. Am. & W.I., 1693–1696,* No. 88.

as far as Boston. Next day he lay to in a light breeze alternating with a dead calm, anxiously awaiting the arrival of Bonaventure, for he did not relish the idea of entering the harbor alone, especially as there was not enough wind for a speedy retreat if he should find the place too hot for him. On the night of the sixteenth a strong wind arose from the north-northwest, with sleet and snow to add to the general discomfort, and he was obliged to head for the open sea. The storm drove the vessel to the Nantucket Shoals, where at a point estimated as eighty leagues from land the commander paused to take stock of the situation. He found his foremast sprung; many of his men were ill from exposure; some lacked proper clothing; most of them were without shoes or stockings; and to make matters worse, the bread, chief source of nourishment, was moldy. There was nothing to do but to abandon all thought of further cruising along the New England coast and head for home.

The journey back to France was made in rapid time. Bowling along under a steady southwest breeze, the *Poli* reached Rochefort on the sixteenth of December, a pleasant contrast to the three months spent in making the westward passage. On the way Iberville made a capture, which was regarded as of little importance at the time but which led to his acquiring information that was to have considerable influence on his future plans. He seized an English flyboat coming from Newfoundland with a cargo of cod. Among the crew was a Frenchman who had lived on the island for six years, and from him as well as from the others, who seemed willing enough to talk, he gleaned valuable knowledge of Newfoundland. The Frenchman said he did not believe that there was a fortified post in the English settlements—at least none worthy of the name—and that there were no more than six or seven hundred men in the entire colony. These were scattered among twenty villages, the largest being St. John's with only twenty-five, by which is probably meant *habitans* or heads of households, for the place actually had some two hundred men, most of them employees of the *habitans*. This year a force of only two hundred fishermen had caught 30,000 quintals at Carbonear alone, an amount equivalent to over 6,500,000 pounds, while those living within a radius of six miles from this place had taken in 40,000 quintals. All this Iberville learned, not entirely from sailor's gossip—which might have been grossly exaggerated—but from a memorandum he found among the ship's papers. Nevertheless, he gained the impression from the way in which the harbors were situated that it would be no easy task to capture them from the sea, though in winter, when the ground was frozen and covered with snow, the settlements could be taken from the land side even more easily than Port Nelson could be captured. Iberville questioned the Frenchman closely and obtained from him a mass of details that will be discussed later; in fact from now on the commander was almost as eager to lead an expedition against Newfoundland as Port Nelson.

On December 16 the *Poli* anchored off Rochefort.[16] Iberville was favorably received by the authorities; his somewhat meager achievements do not seem to have lost him the royal favor; perhaps the reasons he gave for his failure before Pemaquid were considered valid. Then, too, he had brought back an enormous quantity of information about Newfoundland, all of which was of great interest to the government, for the capture of that island was part of the general plan against England in North America. Yet he was not ready to forsake his pet project, the capture of Port Nelson, for a campaign in Newfoundland, despite the interest he displayed in the latter. Nor would the government or the company have considered it if he had; furs were more interesting to them than codfish. From his residence in La Rochelle, Iberville now wrote to an influential member of the company [17]

---

[16] Iberville to Minister, Dec. 16, 1692, Archives des colonies, $C^{11}A$, 12.1, 206–218.

[17] Letter of Feb. 6, 1693, *ibid.*, $C^{11}A$, 12.2, 639–657.

expressing his eagerness to be off to Hudson Bay, but his willingness to attack Newfoundland was a second choice. The company needed no prodding for an attack on Port Nelson. They were already at work urging the Ministry to take the necessary steps, and the Ministry, as a matter of course, selected Iberville as the leader.

Iberville had ideas of his own about the business. He asked to command the *Poli* again, to take the *Sainte-Anne* as consort, and to be given a third ship, the *Indiscret*, a thirty-four-gun vessel then at Rochefort, which carried a crew of forty or fifty men. He wanted his old companion, Pierre de Lorme, to command this ship, and to accompany him to Quebec, where they would take on board one hundred men and one hundred soldiers. His plan was to reach Port Nelson in the middle of August, before the English fleet appeared, enter the Hayes River, batter down the fort; and if the fleet came in later he might be able to seize a ship or two. He would also take with him his brothers Joseph de Sérigny and Louis de Châteauguay, the latter a youth of eighteen who had been with him in the north and who, so he says, was able to navigate a ship. Iberville wanted a twelve months' supply of provisions for the *Poli*, above all whisky and flour, two articles not readily obtainable in Quebec. The crews were to be paid four months in advance so that they might procure suitable clothing, for Iberville well remembered how his men had suffered from exposure on the previous voyage. Once he had taken Port Nelson he expected to remain there during the winter, keeping only the *Sainte-Anne*, while Sérigny and De Lorme brought back the *Poli* and *Indiscret*, well freighted with furs, it was hoped, to the great satisfaction of the company.

Although the French government was concerned over the impending British attack on Quebec and Montreal, it was sympathetic to Iberville's plans for capturing Port Nelson, and the King ordered the *Poli* and the other two ships to make ready to sail for Canada in March.[18] Owing to hostilities on the seas, however, Iberville was obliged to act as escort, across the Atlantic, to four merchantmen that were then loading their cargoes in nearby ports. This meant delay, and he chafed under it, but he could not leave the merchant ships behind without express permission.

To strengthen Quebec against the coming attack, Iberville's ships were to carry the munitions, supplies, and a force of five hundred soldiers recently recruited for the Canadian service; this was all His Majesty could spare at that time for the defense of his great colony.[19] Iberville was placed in charge of the entire expedition. The government did all it could to hasten the preparations, even threatening to cancel the clearance papers of the merchantmen if they were not ready to sail with the escort, for word had been received that the English fleet, then at Boston, would leave during the latter part of April or early part of May, and it was necessary for the French ships to reach the St. Lawrence before the enemy arrived.[20]

Expeditions for Canada at this time were organized at Rochefort, a town situated at the mouth of the Charente River. It was the site of one of the principal French shipyards, which engaged chiefly in building ships for the Royal Navy. The intendant charged with the work was Michel Bégon, an able, industrious, and patriotic citizen who supervised the construction, equipping, and manning of the King's vessels for some twenty years. It was to him that most of the correspondence regarding Iberville's present expedition, as well as his later ones, was addressed by the Minister of Marine, either in his own name or in that of the King. Twenty miles north of Rochefort lies the port of La Rochelle, famous in history as the great Huguenot stronghold. It possessed better harbor facilities than Rochefort, and for this

[18] Minister to Bégon, Jan. 3, 1693, *Report on Canadian Archives, 1899, supplement,* p. 295.
[19] Minister to La Vograde, Jan. 20, 1693, *ibid.,* p. 295.
[20] Minister to Bégon, Mar. 4, 1693, *ibid.,* p. 298.

reason ships fitted out in the latter place frequently congregated at La Rochelle while waiting for a favorable breeze. These places were the starting points of all Iberville's expeditions.

When the King had given his orders, the Minister of Marine wrote Michel Bégon telling him to dispatch a fast-sailing ship to Acadia before the middle of February—a vessel of 150 tons manned by a crew of fifty sailors and placed under the command of Denys de Bonaventure. This ship was to carry back to Canada a detachment of twenty men brought over by Iberville on his last crossing,[21] and to transport forty soldiers and a supply of munitions to Villebon at Fort Naxouat. Bonaventure was then to proceed to Quebec; later this part of the order was changed and he was instructed to return directly from Acadia to France.[22]

Although Quebec and Montreal were subject to attack, the King kept his interest in Port Nelson. It was not only the capture of Port Nelson itself that turned the government's attention northward, but also a well-grounded fear that the Company of the North might lose the three posts on James Bay. During the previous summer the Hudson's Bay Company, fully determined to recover the lost forts, had appropriated £20,000, with which they equipped an expedition and sent it forth under the command of Captain Michael Grimmington; it is hardly possible that this could have been done without news of it reaching the French government. Thus Iberville's campaign might turn out to be something more than capturing Port Nelson. At the same time Count Frontenac was briefed by a memorial throwing much of the responsibility for the expedition on his shoulders. He was informed of the King's pleasure in appointing Iberville to the supreme command. The Company of the North, he was told, was to underwrite the business end of the undertaking, furnishing fifty men and enough provisions to last eleven months, as well as various miscellaneous supplies needed for such a venture. To

[21] Same to same, Jan. 14, 1693, *ibid.*, p. 295.
[22] Minister to Bonaventure, Mar. 14, 1693, *ibid.*, p. 298.

reimburse itself the company was entitled to keep everything taken from the enemy, in return for which concession it was obliged to maintain the captured post at its own expense. The governor was to see that these arrangements were carried out.

Iberville was to return to France as soon as he had completed his mission, bringing the *Poli* and the *Indiscret* with him; but if circumstances required his presence in the Bay, he was to send the former back to France in the charge of Pierre de Lorme, keeping the latter for his own use.[23] The *Sainte-Anne*, as will be seen, did not accompany him.

From the general tone of the correspondence and the documents covering the preparations for this expedition—a tone expressing nervousness and excitement—it is evident that the situation in Canada was considered very serious indeed, and that the King had become weary of the continual failures to capture Port Nelson or even to get ships into the Bay. This time he was determined to make sure that no unnecessary delays should occur either in France or in Canada; to insure undivided attention to the work at hand, Iberville and Bonaventure were strongly urged not to avail themselves of their leaves of absence but to remain at Rochefort. It was imperative now to get help to the colony with the least possible delay. Everything must be pushed forward with the greatest haste.

Meanwhile the company was rent by a factional split between the stockholders residing in France and those living in Canada, the former holding the majority of shares. In a memorial to Count Pontchartrain the French owners pointed out that it would be better for Iberville to return directly to France from the Bay in order to avoid the enemy who might be lurking in the St. Lawrence. The true reason, as the memorial goes on to say, was that they wished to have the furs come directly to La Rochelle, instead of passing through Quebec, as this would reduce expenses.

[23] Instructions for Iberville and memorial to Frontenac, Mar. 28, 1693, *ibid.*, p. 300; *Rapport de l'archiviste de Quebec, 1927–1928*, pp. 136–138.

Furthermore, it seemed unjust to the French stockholders that their Canadian colleagues should themselves be contractors for supplies to the company, a practice which led to the company paying a 60-per-cent profit to the merchants of Quebec.[24]

By the middle of February notice was sent to the merchantmen that they must be ready to sail with the escort or they could not go at all. Yet despite all the bustle there seem to have been causes which held up the expedition for several weeks. At the end of March the commander was still at Rochefort, complaining of the unfitness of his crews, who must be replaced before he could venture forth.[25] Another month passed and yet he did not move, and we find him later still in port with the season so far advanced that the Minister was constrained to write Frontenac expressing his fears that contrary winds might prevent the fleet from reaching Canada in time to go to the Bay. If this turned out to be the case, the governor was requested to order Iberville back to France or send him to destroy the English settlements in Newfoundland.[26] At last the flotilla set forth, the *Poli* and the *Indiscret*, with the convoy of merchantmen; but the start was so late that it was July 23 when they reached Quebec. On the way over Iberville had stopped long enough to capture an English trader, the *Mary-Sara*, which had sailed from Boston with a cargo of tobacco. As reinforcements for the Canadian army he had brought over the five hundred recruits we have mentioned, but upon inspection they were found to be chiefly youths of fifteen or sixteen years of age incapable of standing up under the rigors of Canadian warfare. Many had died on the way over and one hundred others were so ill that they were sent directly from the ships to the hospital when they landed in Quebec.[27]

[24] Memorial to Pontchartrain, Feb. 25, 1693, *Report on Canadian Archives, 1899, supplement*, p. 301.

[25] Minister to Bégon, Mar. 28, 1693, *ibid.*, p. 299.

[26] Minister to Frontenac, Apr. 18, 1693, *ibid.*, p. 302.

[27] Lorin, *op. cit.*, p. 406.

The late arrival of the fleet caused Frontenac to abandon for the third time the idea of attacking Port Nelson, though he did for a moment consider the feasibility of sending the *Indiscret* with the newly acquired *Mary-Sara* in place of the *Poli;* but Iberville did not feel that the *Indiscret* was capable of accommodating the men to be supplied by the company in addition to her crew, while the *Mary-Sara* was too small and a poor sailer to boot. Iberville might, so Frontenac wrote the Minister, have accomplished his purpose in the Bay by taking the entire fleet, but since the Minister's orders were to have the *Poli* back in France before winter set in, this could not be considered, and it was believed to be too hazardous to make the attempt with only two ships.[28] The question, as in 1691, was referred to a committee, which, after making a thorough examination of the facts, reported in favor of abandoning the enterprise. History was repeating itself with a vengeance.

The reasons advanced by Iberville for refusing to make the attempt on Port Nelson did not fail to rouse Count Frontenac's wrath. In a letter to M. de Lagny, Intendant-General of France, he bluntly accused the commander of subordinating his interest in Hudson Bay to a supposedly more lucrative expedition against the English settlements in Newfoundland; and to cap the climax he even denounced Iberville as a garrulous and presumptuous ass, comparing him unfavorably with Denys de Bonaventure. Others joined in the hue and cry, some accusing the unfortunate leader of having had his head turned by his recent appointment in the Navy, and of wishing to remain nearer home where he could hope for further promotion.[29] The absurdity of such accusations was manifest to any impartial observer, if for no other reason than the booty to be had at Port Nelson was probably greater than any that could be taken in Newfoundland, and the Court paid no

[28] Frontenac to Minister, Aug. 14, 1693, *Report on Canadian Archives, 1899, supplement,* p. 91; *Rapport de l'archiviste de Quebec, 1927–1928,* pp. 148–151.
[29] Guy Frégault, *Iberville le Conquérant* (Montreal, 1944), pp. 170–173.

attention to these charges. When Iberville arrived at Versailles some time later he was promptly entrusted with another expedition.

As the main purpose for which Iberville had come to Canada had been shelved for another year, Iberville found time hanging heavily on his hands. It was then, at the age of thirty-two, that he decided to bring to a conclusion a romance he had been carrying on for several years with Marie-Thérèse, a young lady eleven years his junior, daughter of the late François Pollet de la Combe Pocatière, a captain in the famous Carignan-Salières regiment, and Marie-Anne Juchereau, his wife. It is difficult to say how long the courtship had been going on, but it probably began shortly after the hero's return from his first expedition to Hudson Bay, as we find that M. de la Mollerie, guardian of Mlle de Belestre, had entered a protest against Iberville's marriage before the Council as early as June, 1688, insisting that he should marry his ward.[30] But although La Mollerie was able to delay the ceremony, he was not able in the end to prevent it. By this time the Lemoyne family was one of the most prominent in Canada, and its members may well have persuaded the authorities not to force their distinguished kinsman into an alliance that resulted from a scandal.

The marriage contract was signed in Quebec on October 8, 1693, at the home of François Viennay Pachot, uncle of the bride, in the presence of a large number of notable persons. Among the witnesses for the bridegroom we find Count Frontenac—whose name appears with all his titles—Joseph de Sérigny, and François de la Forest, styled governor of Louisiana. For the bride the witnesses comprised the Intendant Champigny and several members of the Juchereau family. The financial arrangements for the marriage were set forth in great detail. Of his fortune—and Iberville was by now a well-to-do man—the bridegroom reserved 10,000 *livres* for his own family, the remainder to go, of course, to the new community property created by the

[30] *Ibid.*, pp. 171–172*n*.

marriage. Marie-Thérèse, at the death of her husband, was to have the choice of the usufruct of his estate or an annual income of five hundred *livres,* unless she should contract a second marriage and have children by the same—which she eventually did—in which case the income should be cut in half.[31] After signing the contract the wedding party proceeded to the church, where the marriage was properly solemnized. Three weeks later the couple started on their honeymoon, and the commander took his bride on board the *Poli* and set sail for France. On landing at La Rochelle he found still another expedition being organized for him, for there was no limit to the determination of the government to acquire Port Nelson.

We wish we could give the reader some information about Mme d'Iberville—her appearance, her character, and the details of her life with her husband—but there is scarcely any mention of her in the records. We know that she accompanied her husband back to Canada the following year and that she returned to France, probably the next spring, never to see her native Canada again. For the next eight years Iberville was busy making repeated voyages to America, and probably saw little of his wife; but from 1701 to 1706, he resided continually in France, and it was then that he was at last able to enjoy domestic life with Marie-Thérèse. There were children of this union, but the information concerning them is so unsatisfactory that we have relegated it to an appendix [32] together with our critical comments. The children were born too late to play an important part in their father's life. After Iberville's death Mme d'Iberville married Count Louis de Bethune, and thus entered the higher French nobility.

While Iberville was thus busy sailing back and forth across the Atlantic, Captain Michael Grimmington struck. After wintering in the northern part of the Bay he moved south and seized, ap-

[31] Heloise H. Cruzat, "Marriage Contract of d'Iberville," *Louisiana Historical Quarterly,* XVII (1934), 242–245.
[32] See Appendix A.

parently with little effort, the posts on James Bay, namely, Ste. Anne, St. Jacques, and St. Louis. They were never recaptured by the French, who from now on concentrated their efforts on Port Nelson.[33] The English fortified and held the post on the Albany River and appear to have abandoned those on the Rupert and Moose, at least these posts occupied a very subordinate position. On two occasions Iberville planned to recapture his old Fort Ste. Anne, but the plans never materialized. As for the British expedition against Quebec, heralded with so much fanfare, it simply petered out. The fleet which was to have sailed from Boston in May or June had been sent to the West Indies during the winter to assist in the reduction of the island of Martinique. Here the crews were stricken by disease, so that by the time they reached Boston more than half of them, including also the soldiers, had perished. Thus the attack on Canada was postponed to a more propitious occasion.

[33] *C.S.P. Am. & W.I., 1699.* Document No. 1358 gives the date of the expedition as 1693 and so do other sources. Documents No. 570 and No. 1024 give 1692, but this refers to the year when it sailed from England.

CHAPTER V

Port Nelson and Pemaquid

THE English were now in complete possession of Hudson Bay, and it seemed as though the work of the French during the past eight years had been undone. Four times during that period had King Louis dispatched an expedition to capture Port Nelson, and all these attempts (three of which got no farther than Quebec) had failed because of a variety of causes, most of them, it is true, unavoidable. Yet fortunately these reverses, even the failure before Pemaquid, did not diminish Iberville's favor at Court, and we find him during the winter busily engaged in completing arrangements for another campaign in Hudson Bay. At this time, it is interesting to note, a change took place in the Ministry of Marine. Count Pontchartrain, on December 27, 1693, took as his associate his son, Jerome, Marquis de Phélypeaux, with the understanding that Jerome would succeed him when he died or retired. Four years later Jerome changed his title from Marquis de Phélypeaux to Comte de Maurepas, under which name we shall have occasion to refer to him when we take up Iberville's expeditions to Louisiana. From now on he plays an important part in Iberville's undertakings.

Though the Company of the North had continually clamored for Port Nelson, it did not care to supply funds for capturing the post; probably it was discouraged by the failure of the other attempts. According to the plan now determined upon, the financial burden of the expedition was to be borne entirely by Iberville and such persons as he could persuade to help him by holding out to them the possibilities of a profit. For his part, the King would furnish two ships, properly manned, and guarantee the wages of the crews if the hoped-for booty were insufficient; but more than this he would not do, for the war in Europe took nearly all his men and most of his money. He did, however, send orders to Frontenac and Champigny to assist Iberville with their resources and to take measures for keeping the posts after they had been captured.

Arrangements for the financing of the enterprise were somewhat complicated; there had to be due regard for the rights both of Iberville and of the company. The ships which the King agreed to furnish were the *Poli,* now the commander's favorite, and a twenty-gun frigate, the *Salamandre,*[1] both to be fitted out by him with guns, bombs, munitions, and all the necessary apparatus for a northern expedition. Iberville, with whatever associates he could induce to join him, was to man the vessels with seventy-eight sailors on the *Poli* and thirty on the *Salamandre.* He was to pay these men and their officers out of his pocket and also supply them with food. At Quebec he was to take on board 100 to 120 men collected for him by Governor Frontenac under orders from the King. As reimbursement and profit for his outlay Iberville was to get all the furs and other merchandise he might seize in the English posts the same to be divided according to the arrangements he made with his associates. In case the amount thus obtained came to more than double the sum advanced for the expedition, the wages of officers and crews should be deducted from such surplus;

[1] Nicolas Jérémie (*Twenty Years at York Factory,* ed. by R. Douglas and J. N. Wallace [Ottawa, 1926]) says that the *Charente* was the companion ship (p. 25); but we know from Iberville's letter it was the *Salamandre* (letter of Aug. 8, 1694, Archives des colonies, C¹¹A, 13, 137–139).

but if the amount fell sort of twice the sum advanced, then the King would take care of the payroll. This, of course, guaranteed a good profit for the adventurers if the expedition should succeed; and in order to make sure that there would be no mistakes in the accounting the King sent along his own supercargo. The government even went further. It provided that in case the English destroyed their property before the forts were taken, so that the victors got nothing or not more than twice the amount of their expenses, the King would then grant Iberville and the Company of the North exclusive rights of trade in the Bay until the year 1697. But should Iberville and his associates get their allotted share, the company would enter into possession of the posts and all their equipment, with the understanding that they would maintain them at their own cost. The King therefore ordered Frontenac to call a meeting of the Canadian stockholders before Iberville left Quebec and sound them out as to their willingness to take over the property under these terms, for if they declined to assume the burden Iberville and his associates were to take over the posts under the same conditions.[2] In closing his correspondence the King ordered Iberville to send a report of his success by special messenger overland to Quebec if he should be obliged to winter in the Bay.[3]

With this understanding Iberville set sail from La Rochelle on May 15, 1694, in command of the *Poli*, while to Joseph de Sérigny was given the *Salamandre*. Mme d'Iberville accompanied her husband. After weighing anchor the two ships picked up a convoy of twelve fishing vessels, which they were to escort to the Grand Banks, and set sail across the Atlantic. The voyage was made in less than two months, not a bad run for the westward passage, and Iberville came in sight of Quebec on July 11. On the way over an

[2] Articles drawn up by the King, Apr. 6, 1694, Archives des colonies, C¹¹A, 13.
[3] King to Iberville, Apr. 21, 1694, *Report on Canadian Archives, 1899, supplement*, p. 305.

important event occurred. When crossing the banks of New-foundland Mme d'Iberville gave birth to a son, who was presently baptized at Quebec under the name of Pierre-Louis-Joseph; his uncle, Sérigny, acted as godfather, and his maternal grandmother, Marie-Anne Juchereau, as godmother. This, together with the taking of a one-hundred-ton English vessel, was the only incident worthy of record on the outward voyage.

The two brothers landed at Quebec and at once set to work on the difficult task of securing men for their expedition, for the men Frontenac had been ordered to provide do not seem to have materialized in any great numbers. Sérigny went to Montreal to confer with the governor and see what could be done, while Iber-ville remained in Quebec. The latter worked hard to induce men to enlist and even tried to get some members of the company to join him, for they, after all, best understood the fur business and were in a position to handle the large volume at Port Nelson. The company stockholders as a group showed no particular en-thusiasm for the business; they did not wish to risk their money in the enterprise and were quite willing to let Iberville occupy the posts for the next three years. In the end a sort of compromise was reached by which the brothers pledged 6,000 *livres* in behalf of their father's heirs, to be paid when the company took over in 1697, while the stockholders selected one of their number in whose name they pledged 15,000 *livres*.

Meanwhile, the work of recruiting went on. Volunteers do not seem to have been plentiful, if we can judge by the liberality of the terms Iberville was obliged to offer, but he succeeded in get-ting together 110 hardy Canadian woodsmen, including six Iro-quois Indians, ready to take a chance for the sake of the large remuneration offered. These men were obliged to furnish only their guns and clothing, everything else was supplied them. As pay the men were to receive half the plunder taken from the time the expedition left Quebec and one-half the profits of trade at the Bay until July, 1697. Each man was to get an advance of forty *livres* before leaving home, which sum was to be paid back from the profits of the undertaking. Each was also allowed to take with him one hundred pounds of goods for purposes of private trade. Should the booty exceed 140,000 *livres*, the wages of the crews were to be paid out of such excess, the rest allotted to the Canadians. Only the forts, artillery, and ammunition should become the property of the King. In all, Iberville claimed to have advanced 110,000 *livres* for the expedition.[4]

Iberville hoped to reach Port Nelson by the middle of September in time to capture the Hudson's Bay Company's ships before they set sail for England. Here, then, would be a rich booty. During the winter he would attack, and no doubt take, the fort. When spring came he would send boats to the Albany River to intercept the Indians coming down to trade at Fort Ste. Anne. Then he would place one hundred men on board the *Salamandre* and send them to take this post before the fleet arrived on its annual visit from England; or he might arm the *Poli* and anchor off Port Nelson to await the English fleet. If he took the fleet, he would load the *Poli* with the booty and send her with eighty men to France or to Quebec. With the *Poli* out of the way and Port Nelson in his hands he would winter in James Bay and in due course of time seize Fort Ste. Anne. It was a noble plan, well thought out, and in some ways it proved successful.[5]

The fleet set sail on August 10. Among the officers were Louis de Châteauguay, Gabriel Testard de la Forest, Lemoyne de Martigny, Nicolas Jerémie, Father Pierre Gabriel Marest (a new arrival in Canada who has left us a detailed account [6] of the expedition), and, of course, Joseph de Sérigny. For the first few days

[4] Iberville to Pontchartrain, Aug. 8, 1694, Archives des colonies, C¹¹A, 13, 137–139; Conventions of Aug. 8, 1694, *ibid.*, F3, 7.2, 716; "Procès verbal de l'assemblée," *ibid.*, F3, 7.2, 707; Le Jeune, *op. cit.*, pp. 90–91.

[5] Letter of Iberville, Aug. 8, 1694, Archives des colonies, C¹¹A, 13, 137–139.

[6] Letter of Marest to Lamberville concerning Iberville's expedition, in Tyrrell, *op. cit.*, pp. 105–129.

the adventurers endured an irritating calm; then after ten days' sailing they passed through the Strait of Belle Isle and bowled along northward over the rough waters of the North Atlantic. By the end of August they had reached Hudson Strait and were working their way slowly westward through ice-laden waters when calm once more beset them. After this came adverse winds, until in despair the Canadians approached Father Marest suggesting they make a vow to consecrate a share of the profits of the enterprise to Saint Anne as a token of gratitude for more favorable weather. In this pious promise officers and sailors joined, and Father Marest gave them his blessing, warning them at the same time to think more of the purity of their conduct. Their vows were soon answered, and a following breeze sprang up; Saint Anne, as on the occasion before the fort on the Albany River, had not failed her votaries.

On September 24, toward six o'clock in the evening, the vessels anchored at the mouth of the Nelson River. Rejoicing at the happy outcome of the voyage, the crews bared their heads and gave thanks, singing the *Vexilla Regis* and the *O Crux Ave*. The latter, Father Marest tells us, was repeated many times "to do honor to the adorable cross of the Saviour, in a country where it is unknown to the aborigines, and where it has been so often profaned by heretics, who have thrown down with derision all the crosses which our Frenchmen formerly raised."

The fortification Iberville was now to attack was situated on the northern shore of the Hayes River about four miles from its mouth and half a mile below the present York Factory. The structure was fairly new, as three years before its commander had set fire to the original post on the appearance of some French vessels in the offing, and it had been necessary to rebuild it. The fort was in the form of a square thirty feet on each side [7] with a bastion at each corner. One of these bastions contained the trading store,

[7] It seems strange that it should have been so small, but these are the dimensions given in the records.

another a supply store, while the other two were used as guardhouses for the garrison. Inside the palisade was a warehouse two stories high. In line with the first palisade were two more bastions facing the river, one of which served as officers' quarters, the other as a kitchen and forge. Between them was a space shaped like a half-moon in which were placed eight cannon, and below this space, level with the water's edge, was a platform supporting six more. Thus the side facing the water front was well protected against attack by sea. The rest of the artillery, for there were all told thirty-two cannon and fourteen swivel guns, were mounted on the bastions. The entire structure was, of course, built of wood like the other forts on the Bay—the palisades were constructed from a double row of logs.

The garrison consisted of fifty-three men commanded by Governor Thomas Walsh, with Philip Parsons as his deputy. Among the officers we must also note Henry Kelsey, to whom we are indebted for the only account of the siege written from the English point of view by an eyewitness.[8] The rear of the fort, that is the one facing away from the river, was unprotected; it was the post's most vulnerable spot. The country around about was flat, marshy, unproductive, and nearly devoid of trees, save a few scrubby ones—altogether a bleak, uninviting locality, especially at this season, for cold weather here began in September.

September 24 had been stormy; a cold northerly gale had piled up drifts of snow, making it difficult for the garrison and their Indian friends to indulge in their favorite sport of hunting wild geese in the neighboring marshes. Toward evening, however, the weather cleared, disclosing a view of the sea, and a few bold hunters who had ventured across the peninsula to the mouth of the Nelson River saw two ships flying the French flag. Quick to sense the meaning of this unexpected apparition, they hastened back to the fort to rouse the garrison. Governor Walsh at once

[8] *The Kelsey Papers*, ed. by A. G. Doughty and Chester Martin (Ottawa, 1929).

dispatched a man down the Hayes River, to the outpost where a watch was kept throughout the night. The following day some hunters and Indians started out early to make a reconnaisance toward the Nelson River and returned presently with news of the landing of a detachment from the ships. Arms were at once distributed, ammunition cases were opened, and preparations were made for a stout defense.

Meanwhile, Iberville had been preparing a surprise attack. He managed, after maneuvering his vessels as close to shore as the shallow waters would permit, to land a body of forty picked men whom he proposed to march overland and attack the fort on its unprotected side. But thanks to the warning given by a lookout, the surprise failed, and the scouting party returned on board with only a couple of Indian prisoners for their trouble. And now before taking any further step to reduce the fort, Iberville decided to look for winter quarters, as the season would be too far advanced to think of going to James Bay after he had captured the fort. Since the Nelson River was deeper than the Hayes, he decided to lay up the *Poli* in the former while he took the *Salamandre* to find suitable shelter in the latter stream. Ensconced here, the *Salamandre* would naturally become the French headquarters in the coming operations against the fort. Sérigny was therefore transferred to the *Poli* with orders to take her to the berth selected for her, while Iberville took over the *Salamandre*. In order to find a place where she could ride safely through the winter, Iberville steered her slowly up the Hayes, taking careful soundings. After two days he found, at a league and a half above the fort, a bay formed by a point of high land jutting out into the river where the ship would be sheltered from the ice that flowed downstream in the spring; and the men already on shore were told to come here and locate their camp. But bringing the ship upriver to her anchorage proved a more difficult matter. Wind, ice, and snow had been increasing daily, and now an adverse breeze sprang up at low tide to hold her back. At last, when the wind died down, a boat manned by sixteen oars took her in tow and helped by a fair tide managed to bring her opposite the fort, which opened fire with several volleys that fortunately dropped short of their mark. And now real obstacles arose. Masses of ice swept down the river, crashing into the ship with such force as to break through her hull in several places. To prevent her from foundering, a dozen guns were jettisoned, together with such other articles as would not suffer from a few months' immersion. When the bad weather subsided, Iberville was able to unload his ship with the help of some canoes he had brought from Quebec.

During this time intermittent skirmishes were taking place between the English in the fort and whatever Canadians chanced to come within range of their guns; and it was in one of these engagements that the tragic death of young Châteauguay occurred. Father Marest in his account gives us only the barest details:

Monsieur de Châteauguay, a young officer nineteen years of age, M d'Iberville's brother, had gone to skirmish at the English fort to divert their attention and keep them from learning the difficulties we were in. Approaching too near it, he was wounded by a ball which pierced him through. He desired I would come to hear his confession, and I went at once. We thought at first the wound was not mortal. We were soon undeceived for he died the next day.

During all these misfortunes the gallant commander kept up his courage. As Father Marest goes on to say:

He was very much affected by the death of his brother whom he had always loved tenderly, but he resigned himself to God in whom he placed all his confidence. Foreseeing that the least sign of uneasiness in his countenance would put all his men into consternation, he still bore up with wonderful resolution, setting all the men to work, acting himself and giving orders with as much presence of mind as ever.

When the ships were safely anchored, Iberville turned his whole attention to the siege. A camp was pitched near the fort and a good road constructed through the underbrush to the river's edge for the transportation of cannon, mortars, and bombs. There had been shooting for several days, but on October 12 an Indian arrived at the fort with news that the French had placed their artillery in position. A light bombardment began in the evening, though no harm was done, as the range was too great and the missiles fell short of their objective. The following day a French officer advanced under a flag of truce with a threat to bombard the place and reduce it to ashes unless the defenders surrendered at once. An answer was requested for eight o'clock the following morning. If the reader expects to hear an account of a thrilling battle against overwhelming odds he will be disappointed, for the English garrison acted as English garrisons had acted before on similar occasions. Since they were given until morning to make their decision they requested as a further concession that they might be permitted a good night's sleep, undisturbed by the barking of guns. Reassured on this point, they retired early to bed like good burghers, and the next day after a leisurely breakfast they presented their terms, sending Henry Kelsey and a companion to the French camp as envoys. Iberville glanced at the terms, altered those he did not like, and ordered the governor to surrender at four o'clock.

Thus it was that at the appointed hour on October 14, 1694, Governor Walsh surrendered his post to the French commander, who immediately sent a lieutenant to take possession. In honor of this bloodless victory the place was renamed Fort Bourbon, and the Hayes River, Ste. Thérèse, after the saint on whose day the victory took place. In accounting for the ease with which the capture was made Father Marest says: "They had been in a fright ever since our arrival and had all the while kept close indoors, without daring to go out even at night to fetch water from the river which washes the foot of the fort." Father Marest continues his explanation by saying that the commander "was better skilled in trade than in martial affairs, having never been a soldier, which was the cause of his surrendering so easily." Even so one would imagine that self-respect would have dictated a more pugnacious policy than the meek surrender which reflected so little credit on British arms.

The terms of the capitulation were mild and provided for the comfort of the fallen foe. It was agreed that the governor and his officers would be allowed to remain in the fort during the winter, while the garrison would be treated on the same footing as the French rank and file, that is, they would receive the same amount of provisions. They were also allowed to retain their own property and were guaranteed freedom from insult and injury. The following year they were to be transported to France, whence they could make their way to England as best they could, unless they preferred to sail directly there in their own ships.

From the testimony later given in England the French did not live up to their obligations. Deputy-Governor Parsons made an affidavit stating that the officers and garrison, who were to have wintered in a building within the fort known as Fox Hall, were driven out three or four days after the surrender and compelled to build shelters in a neighboring wood; only four officers and a boy were allowed to remain in the fort. To this complaint was added a list of atrocities compiled by various persons who had witnessed them or had suffered them. It was alleged that men were cruelly beaten by the French; that some had their fingers burned by the Indians; that five Englishmen were harnessed to sleds and forced to draw them through the deep snow; that the French surgeon had robbed the British surgeon of his instruments. All this makes doleful reading; but the strange part of it is that Governor Walsh filed a counterstatement to the effect that Iberville had loyally lived up to the terms of the capitulation, and in this he was backed up by three witnesses. He also denied categorically the evidence of those who testified to bad treatment. Parsons, however, would not let it go at that. He had been taken with the garrison to La Rochelle, where he had been obliged to borrow the tidy sum of two hundred pounds to supplement the meager

allowance granted his people for their support, and he tartly
observed that Governor Walsh in his statement complimenting
Iberville for faithful adherence to the terms of the treaty should
remember that it would not have cost him (Parsons) two hundred
pounds if the French commander had kept them. It is confusing
to read such conflicting testimony, and extremely difficult to pass
judgment on the merits of the case. In all probability brutalities
occurred, the recital of which bored the governor, for one of the
witnesses affirmed that the governor had declared himself weary
of the complaints and had betaken himself to the Nelson River,
where he could no longer be importuned by them.[9]

Was Iberville responsible for these alleged infractions of the
treaty? Probably not. Walsh and his three compurgators absolve
him, testifying that he had kept the terms. The incidents related
were, no doubt, isolated occurrences, the work of irresponsible
individuals whose actions were not brought to the notice of the
commander. This is quite understandable when we consider the
precarious condition of the French forces who, quite as much as
the English, were suffering from disease and malnutrition.

During the long winter Iberville whiled away the time by interesting himself in that time-honored project—the discovery of
the Western Sea. This project had gone through several phases
during the past two centuries, and by now the Western Sea was
regarded by some French geographers as a vast gulf indenting the
Pacific coast in the regions now covered by British Columbia,
Washington, and Oregon, and connected with the Pacific by a
strait. Reports of the accessibility of this sea by a river route had
been gathered by various explorers, and now Iberville heard similar news from the Indians loitering around the fort, as well as from
the English garrison. The route, from what he was able to gather,
lay in the northern part of the Bay, a sort of strait connecting the
two bodies of water. The English had already attempted the discovery, but had only succeeded in losing two ships in the ice.

[9] *C.S.P. Am. & W.I., 1696–1697,* Nos. 524, 560, 561.

Now Iberville suggested that the proper way to handle the business was to winter at Fort Bourbon and get an early start in the spring, for it was necessary, so he was told, to go as far north as the eightieth parallel, or even higher, in order to find the passage. Not only did he advocate such a plan but he also attempted to put it into practice. He sent out one of his officers, a man named Renaudot, with a party to see what could be found. Renaudot managed to discover a gulf in the northern part of the Bay—possibly Chesterfield Inlet—and sailed into it for some twelve leagues—but that was all. The French government was not interested in the problem at this time; the war in Europe needed too much attention. But after the Treaty of Utrecht in 1713 the desire to find a route to the Pacific was revived, and the Canadian intendant, Claude Bégon,[10] wrote the government about Iberville's plan. The plan, however, excited little interest; even if a connecting strait were found, in this northern latitude it would be useless for trade.[11]

The winter passed slowly as time always does when men are suffering. Lack of food became painfully evident early in the season, and scurvy, the curse of northern explorers, soon broke out. The French crews suffered greatly from it, Iberville losing no less than twenty men. During this trying period Father Marest, who seems to have tried to comfort the stricken men, made many crossings of the peninsula between the fort and the *Poli*, never asking for a respite even during the severest part of the winter.

When warm weather returned, the Indians, as was their custom, came down to trade, bringing this time a noble haul of 45,000 pounds of beaver skins. As the ice broke up, Iberville got his ships under way, but the season was late and the end of July came before he was able to anchor the *Salamandre* at the river's mouth. Here he intended to await the arrival of the English fleet, which

[10] Claude Michel Bégon, Sieur de la Picardière, not to be confused with the Intendant of Rochefort.
[11] Margry, *op. cit.*, VI, 497–500.

he fully expected to capture. Then he would send the *Poli* back to France with a rich cargo, proceed with the *Salamandre* to Fort Ste. Anne, take it, and spend the winter there. But the English vessels did not come, and after waiting until September 7,[12] he turned Fort Bourbon over to Gabriel de la Forest with Lemoyne de Martigny for his lieutenant and Nicolas Jérémie for his ensign. He gave them seventy Canadians to form a garrison and set sail in the *Poli* for Quebec. Contrary winds off Labrador and a renewed attack of scurvy compelled him to change his plans and proceed directly to La Rochelle, which he reached on October 9.[13] The *Salamandre* arrived later.

Lemoyne d'Iberville not only had covered himself with glory by capturing the much-desired Port Nelson but had also brought a substantial booty in skins, which he had found at the fort and had obtained by trade from the Indians. He unloaded 51,997 pounds from the *Salamandre* and stored them in La Rochelle for safekeeping. Shortly after landing he went to Paris, where he took lodgings at the Image de Nôtre Dame on the Rue Saint-Honoré. Here he set about disposing of his furs. He sold them to Pierre Pointeau, a farmer-general of the King, for the sum of 60,000 *livres*, 10 per cent down, the balance to be paid within a year.[14] This, of course, did not cover the outlay on the expedition, but he hoped to reimburse himself—and in the course of time he actually did—by the trade of the next few years. Pierre d'Iberville was now on his way to becoming one of the wealthy men of Canada.

While Iberville was absent in Hudson Bay, the King had been making plans for a bold stroke that would re-establish French

[12] Jérémie says that Iberville sailed on July 20, but this is an error, as other records put the date early in September. Moreover, since he reached France on October 9, he could not have spent ten weeks in making the journey.

[13] For accounts of this expedition see Father Marest's letter in Tyrrell, *op. cit.*, pp. 105–129; relation of Iberville, Oct. 13, 1695, Archives des colonies, C¹¹A, 13, 481 ff.; Jérémie, *op. cit.*; and *Kelsey Papers*, pp. 40–44.

[14] Le Jeune, *op. cit.*, p. 107.

influence over the Indians in Acadia, influence that had been badly shaken when the English built the new fort at Pemaquid, now considered one of the strongest posts in New England. As early as April, 1695, he considered attacking Pemaquid the following year.[15] Fear of a combined attack by New England and New York on Quebec and Montreal had by this time evaporated, and there was no reason why the French could not carry the war into the enemy's territory. Intendant Champigny considered French-sponsored Indian raids as on the whole ineffectual, since they consisted merely of surprise attacks on outlying settlements, and he strongly urged that the next offensive move be made by the French themselves and directed against a strategic post.[16] During the summer of 1694 Bonaventure had been sailing the *Envieux* up and down the Acadian coast, visiting various settlements, and on one occasion he enjoyed a successful brush with an English man-of-war. Now he was back in France to tell his superiors how greatly pleased the Indians were to see that the French had not deserted them. With Iberville and Bonaventure again in France, the King was able to make careful preparations for what was to be a three-point program.

The campaign of 1696 was to be an extensive one, so extensive, in fact, that it would take two years to complete it. It comprised three objectives: the destruction of the fort at Pemaquid, the conquest of Newfoundland, and the recapture of the posts on James Bay. These projects were to be taken up in the order named. Iberville was, of course, appointed commander-in-chief of the Pemaquid expedition, quite an honor for a man only thirty-five years old. His brother Jean-Baptiste de Bienville, Du Tast, and Pierre du Guay de Boisbriant were to be his personal aides.[17] The last now appears in our story for the first time. He was to

[15] Minister to Villebon, *Collection de manuscrits*, II, 176–179.
[16] Champigny to Minister, Nov. 6, 1695, *ibid.*, p. 189.
[17] List of officers, Mar. 17, 1696, *Report on Canadian Archives, 1899, supplement*, p. 318.

serve under Iberville in Newfoundland, in Hudson Bay, and later in Louisiana. Iberville's flagship was to be the *Envieux*, his consorts the *Profond*, commanded by Bonaventure, and the *Wesp*, under Jean Leger de la Grange. The latter was to accompany him across the ocean, then proceed to Quebec to obtain recruits for the Newfoundland venture while Iberville directed his attention to Pemaquid. Iberville was to go first to Sydney Harbor to take on board a band of friendly Indians and learn what he could about possible English vessels in the Bay of Fundy, for he was to destroy such vessels before venturing against Pemaquid. If the coast were clear, he should go at once to the Penobscot River, sinking all fishing boats on the way in order that no news of his presence could be carried to the English colonies. If on reaching the Penobscot he should not find the Indians assembled there, he was to go to Fort Naxouat, where he was to land the guns, munitions, and men sent by the King to reinforce this post, and there he should take on board two officers, Claude Charles de Villieu and Jacques Testard de Montigny, the latter Iberville's boyhood friend and a younger brother of the La Forest who had been left in command of Port Nelson. These officers, with twenty picked men who were to accompany them, were to be sent back to Naxouat after the capture of the British fort. Iberville also had the good fortune to have as his chaplain Father Jean Beaudoin, an ex-musketeer turned Sulpitian, who has left us a valuable account of the campaigns in Acadia and Newfoundland. On the other hand if the Indians were at the Penobscot rendezvous he was to sail for Pemaquid, sending word to Villebon that he was about to commence operations.[18]

Thus far the orders were fairly explicit, but when it came to the actual conduct of the siege the commander was left to his own devices. At the same time Villebon received a letter from the Minister promising him additional forces that would bring

[18] Iberville's instructions, Mar. 28, 1696, *Collection de manuscrits*, II, 216–218.

his command up to one hundred men. He was instructed to remain at Fort Naxouat and devote his energies to strengthening the post while Iberville attended to the business at Pemaquid.[19]

The attack on Pemaquid was an important part of the over-all program, for the King was anxious to secure the allegiance of the savages in Acadia in order to thwart the British plan of overrunning that country, perhaps as far as Quebec. This fort was the key to the situation, for it was a powerful structure, capable of overawing the Indians and keeping them loyal to the English. The French authorities were well posted on the state of affairs. Governor Villebon in a letter to the Minister (August 20, 1694) gave him a complete description of the newly built post, its exact location, its ground-plan, its structural strength, and the details of its armament, which he had obtained from a native of Port Royal who had twice visited the place. The man had also frequented Boston, where he had picked up scraps of information, and by piecing these together Villebon managed to draw up plans for an attack. The best time to strike, he advised his superior, was early in June. The British usually fitted out a frigate in May to patrol Port Royal and Cape Sable; thus it would not be near Pemaquid in June. At the same time the New Englanders seldom received communications from England; hence there was little likelihood that they would know of the French plans. The second choice for an attack was toward the end of August, though Villebon listed several reasons why this time was less favorable than June.

The French force, he went on to say, should be composed of three ships: one, a powerful vessel of forty-eight guns, the second, a frigate of thirty-six, the third, a flyboat to carry munitions and supplies. As to the number of men in the expedition, he suggested one hundred soldiers backed by an equal number from the combined crews, and to these should be added two hundred Indian allies. He then gave a list of the pieces of artillery required for the

[19] *Ibid.*, pp. 213–215.

siege. The landing should be made in the harbor three-quarters of a league from the fort, where a wagon road leading to it would be found. Villebon ended his memorandum by recommending Denys de Bonaventure for a command in the expedition as he was well acquainted with the territory.[20] The government attached considerable weight to Villebon's views, especially as he was said to have visited Pemaquid in person disguised as an Indian.[21]

When Iberville had completed his campaign in Acadia—successfully, it was hoped—he was then to apply himself to the second point in the program, namely, the conquest of the English settlements in Newfoundland. Four years before, it will be recalled, he had obtained much information about this island which he embodied in a letter to a member of the Company of the North.[22] As one reads this letter one is amazed at the enormous mass of precise detail which the writer sets forth: the names of harbors, their positions in relation to each other, the distances between them, the depth of water in the principal ones, and the names and locations of the villages with the number of *habitans* living in them, as well as their total populations. Then he describes the nature of the terrain and its probable condition in winter when the time for a campaign would be most favorable. It is probable that Iberville found a map among the ship's papers, for it is hardly possible that he could have compiled all his data from information given him verbally, or even from written records. In addition to all this information, the French had the advantage of having a small colony on the island situated in Placentia Bay whence they could start their operations. This colony had been governed for the past few years by the Sieur François Jacques de Brouillan, a man of some ability but an irascible fellow, quarrelsome, stubborn,

[20] *Docs. Rel. Col. Hist. N.Y.*, IX, 574-577.
[21] Certain interesting documents about this proposed expedition are to be found in J. H. Cartland, *Twenty Years at Pemaquid* (Pemaquid Beach, Me., 1914), pp. 183-189.
[22] Letter of Feb. 3, 1693, Archives des colonies, C^{11}A, 12.2, 639-657.

and above all touchy on the subject of his authority. In all probability there would be trouble between him and Iberville.

To meet this delicate situation, the Minister outlined a plan in a letter to Governor Frontenac. The King, he said, was resolved to attack the English settlements in Newfoundland by land and by sea with sufficient forces to insure success. The naval part of the program was to be entrusted to M. de Brouillan, but as there would be little chance of success without an attack by land, this part of the business would carried out by Iberville. During the winter—for it would be winter before he could get there from Acadia and begin operations—he would take such posts as Brouillan's ships had been unable to capture and destroy them. Since this work could be carried out only by men accustomed to forest warfare, Iberville was ordered to bring with him fifty or sixty Indians from Acadia under the command of Montigny, while a band of eighty Canadians was to be recruited by Paul de Maricourt at Montreal and by the Sieur d'Auteuil at Quebec.[23] Iberville was also empowered to take command of the fort at Placentia as well as the various posts on the island while Governor de Brouillan was absent because of his naval activities.[24] Nevertheless, and this was a sop to the governor's feelings, Brouillan was to be in supreme command of the combined forces, though he was strongly urged, if not actually commanded, to allow his subordinate a free hand in the management of his part of the campaign. If the expedition were successful, the French leaders were to take the English colonists on board their ships and transport them to England with as much humanity as circumstances would permit.[25] It was evidently the intention of the French government to take complete possession of the island.

[23] Minister to Frontenac, Mar. 31, 1696, *Collection de manuscrits*, II, 210–212.
[24] Instructions and commission of Iberville, Mar. 31, 1696, *Report on Canadian Archives, 1899, supplement*, pp. 314–315.
[25] Memoir of Minister, Apr. 21, 1696, *ibid.*, p. 94. See also p. 315.

The third part of the general plan was, as has been said, the capture of the English-held posts on James Bay. Since Iberville would be too much occupied with his operations against Pemaquid to attend to this, the King permitted him to place the expedition in the hands of Joseph de Sérigny, who had served under him at Port Nelson two years before. Sérigny's sole orders were to follow the advice of his older brother, whose experience in such matters made him a reliable authority. But Iberville was to bear the expenses of this venture, and also that of Newfoundland, and reimburse himself with whatever booty he and Sérigny might be able to take. What interested the King in this undertaking was to have the forts so completely destroyed that not a vestige of them would remain.[26]

Sérigny's story is quickly told. He set sail in the *Dragon* with the *Hardi* under La Motte-Egron as consort and betook himself to the Bay. His first stop was to be at Fort Bourbon (Port Nelson), where he expected to make contact with La Forest; but when he came in sight of the harbor he saw to his consternation a fleet of five ships flying the English flag. It was the expedition of Captain William Allen come to retake Fort Bourbon. In the face of such superior numbers Sérigny saw the folly of attempting to relieve the post; even the capture of the forts on James Bay would hardly be worth the trouble, since Allen could easily retake them and, perhaps, Sérigny's two vessels also, if he stayed too long in the vicinity. Seeing the hopelessness of the situation, he discreetly put about and returned to France. Governor de la Forest surrendered at discretion on August 31.[27] Thus the English regained complete control of Hudson Bay: Iberville's work of the last ten years was now undone.

Since February, Michel Bégon had been busy getting the *Envieux*, the *Profond*, and the *Wesp* ready for the coming cam-

[26] Instructions for Sérigny, Apr. 4, 1696, *Collection de manuscrits*, II, 212–213.

[27] *C.S.P. Am. & W.I., 1696–1697*, No. 471.

paign. He placed on board a plentiful supply of presents for the Indians who were to be won back from English influence, besides the usual equipment of guns and munitions for the warlike part of the enterprise. In May the little fleet set sail. After an uneventful crossing it reached Sydney Harbor on June 26, and the following day the *Wesp* left for Quebec. A few days later a Canadian *habitan*, named Germain Bourgeois, arrived from the St. John River bringing letters from Villebon. From them Iberville learned that New England ships were cruising off the coast awaiting the arrival of the French squadron. He at once weighed anchor and started for the Bay of Fundy, accompanied by a brigantine under the command of the said Bourgeois. He also took on board some Micmac Indians eager for the attack on Pemaquid.

Off St. John, which he reached on July 14, he saw in the distance three vessels lying in wait for him: the *Newport* (twenty-four guns, Captain Paxton), the *Sorlings* (thirty-four guns, Captain Fleetwood Eames), and the *Province*, a trader. It was two o'clock in the afternoon when he first sighted these two ships, well up to windward and bearing down on him. Caught by a superior force he decided on a ruse. The *Profond*'s guns were drawn inboard, her ports closed, the English flag hoisted, and everything done to give her the appearance of a prize recently captured by the *Envieux*. Believing that they had only one ship to contend with, the Englishmen quickly closed in; but when they had come within range, the *Profond* threw open her ports and poured in a volley, ably seconded by the flagship. This unexpected resistance threw the enemy into confusion, especially when the *Newport*'s maintopmast went by the board. In order to escape the fury of the cannonade, Paxton headed downwind; Iberville followed closely, as fast as the *Envieux* could plow her way through the water, keeping up a continuous fire until the Englishman struck his colors. Turning his prize over to the *Profond*, Iberville continued after the *Sorlings*, hoping to cripple her by firing at long range. For hours the chase continued until at last darkness fell and a blanket of fog spread its protecting mantle around the fleeing vessel, leaving the disappointed Frenchman to put about and proceed to the St. John River for the night.

Early next morning when the fog had cleared, Iberville saw anchored near him his prize of yesterday, the *Newport*. On examination she proved to be leaking badly, but after considerable effort and much pumping her crew managed to get her up the river to the place where Villebon was impatiently awaiting his supplies. Here for two weeks the carpenters worked hard to get her once more in a seaworthy condition, while the supplies for the fort were unloaded from the *Envieux* and the *Profond*. On August 2, Iberville and Bonaventure set sail for the Penobscot, taking with them M. de Villieu and a company of twenty-five soldiers. They arrived at their destination five days later. Here they were met by the Baron de Saint-Castin, who had collected a band of two hundred Indians, and Iberville quickly purchased their loyalty by distributing the King's presents among them. The expedition then proceeded to Pemaquid, strengthened by the Indian contingent which accompanied the ships in their canoes. On August 14, the vessels anchored at the mouth of the Pemaquid River just outside of St. John's Island.

The fort, known as William Henry, was one of the strongest in New England. It had been built by order of the home government at a cost of 20,000 pounds, which expense was borne by the colony of Massachusetts, to the great annoyance of the taxpayers. Yet despite complaints the authorities felt justified in erecting such an expensive structure, as it was to be situated near the line claimed by the English as the boundary between their colony and Canada; and it would protect, so it was believed, the New Englanders from attacks which Count Frontenac was preparing to launch against them. When he had first come to Boston as governor, Phips had raised a force of 450 men, which he sent to the Little Pemaquid River, where on a promontory near its mouth they laid the foundation on the site of a former fort which had been recently destroyed. Cotton Mather described it as follows:

The fort, called William Henry, was built of stone, in a quadrangular figure, being about 737 foot in compass, without the outer walls, and an 108-foot square, within the inner ones; twenty-eight ports it had and fourteen (if not eighteen) guns mounted, whereof six were eighteen-pounders. The wall on the south line, fronting the sea, was twenty-two foot high, and more than six feet thick at the ports, which were eight foot from the ground. The greater flanker or round tower at the western end of this line, was twenty-nine foot high. The wall on the east line was twelve foot high, on the north it was ten, on the west it was eighteen. It was computed that in the whole there were laid above two thousand cart-loads of stone. It stood about a score of rods from the high-water mark; and it had generally at least sixty men posted in it for its defense, which, if they were men, might easily have maintained it against more than twice six hundred assailants.

Yet this powerful bastion, because of its excessive cost, was not popular with the colonists. Mather goes on to say:

The murmurings about this fort were so epidemical, that, if we may speak in the foolish cant of astrology, and prognostigate from the aspect of Saturn upon Mars at its nativity, "Fort William Henry, thou hast not long to live! Before the year ninety-six expire, thou shalt be demolished." [28]

But whatever may have been its cost it was, in the governor's opinion, well worth the outlay, for it so impressed the Indians that he was able to sign a treaty of peace with them the following summer, to the great relief of the colonists.[29]

As soon as he had come to anchor, Iberville saw that Saint-Castin had already set up a few pieces of artillery, and he thereupon attempted to persuade the commander to surrender before

[28] *Magnalia Christi Americana* (Hartford, 1853), II, 619–620. A reproduction of the ground-plan of the fort may be found in Cartland, *op. cit.*, facing p. 172.

[29] *C.S.P. Am. & W.I., 1693–1696*, No. 545.

he attacked the place. The fort at this time was manned by a garrison of ninety-two soldiers under Captain Pasco Chubb. These men were well armed and could, one would think, have given a good account of themselves, entrenched as they were behind walls of stout masonry. Between three and four o'clock in the afternoon the French commander sent a boat ashore with a flag of truce and a drum. The party was met at the landing place by a file of musketeers who led the two messengers blindfolded into the captain's presence. The letter they brought was written in French and was unintelligible to the Englishman, but the messengers had no trouble in making him understand that their commander demanded an immediate and unconditional surrender. To this Chubb replied with spirit, saying he would not yield the fort though "the sea was covered by French vessels, and the land with Indians," though he modified this somewhat by adding that if pressed too hard he hoped to find good terms from a Christian nation.

When the envoys had left, the Indians opened up a desultory fire to which the English replied in kind. That night Iberville landed two cannon and two mortars half a league from the fort, and the next morning he proceeded to move them within range. By noon he was in position. Meanwhile the *Newport*, now commanded by the Sieur de Lauson, had arrived with additional men and a band of Indians estimated at five hundred. The bombardment now began. The inmates of the fort, it seems, had no bombproof covers, the powder magazines only had been furnished with this protection. Moreover, they did not seem to be able to return the fire successfully; possibly because the French had placed themselves skillfully, they could bring only one gun to play on the enemy, and this was put out of business when the flanker supporting it collapsed.

As the situation became more and more disheartening, Captain Chubb was handed a letter which the Baron de Saint-Castin had managed to smuggle into the fort. This letter was a last summons to surrender and contained a threat that if an assault were made it would be led by savages who would show no mercy; and Saint-Castin assured the captain that Iberville's instructions from his King urged him to be ruthless. The letter had its effect, for the English well knew that their own cruelty to the Indians in recent times would be repaid tenfold. Chubb accordingly sent out a messenger, Sergeant David Francis, under a flag of truce to sound out Iberville as to terms. Francis was led to the French camp, where he saw the size of Iberville's forces: one hundred soldiers, over five hundred Indians, two mortars, and a field piece, and the French assured him that back in the harbor were six more pieces of artillery. Francis was handed a letter from the French commander demanding surrender in half an hour. In such circumstances Chubb had little choice, and after a brief consultation with his officers he agreed to capitulate on condition that his people might keep their clothing and be transported to a Christian shore. These terms were quickly granted and the fort was at once surrendered.[30]

Captain Chubb's tame surrender met with general condemnation, though it is difficult to see how he could have pursued a wiser course. He was surrounded by a vastly superior force, consisting for the most part of vengeance-seeking savages who would have shown the garrison no mercy, and while he could have held out longer, the end would have been the same; all he would have gained would have been the credit of making a heroic stand. One can, of course, understand and even sympathize with the feelings of the officials at Boston when they learned that the fort they had erected at so great a cost and which they hoped would protect them against the attacks of the French was thus given up with

[30] *C.S.P. Am. & W.I., 1696–1697*, Nos. 257i, 146, 422; Thomas Hutchinson, *op. cit.*, II, 92–93; P. F. X. de Charlevoix, *History and General Description of New France*, tr. by J. G. Shea (New York, 1866–1873), V, 25–26; *Docs. Rel. Col. Hist. N.Y.*, IX, 658; Jean Beaudoin (Baudoin), *Journal d'une expédition de d'Iberville*, ed. by Auguste Gosselin (Evreux, 1900).

only a routine defense. Captain Chubb was denounced as a "cowardly villain" and thrown into prison when he reached Boston, but he was released with no further punishment than being retired from the service.[31]

Having captured Fort William Henry, Iberville proceeded to destroy it. The guns were removed to the ships, while the small arms consisting of some two hundred muskets were given to the Indians in consideration of their services. He sent part of the garrison to Boston under Bernard Damours des Plaines with a message to the governor informing him that if he wished to get back the rest of his men and the crew of the *Newport* he would have to surrender all French prisoners in his jails. This request was backed up by a threat that he would hand over ten of his more prominent captives to the tender mercies of the Indians unless the French were promptly released. But it was no use; the governor would do nothing. Later, when he received no answer, Iberville sent another batch of prisoners to Boston, an act dictated not so much by a desire to gain the governor's good will as by a wish to spare the inroads these captives were making on his fast-diminishing supply of provisions. At last, unwilling to wait any longer, he placed a wealthy Boston merchant and an Indian chief who was friendly to the English, both of whom he had found on the *Newport,* in the hands of Saint-Castin for safekeeping. Turning the officers over to Villieu, Iberville set sail on September 3 [32] and went to the Penobscot.

When news of the disaster reached Boston, the governor acted quickly. Five hundred men were dispatched to Piscataqua, where the French were expected to strike next, and two warships, the *Arundel* and the *Orford,* together with the *Sorlings,* the *Prudent-Sara,* which Iberville had once captured, and also a merchantman

[31] Hutchinson, *op. cit.,* II, 93, shows that Chubb could have done no better.

[32] Iberville to Minister, Oct. 26, 1696, Archives des colonies, C[11]A, 14, 360–370.

of twenty guns and a fireship were sent to attack the French fleet.[33] The squadron arrived at the Penobscot just as Iberville was leaving. Signaling his consorts, the French commander altered his course to hug the shore toward Mount Desert, and as twilight came on he gradually drew away from his pursuers. By daylight they had disappeared and he was able to steer for Cape Breton. When off this island he ordered the *Newport* to stop there and land the Indians he had picked up at Sidney Harbor on his outward voyage, while he proceeded to Placentia Bay for the coming campaign in Newfoundland.

While Iberville was at Pemaquid, his Indian allies, greatly impressed by the success of the French arms, approached him with a proposition for a joint attack on Boston. The idea appealed, of course, to the victorious commander; but as he had no authority to take such a step at this time, he satisfied himself with drawing up a plan of campaign which he took with him to Newfoundland and sent to France at the first opportunity. Unfortunately, the ship carrying the document was lost.[34] In some other way, however, Iberville's ideas in regard to Boston reached France—he may have discussed them with some of his officers—for the Intendant-General of France, De Lagny, wrote the Minister of Marine under date of January 20, 1697, giving him the gist of the plan. "I have taken the liberty," he said, "to submit this project to you, my lord, because M d'Iberville drew it up during the voyage he made last year to Acadia for the capture of Pemaquid." The idea of a concerted attack on New England and New York was not a new one, as we have seen from the expeditions launched by Frontenac when he assumed the governorship. The present plan was merely a variant of an old theme, first broached by Callières, which had Fort Orange and Manhattan as its objectives. The scheme now advocated by De Lagny was to sail against Boston first, then proceed to Manhattan:

[33] *C.S.P. Am. & W.I.*, *1696–1697*, No. 136.
[34] *Docs. Rel. Col. Hist. N.Y.*, IX, 735.

The design against Boston has special objects as regard Canada in general, and for the preservation of Acadia in particular, and the establishments to be necessarily found there. Its execution is of greater utility than [that of] Manhattan, and of infinitely more importance for the state and of incalculable injury to old England and to all the western and southwestern colonies.

Iberville was for this plan heart and soul, and he would, of course, be at least second-in-command of the expedition, that is, if he could be spared from Hudson Bay, though this could hardly be expected considering his experience in the northern regions.[35] In the end nothing came of this, for the war was brought to a close before any action could be taken.[36]

[35] *Ibid.*, pp. 659–662.

[36] For an account of the Acadian expedition see Beaudoin, *op. cit.*, pp. 31–38, and also Iberville's letter to Pontchartrain, Sept. 24, 1696, *ibid.*, pp. 71–81.

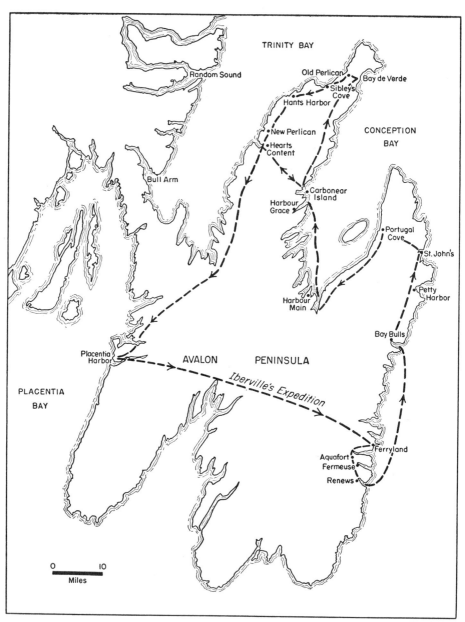

TRINITY BAY

Random Sound

Old Perlican
Bay de Verde
Sibleys
Cove
Hants Harbor

CONCEPTION
BAY

New Perlican

Hearts
Content

Bull Arm

Carbonear
Island

Harbour
Grace

Portugal
Cove

St. John's

Petty
Harbor

Harbour
Main

Bay Bulls

Placentia
Harbor

AVALON   PENINSULA

Iberville's Expedition

PLACENTIA
BAY

Ferryland

Aquafort
Fermeuse

Renews

0   10
Miles

Map of Newfoundland, showing Iberville's route.

CHAPTER VI

The Ravaging of Newfoundland

THAT part of Newfoundland where Iberville was about to launch his campaign is known as the Avalon Peninsula and is connected with the island at its southeastern extremity by a narrow isthmus. This isthmus separates Placentia Bay to the southwest from Trinity Bay to the northeast. The peninsula itself is indented by huge gulfs whose shore lines in turn are broken by numerous small bays and harbors. Its terrain is drained by many rivers and dotted by innumerable lakes, little known to the settlers, who almost to a man dwelt along the coast, where they plied their trade as fishermen. The English had complete control of the eastern portion of the peninsula, their colonists having settled in some thirty-five coastal villages. Their capital was St. John's, situated on the side of a splendid harbor on the Atlantic shore line. The entire population at this time numbered slightly more than 2,000 men, besides women and children of whom no accurate record has been kept.[1]

In contrast to this numerous colony the French had only a small settlement at Placentia Harbor, a small gulf on the eastern side of the great Placentia Bay. Yet it was important to France. "Of all our settlements in North America," wrote Baron de la Hontan,

[1] Letter of Bacqueville de la Potherie, in Tyrrell, *op. cit.*, pp. 181–183.

"Placentia is the post of greatest importance and service to the King, in regard that 'tis a place of refuge to the ships that are obliged to put into a harbor, when they go or come to Canada." [2] At the head of Placentia Harbor one comes to a narrow passage "sixty paces over, and six fathoms water deep," which leads to an inner harbor capable of sheltering 150 ships, safe from outside attacks because of its narrow entrance. The colony itself was a wretched affair of a few houses and a handful of poverty-stricken inhabitants. To protect the settlement, Fort St. Louis had been erected on the crest of the hill flanking the northern side of the entrance. It was none too good a fortification, difficulty of access being its chief source of strength. The garrison consisted of eighteen men under the Sieur de l'Hermitte, to which eighty fishermen could be added in a pinch. While it was doubtful if the place could resist a determined attack, it would do as a base of operations against the English colonies on the island.

When Pierre d'Iberville dropped anchor in Placentia Harbor on September 12, 1696, he found to his surprise that Governor Brouillan was not there. Three days before a formidable fleet of seven ships [3] and some lesser craft, under the command of Joseph Danycan du Rocher, had arrived from St. Malo, where it had been assembled, manned by over 1,000 sailors and soldiers, for the purpose of making a clean sweep of the English settlements, while Iberville was to carry on operations by land. According to the plan outlined by the government, the two leaders were to destroy the colonies, send their inhabitants back to England, and seize what booty they could. Then Brouillan was to turn over the command to Iberville and return to France with a good share of the loot; for it was the government's intention to divide it be-

---

[2] La Hontan, *New Voyages to North America*, ed. by R. G. Thwaites (Chicago, 1905), I, 335.

[3] *Pelican, Harcourt, Diamant, Comte de Toulouse, Phélipeaux, Marie, and Vendôme* (Charles de la Roncière, *Histoire de la marine française* [Paris, 1899–1932], VI, 271).

tween the backers of the expedition—the King, the ship owners at St. Malo who had underwritten Brouillan's share, and Iberville, who was paying his own way.[4]

No sooner had Iberville dropped anchor than he got in touch with the officer in command of the settlement during the governor's absence, one Pastour de Costebelle, asking him for provisions in order that he might join Brouillan in the present campaign, for his own supplies had been exhausted during his cruise along the Acadian coast. To this Costebelle was indifferent; he blandly shrugged his shoulders saying he had no supplies to spare—which was probably true. And even if Costebelle had been able to furnish the ships Iberville could not have marched against such a well-defended place as St. John's with only one hundred men ready for action. He was therefore obliged to possess his soul in patience and await the coming of the *Wesp* with the contingent of men and cargo of provisions that Auteuil and Maricourt had been trying to raise in Quebec and Montreal. But in attempting to carry out their mission, these men had met with difficulties. Governor Frontenac was away on a campaign against the Iroquois, and during his absence Champigny had opened letters addressed to the governor, letters containing copies of the instructions for Iberville and Brouillan. Realizing that haste was necessary, he had set the ball rolling by helping Auteuil enlist some sixty men; but Champigny was also short of provisions and could not allow Auteuil to take enough for both these men and the sixty Indians to be taken on board in Acadia. Fortunately there arrived from France at this time the *Postillon*, carrying a two months' supply for *Profond* and the *Envieux*. This, of course, could be sent directly to Placentia.[5]

On his return to Montreal, Frontenac at once set to work ob-

[4] Brouillan's instructions, Apr. 4, 1696, *Report on Canadian Archives, 1899, supplement*, p. 315.

[5] Champigny to Minister, Aug. 18, 1696, Archives des colonies, C^{11}A, 14, 279–285.

taining twenty more men. He drew from the military as well as from the civil population, as he felt that the *habitans* were for the most part in need of rest after the Iroquois campaign and, moreover, were at this time busy with their crops. Thus of the eighty men required by Iberville thirty were *habitans*, the rest soldiers. They were a picked lot, the choice of over three hundred volunteers. The company was placed under the command of an officer named Nicolas Daneau de Muy, a man of considerable experience and well qualified for the task at hand; he was ordered to report to Brouillan.[6]

On October 3 the *Postillon* arrived in Placentia Bay with her precious cargo. She had left Quebec in company with the *Wesp* on September 16 but had become separated from her and could give Iberville no information as to her whereabouts. While awaiting the *Wesp*'s arrival Iberville spent his time in exploring the neighborhood, getting the lay of the land, and gaining all the information he could about local conditions to help him in the coming campaign. When the *Wesp* finally entered the harbor, the commander found to his dismay that he was no better off than before, as De Muy had been ordered to place himself under the governor, and his contingent, therefore, could not be moved until that official's return. Nothing daunted, Iberville made plans for an attack on Carbonear, an important settlement second only to St. John's in population and situated on the western side of Conception Bay, fifty miles northeast of Placentia Harbor.

The arrival of Brouillan on October 17, however, nipped this plan in the bud. The governor had not been too successful in his own campaign, having failed before St. John's; in fact, owing to misunderstandings and miscalculations he had not even been able to attack it and had been obliged to content himself with the capture of such small places as Aquafort, Fermeuse, and Renews. The campaign had ended in recriminations between him and the

[6] Frontenac to Minister, Oct. 25, 1696, *Rapport de l'archiviste de Quebec, 1928–1929,* p. 311.

men from St. Malo, who promptly left for home, so that his state of mind when he anchored in Placentia Harbor was not such as to lead to pleasant relations with his colleague. Trouble broke out at once. In the first interview, held on board the governor's ship, Iberville learned that Brouillan was displeased with him because he had not joined him before St. John's, a failure he attributed to Iberville's reluctance to be under his orders. He also asserted his right to command the men brought in by the *Wesp*. Since nothing could be gained while the governor was in this frame of mind, Iberville dropped the subject for a brief while, then sought a second interview. At first Brouillan proved as intractable as ever. He insisted in keeping the Canadian contingent, he refused to read Iberville's instructions, and he acted in such an unreasonable manner that the latter was on the verge of giving up the business and returning to France. When news of this reached the Canadians, they rebelled, vowing they would serve under no other than Pierre d'Iberville and would desert if any attempt were made to place them under Brouillan's control.

In the end the governor yielded. He saw the impossibility of coercing these independent pioneers and the necessity of coming to terms with their leader if he wanted their co-operation. An agreement was accordingly reached by which an immediate attack was to be made on St. John's, Iberville going overland with his Canadians, Brouillan going by sea with the French regulars. Brouillan was to have supreme command of the two forces, but Iberville was to get the lion's share of the booty as he had borne most of the expense. When St. John's had been taken, Iberville was to be left free to attack the northern settlements, Carbonear, for instance, while the governor returned to Placentia Harbor. The *Profond*, still under the command of Bonaventure, was to convey the governor and his followers to the rendezvous at Renews, forty-five miles south of St. John's, with ample provisions for Iberville's men when they got there and for a detachment Brouillan had left at near-by Fermeuse. Strange to say,

Brouillan persuaded Daneau de Muy to join him instead of accompanying Iberville; perhaps he had lured him with some hopes of preferment.

Eager to do a thorough job of destroying the English fishing industry, Iberville seized the occasion to write the Minister asking that a forty-gun ship with a crew of 120 men be off the coast of Newfoundland the following March in order to intercept any ships coming there from England. The command of this ship, he earnestly hoped, would be given to Ensign du Guay de Boisbriant, whom he mentions as an able officer well acquainted with Newfoundland waters. He closes his letter with a delicate hint that he has been promised promotion to the rank of full captain.[7]

On the first day of November, the festival of All Saints, Iberville with 120 men set out from Placentia. The campaign was to be a long one—according to indications it would probably last all winter—and in view of the dangers that lay ahead Father Jean Beaudoin was to accompany them as chaplain. Among the more prominent members of the undertaking was the Abnaki chieftain, Nescambiouit, whose greatness of soul, according to the historian La Potherie, was shown by the fact that he had taken upward of forty scalps during his lifetime. Iberville selected from his inexhaustible supply of younger brothers Jean-Baptiste de Bienville to act as his aide. The route lay nearly due east, and for nine days the little army made its way over the frozen ground, plunging into almost impenetrable woods, and waist-deep in the freezing water, crossing the lakes and rivers that lie at the head of St. Mary's Bay. They were nearly destitute of provisions when they reached Ferryland—Forillon the French called it—on the east coast of the island, eight miles north of Renews. Here they were fortunate

---

[7] Iberville to Pontchartrain, Sept. 24, 1696, Jean Beaudoin, *op. cit.*, pp. 71–81; same to same, Oct. 26, 1696, Archives des colonies, C¹¹A, 14, 360–370; Charlevoix, *op. cit.*, V, 35–39; letter of La Potherie in Tyrrell, *op. cit.*, pp. 161–163.

enough to find a dozen horses which, *faute de mieux*, they used as food.

Meanwhile, Brouillan had arrived at Renews with the *Profond*. His first act was to send out the Chevalier de Rancogne with three or four men to make a reconnaissance in the direction of St. John's. Somewhere along the road the chevalier managed to capture an English fisherman, who quickly made his escape and hurried to St. John's, where he informed the commander, Governor Miners, that the French had landed. Governor Miners immediately sent out a detachment to seize Rancogne, but he managed to elude them after a struggle in which he lost one of his men and arrived at Ferryland after a journey marked by severe hardships. The English at St. John's were therefore well aware of the presence of the French and what might be expected from them.

Within a day or two Iberville went to Renews, where the old bickering between him and Brouillan flared up anew. The governor now informed his colleague of his intention to take half of all the plunder from such places as they might capture together, a division of booty which, as Iberville pointed out, was in direct contravention to the agreement they had reached at Placentia, and as witnesses to this he called on his brother-in-law, Pierre Payen de Noyan, and Ensign du Guay. But the governor was obstinate, and when they returned to Ferryland the quarrel broke out again. Here Iberville decided to review his men, and for this purpose he lined them up in groups of twenty-five for inspection. At this, the Sieur de Muy, without so much as asking Iberville's leave, selected two dozen volunteers, claiming he had brought them from Quebec to serve under the governor. To make matters worse, Brouillan himself asserted that Frontenac had given him Iberville's entire contingent and that he was master of all the forces. Feeling ran high. The governor and De Muy drew their swords and threatened to stab all objectors, saying that if Iberville wished to make war he could do so on his own hook with any volunteers that Brouillan did not need. Enraged at this high-handed action, Iberville read the King's commission appointing him commander during the winter season; but the governor of Placentia would have none of it. It soon dawned on Iberville that the avaricious Brouillan was interested in plunder rather than the honors of supreme command; so setting aside his own personal rights as guaranteed by the agreement at Placentia, he offered his colleague an equal share of the loot. The offer was at once accepted: Governor Brouillan returned the soldiers to Iberville's ranks; a truce was patched up; and the two proceeded with their plans to capture St. John's.[8]

The leaders thus reconciled, or perhaps we had better say having adopted a policy of unfriendly neutrality, they now prepared to move northward. Before starting, however, they received a scouting party which had been prowling about the neighborhood for some time in search of information concerning the enemy. These scouts under the leadership of Damours des Plaines brought in some prisoners they had picked up at Cape Broyle, and from these men the commanders heard the interesting news that about one hundred fishermen were scattered along the coast as far as Bay Bulls, a harbor halfway between Ferryland and St. John's, all busily engaged in rebuilding the homes Brouillan's men had destroyed during the recent campaign. At this point the governor decided to send the *Profond* back to France with an account of his achievements thus far, and Iberville seized the occasion to entrust a letter to his old friend, Bonaventure, requesting the authorities to send him reinforcements the following spring so that he might complete the subjugation of the island. The prisoners just captured were placed on board the ship and sent to France, whence they might make their way back to England as best they could.

Iberville now embarked his Canadians in a fleet of small boats

[8] Iberville to Pontchartrain, July 5, 1697, Archives des colonies, C[11]A, 15, 216.

and proceeded to Bay Bulls, where he had the good fortune to capture a merchantman. The crew had fled to the woods at Iberville's approach, but fortunately for the French the captain had courage enough to remain by his ship, and on being questioned he yielded the valuable information that two men-of-war, the *Dreadnaught*, seventy-two guns, and the *Oxford*, fifty guns, had just arrived from England and were headed for St. John's. This confirmed the rumors of the coming of an English fleet that had been causing the French commanders considerable anxiety. A few days later Brouillan entered Bay Bulls with the main army.

On November 26, the entire army began its march. Brouillan sent forward a detail of twenty men to St. John's and ordered other small detachments to harass the neighboring settlements; he followed these with the main body commanded by Iberville, who was ably seconded by his lieutenant, Jacques de Montigny. With a small detachment of picked men Iberville now advanced on Petty Harbor, situated eight miles south of St. John's, where he found the road blocked by thirty fishermen. Though greatly outnumbered, he attacked at once, driving them across a foaming torrent that poured its icy waters into the bay. On the other side he found that the defenders had retreated into a trench. The engagement was quickly over, and the French were masters of the place despite the resistance of the villagers, who immediately sent to St. John's asking for help. The town responded with alacrity, sending some thirty men the following day; but bad weather prevented them from reaching Petty Harbor, and they were obliged to return with nothing to show for their efforts. Next day a larger contingent, this time one of over eighty men, was sent to the rescue, for the settlers were determined to check the enemy before the French could reach the capital.

St. John's at this time was, for a Newfoundland settlement, a well-protected, well-fortified place. Access to its spacious harbor, which is a mile in length and half that distance in width, can be had only through a passage 1,400 feet wide, which at one point narrows down to less than 700 feet. This passage is a half-mile long and is flanked by hills rising to a height of 500 or 600 feet. The largest vessels could anchor in the harbor, for it has a depth ranging from five to ten fathoms, and even more in the center, while the tidal variation is only four feet. In Iberville's day the entrance was protected by a battery of eight guns. The inhabitants were scattered along the northern shore for a distance of half a mile, while three forts gave protection to the town: one near the wood on the west side; the second toward the middle of the settlement; the third on a site overlooking the harbor. This last fortification, known as King William's Fort, was situated on a hill to the north of the town. It was a square-shaped structure built of palisades eight feet high with a bastion at each corner. A trench, now filled with snow, was spanned by a drawbridge. In spite of these fortifications the supply of ammunition at this time was too low to permit a protracted defense.

Meanwhile the French were advancing four hundred strong. The van, consisting of thirty Canadians, was led by Montigny, who marched five hundred paces ahead of the main body commanded by Iberville and Brouillan. The going was very rough; snow was falling; the roads, such as they were, proved to be impassable for horses and wagons, thus forcing the men to carry their own supplies. On November 28 they came in sight of St. John's. Suddenly, as the van was passing a wood recently destroyed by fire, it was met by a volley from a detachment of eighty men well concealed behind rocks and boulders. It was the contingent sent out to rescue Petty Harbor. When Montigny gave the order to charge, the Canadians threw down their packs and rushed at the enemy; then as the main body came up on the run Brouillan attacked head on while Iberville advanced on the left flank. The battle, in which the French were victorious, lasted but half an hour and was marked by the personal courage of the governor, who made amends for his past selfish conduct by a display of bravery that was an inspiration to his men. Iberville and his detachment, leaving the governor to follow them with the main body rushed into St. John's close on the heels of the fleeing English, some of whom promptly took refuge in King William's Fort, while a hundred of them sought asylum on a ketch that was riding at anchor in the harbor. Shortly after this, Governor Brouillan arrived with his army and sent De Muy to lead sixty men into the fort nearest King William's while he quartered the bulk of his forces in the neighboring houses. According to Father Beaudoin, Iberville could have taken King William's Fort had he had with him a small division of one hundred men, but lacking these he was compelled to content himself with the capture of a few prisoners. Those on board the ketch do not seem to have had any further interest in the campaign, for they promptly hoisted their anchor and set sail.

Believing themselves to be in for a long siege, the French sent to Bay Bulls the following day for the mortars and ammunition they had left there. While awaiting the arrival of this equipment, the commanders decided to make at least one effort to obtain possession by the time-honored method, so successfully employed by Iberville, of summoning the garrison to surrender. For this purpose a prisoner was sent to the fort with the usual proposal. When he failed to return after a reasonable time De Muy and Montigny were sent out during the night to burn the surrounding houses, a bit of frightfulness that evidently had the desired effect, for the next day a messenger arrived under a flag of truce requesting an interview to discuss terms of surrender. The request was immediately granted, and Governor Miners presently appeared with four of his lieutenants to receive the terms offered by Brouillan. He then asked for a day's time to consider them, hoping that this delay would enable the *Dreadnaught* and *Oxford* to arrive before the surrender took place. But the French saw through the ruse and, anxious to bring matters to a head, decided to force the enemy's hand by an action that was as contemptible as it was brutal. Among their prisoners there was a settler named William

Drew. This man was handed over to the Indians, who "cut all around his scalp and then by the strength of hand stripped his skin from the forehead to the crown and so sent him into the fortification, assuring the inhabitants that they would serve them all in like manner if they did not surrender." [9] This action was accompanied by a list of the terms of surrender which provided that the fort should be evacuated at two o'clock in the afternoon, the garrison to march out without their arms. It was promised them, however, that their lives would be spared, their clothing left them, their wives and daughters protected from insult, and two vessels given them to take them back to England. Major l'Hermitte carried the articles to Governor Miners, who signed and returned them to Brouillan for ratification.

The ceremony of surrender took place on the last day of November, and at two o'clock in the afternoon the wretched garrison and inhabitants to the number of 160, besides women and children, laid down their arms and evacuated the fort. In negotiating the surrender, it is significant to note, Governor Brouillan showed his animosity to Iberville by ratifying the treaty without waiting for the signature of his colleague, a discourtesy which the latter did not forget. The expedition thus far had been successful both from a military and a financial point of view. Father Beaudoin credits the French commanders with having captured or defeated nearly eight hundred men—an exaggeration, perhaps—and having seized 220 boats and over 100,000 pounds of codfish.

It was now deemed advisable to proceed with the destruction of the other settlements where there were further accumulations of fish. West of St. John's lies Conception Bay, and west of this larger Trinity Bay, and on the shores of these gulfs lay the English settlements, the most important being Carbonear, where many panicky fisherfolk had found asylum. To this task Iberville now addressed himself, while Brouillan, who by this time had had

[9] Deposition of Philip Roberts *et al.* in D. W. Prowse, *A History of Newfoundland*, 2nd ed. (London, 1896), p. 229*n*.

enough of the campaign, though indeed it had thus far proved a profitable one, prepared to return to Placentia, much to his colleague's relief. But before doing so he took steps to put St. John's *hors de combat*. His resolution to destroy the settlement was the result of an altercation with Iberville. The commanders in making their plans had, as might be expected, some words in regard to the division of spoils, and the trouble was adjusted only by the mediation of friends.

Brouillan then decided to hold St. John's by putting De Muy in charge of the settlement, an arrangement to which Iberville was willing to agree provided the Canadians were not retained to guard it, as he needed them all for his own expedition. Such an arrangement did not suit De Muy, who promptly declined to stay without his Canadian followers; and as a result of this refusal Brouillan decided to destroy the settlement since he could not hold it. With ruthless thoroughness he ordered the forts and all the houses, save a few sheltering the sick, to be burned. He gave the settlers a fireship lying in the harbor for transporting 250 of them back to England, while the ship captured at Bay Bulls was assigned to take eighty more to France. On December 24 the governor left for Placentia, and the following day the two ships sailed for their destinations.

The campaign upon which Iberville was now to embark does not make for inspiring reading. As a military feat it does indeed deserve praise, for a march over the wastes of Newfoundland in midwinter called for endurance on the part of the men and unusual leadership on the part of the commander; but aside from this we see merely a sorry spectacle of wretched fisherfolk harried from their homes and their property destroyed or confiscated, for it was the policy of France to exterminate the colony by driving out the settlers. Before leaving St. John's, Iberville sent out exploratory parties to give the countryside a taste of what was to come. Montigny was dispatched to Portugal Cove ten miles west of St. John's, just across the peninsula which separates the Atlantic from Conception Bay. Here he captured a boat coming from Carbonear, situated on the west side of Conception Bay, and found the ketch which had sailed from St. John's at the beginning of the siege. In all he took about thirty prisoners there. Other detachments under various leaders, notably René Boucher de la Perrière, moved back and forth along the east coast of Conception Bay, doing what damage they could and taking, all told, about one hundred prisoners. They also destroyed eighty-four boats and succeeded in gaining control of considerable territory.

Iberville left St. John's for Portugal Cove on January 14, 1697, with the main army. Rude snowshoes had been made for the journey, and the men were able to travel over roads that would otherwise have been impassable. Montigny, as usual, led the way, the rest following closely on his heels. On reaching the Cove they remained a few days snowbound, for the snow, so La Potherie tells us, exceeded anything seen in Canada, by which he probably meant that part along the St. Lawrence. Then Montigny with thirty men moved southward along the shore, to be followed next day by the main body. The going was rough; men fell and were buried momentarily in the mountainous drifts to the great amusement of their friends, while Montigny himself went through the ice while crossing a river and was obliged to throw away his sword and musket in order to save himself. At last the van reached the head of the bay, a deep, narrow inlet called Harbour Main, where Montigny called a halt and awaited Iberville and his men.

When Iberville arrived a consultation was held. It was felt that to proceed by land to Carbonear, the next objective, would be a long exhausting journey, for it was thirty miles thither, and such a march over the sort of terrain they had just traversed was something to be avoided at all cost. The leaders therefore determined to make use of some boats they had found at Harbour Main. Three of these and a skiff were put in condition for the voyage; then the entire army, numbering 120 men, was placed on board, and the little fleet set sail under a favorable breeze. Unfortunately they were seen by some fishermen, who fled in their boats to Carbonear to give the alarm. These men were part of a detachment of scouts sent out to reconnoiter the French forces; for since the fall of St. John's none doubted that the French would strike at Carbonear. Unable to overtake these scouts, Iberville led his men to Harbour Grace, where they took over a hundred prisoners, and here was found an abundant supply of cattle that furnished the Canadians with fresh meat. As the inhabitants of the neighboring settlement of Brigus did not come to the help of their fellow countrymen, Iberville sent orders to their leaders to bring him all their arms in token of submission; then, unwilling to burden himself with more prisoners, he decided to leave them behind after demoralizing them by destroying their houses—a brutal act that left them shelterless during the bitter cold of midwinter.

At dawn on January 24 Montigny started with fifty men to seize a small village situated between Harbour Grace and Carbonear, while Iberville led the rest to Carbonear Island. This island must not be confused with the settlement on the mainland bearing the same name. By its formation it was well protected against invasion, being a solid rock rising precipitously from the water with a narrow landing place on its western side, and this the fishermen had covered by a small battery. Here were gathered the people from the various harbors on the mainland and a handful of refugees from St. John's, numbering in all about two hundred; and here, warned of Iberville's presence in the bay, they had laid in enough supplies to withstand a long siege should the French determine to invest the place. After getting the lay of the land Iberville proceeded to Carbonear proper, where Montigny had already seized a few of the inhabitants and driven the rest to Old Perlican on Trinity Bay. But Iberville was eager to capture Carbonear Island and make a clean sweep of all settlements on Conception Bay before leaving it.

Two days later some prisoners, lured by the promise of a handsome reward, disclosed two places where it was possible to land on the island and climb up its sides two abreast. Cheered by this news, the French decided to attempt a landing on the first calm day, for it was impossible to do so in a running sea. For the next few days the weather was unfavorable; then on the thirty-first the wind died down, and Iberville with ninety men in five boats left for the island to land simultaneously on its northern and eastern sides. As they approached, a sentinel gave the alarm and the garrison sprang to arms; but when Iberville's men attempted to land, the recoil of the ground swell as it hit the rocky shore drove back the boats and prevented a landing. "Ten men ashore," says Father Beaudoin, "would have terrified these people. Perhaps one could land in summer when the sea is entirely calm and the surf less." Next day Iberville rowed around the island looking for a vulnerable spot. He found the landing place on the western side, but it was too well manned to be successfully carried.

A few days were now spent sending out parties under Du Guay and Damours des Plaines to destroy some of the smaller hamlets and take their inhabitants prisoner, then on February 3 Iberville started with fifty men in three boats for the settlement of Bay de Verde—a fair-size town numbering about one hundred men—at the northerly tip of the peninsula. Landing at dawn three miles south of the village, the party advanced; at noon they captured two fishermen on their way to Old Perlican on the western side of the peninsula, that is on Trinity Bay, where several boats were being made ready for a speedy getaway. Anxious to capture Old Perlican before it was evacuated, Iberville turned his steps westward and on reaching the village summoned its inhabitants to surrender, a summons they readily obeyed, knowing well the futility of resistance. Old Perlican was, indeed, an important fishing village, inhabited by 150 men in addition to women and children and well stocked with cattle; but the dwellers had not waited for Iberville's arrival and had fled for the most part to Hearts Content, a coastal village twenty miles south of Old Perlican, where they sought safety in a well-built structure capable of withstanding musketry fire and armed with two or three small pieces of ordnance.

While at Old Perlican, Iberville sent a deputation to Cape de Verde to demand its surrender, assuring the natives that he would grant them easy terms. These terms, it appears, were promptly accepted, but in the meanwhile some thirty of the inhabitants had managed to cross the peninsula to Trinity Bay—it is only two miles wide at this place—and make their escape. On February 6, Iberville went to Bay de Verde in person. He sent the leading citizens with Du Guay to Carbonear and left the others in their village without bothering to plunder the settlement. On returning to Old Perlican he gave the order to start. He led his men southward along the coast, marching by easy stages and stopping at night at Sibley's Cove, Hants Harbor, and New Perlican, until he arrived at Hearts Content. "The Canadians," La Potherie tells us, "left most of the people, with a few exceptions, content with their good fortune but very forgetful of the favorable treatment they had received." Iberville's leniency on this march evidently bore fruit, for the inhabitants of Hearts Content were quite willing to surrender at discretion without first putting their little fortress to the test. The fact that there were only about thirty men in garrison may explain why they thought that they could never resist the superior numbers of the French. Leaving ten of his men to guard the captured village under the command of Louis Damours des Chaufours, brother of Damours des Plaines, Iberville now led his army back across the peninsula to Carbonear Island, the only place that had not surrendered to him.

By this time the French had accumulated a large number of prisoners whom they wished to exchange for some of their own men captured in various places and taken to Carbonear Island. There were also among the prisoners held by the English three Irishmen who had sided with the French.[10] After a brief parley

[10] La Potherie says that they sided with the English, but this is obviously a mistake.

with the inhabitants of Carbonear the Canadians agreed to exchange one Englishman for a Frenchman and three Englishmen for an Irishman, a basis exchange by which the English would secure nine of their fellow countrymen at the cost of a little national pride.

Montigny was dispatched with a suitable number of prisoners, among whom was the brother of the commander of the island who, according to La Potherie, would rather have remained with the French. Taking his place on the shore well out of gunshot range, Montigny awaited the arrival of the French prisoners. At last a skiff made its appearance manned by six men but bringing no Frenchmen. When asked the reason for this, the Englishman in command of the boat gave evasive replies and had the audacity to say that the garrison wished to take their commander's brother back to the island where he would find the prisoners and would bring them all safely to Montigny. This request was, of course, turned down. Words ensued, and a scuffle followed in which three English officers were seized by Montigny and taken to Iberville. They begged their release, promising to obtain the return of the French prisoners without any further nonsense, an offer which was promptly declined. Later, these officers proposed to surrender the island and compel those ensconced there to recognize the King of France, with the understanding that they might retain their fishing rights during the summer. One of these men actually did undertake the mission, while his companions were forced to go bond for him, agreeing to pay the French 10,000 *livres* if he failed to return. The mission, however, failed.

Meanwhile, Iberville and his officers had been busy in various ways. Damours des Plaines crossed over to Portugal Cove and thence made his way to St. John's, where he picked up eight Canadians, left there on account of illness, and transported them by sea to Placentia together with sixty Englishmen whom he took along as prisoners. On February 28, Iberville and his army returned to Hearts Content after having set fire to the village (not the island) of Carbonear. On March 1 Iberville ordered Montigny and La Perrière to proceed with two hundred prisoners to the head of Bull Arm, a small gulf in Trinity Bay where an isthmus only two miles wide separates it from the northernmost waters of Placentia Bay,[11] and he gave Du Guay orders to remain at Hearts Content and keep an eye on Carbonear. He himself proceeded overland to Placentia Harbor with a small detachment, for he was anxious to obtain some news from France.

Unencumbered by large numbers, the party traveled rapidly and reached its destination in four days. After a brief stay Iberville turned his steps northward to Cromwell Bay, a northern branch of Placentia, where he met La Perrière coming from Bull Arm with Montigny and his band of prisoners. Placing these men on an island near by, Iberville dispatched his officers, La Perrière, Damours des Chaufours, and Bienville, to Random Sound, a large gulf on the western shore of Trinity Bay, some fifteen miles north of Bull Arm, where they burned two villages and captured forty men, while he returned to Placentia Harbor to enlist an expedition of one hundred men to attack the settlement of Bonavista, northernmost of the English villages and one of the largest. This venture, it appears, was never undertaken, for Iberville insisted on waiting until some news came from France before giving the order to march; and when news did come it was in the form of instructions to leave as soon as possible for Hudson Bay.

In this manner did Iberville's campaign in Newfoundland come to a close. He had taken nearly all the English settlements, captured an immense quantity of booty, destroyed fishing vessels, and seized seven hundred prisoners. Such a large number of prisoners was far too many to look after; many escaped and made their way to Carbonear Island, the only place the French had been unable to capture. Iberville's expedition, however, was little more than a

[11] Beaudoin says that he went to Bay Bulls at the bottom of Trinity Bay. As Bay Bulls is situated on the Atlantic Coast he probably meant Bull Arm.

raid, taking booty and destroying the enemy's property. Nothing permanent was accomplished by it. A cry of rage arose in England over the destruction of the colony and in a few months a fleet was sent over which quickly recovered the territory that had been lost. Meanwhile Iberville and his men had gone to Hudson Bay.[12]

[12] The best accounts of the campaign in Newfoundland are to be found in Beaudoin, *op. cit.*, pp. 38–69, and in Bacqueville de la Potherie's letter published in Tyrrell, *op. cit.*, pp. 161–183. A good secondary account is found in Charlevoix, *op. cit.*, V, 37–46. See also Prowse, *op. cit.*

CHAPTER VII

The Battle for Hudson Bay

THE fleet which the King of France sent out in the spring of 1697 to recapture Port Nelson was the most formidable one he had ever dispatched to Hudson Bay. The loss of this post the previous year had not only been a serious blow to his pride, but had placed the English in complete possession of the Bay and had destroyed the entire work of the past ten years. He was, therefore, determined to take the place at all cost, and he gave the commander strict orders not to hesitate to destroy the fort if he could not hold it himself.

The squadron collected at La Rochelle during the winter was put under the command of Lemoyne de Sérigny, who was told to place it under his brother's orders when it reached Newfoundland. In order to insure the superiority of the French fleet over any armada the Hudson's Bay Company might send out, no less than five vessels were put in commission, and every precaution, including a supply of ten months' provisions, was taken for a successful outcome of the undertaking. The government had begun the organization of this fleet the previous September, with the intention of sending it out to bolster up the expedition in Newfoundland; but because of various delays the sailing date was postponed from time to time, until when the squadron did at last weigh anchor, the campaign was over and the ultimate destination of the ships was changed to Hudson Bay.[1] The flotilla consisted of the *Pelican*, fifty guns (though in action this number was reduced), the largest of the fleet, on which Iberville was to hoist his flag; our old friend the *Profond*, to be given to Du Guay; the *Palmier*, forty guns, under the command of Sérigny; the *Wesp*, Ensign Chartier; and the *Violent*, Ensign Bigot. Besides the regular crews, Sérigny was fortunate enough to obtain some of the veterans of the French garrison captured the year before at Port Nelson and just repatriated to France. Among them were Lemoyne de Martigny and Nicolas Jérémie. These men were all ordered to report to Sérigny for service in Hudson Bay. Fortunately for posterity, the historian Claude-Charles de la Potherie was appointed commissary of the fleet and sailed on board the *Pelican*. To this able observer, who wrote under the name of Bacqueville de la Potherie, we owe the most graphic narrative of the expedition and also a good account of Iberville's campaign in Newfoundland, which he obtained from those who had taken part in it.

On March 9, 1697, the King issued his instructions to Sérigny. They were brief and merely told him to carry out himself the plan of campaign outlined in the orders to Iberville if for some reason or other he was unable to contact his brother. These orders provided that Iberville should go first to the St. John River to deliver the munitions intended for Villebon, capturing on the way any Boston vessels he might encounter. Then he was to return to Placentia, make his final preparations, and go thence to Hudson Bay. If, however, there should be an attack on Newfoundland by the English, he should assist Governor Brouillan in its defense, then go directly to the Bay without visiting Acadia. When Sérigny left France he carried Iberville's orders with him.[2]

The fleet sailed from La Rochelle on Easter Monday, April 8,

---

[1] *Report on Canadian Archives, 1899, supplement*, p. 320.
[2] See various documents dated Mar. 9, 1697, *ibid.*, p. 322.

and for nine days bowled along under a favorable breeze. During a violent storm which sprang up after a spell of fair weather, a collision occurred between the *Palmier* and the *Wesp* in which the latter nearly foundered and was left behind as lost. By the time the fleet was on the Grand Banks, scurvy had broken out, but here the sailors were able to take in a supply of codfish that halted the spread of this dread disease. Ten days later, on May 18, the ships anchored in Placentia Harbor, and three days later the *Wesp* limped in somewhat the worse for her accident.

Iberville now took command of the expedition. The damage done the *Wesp* was considerable, and by the time she was again in commission it was deemed too late to undertake the mission to Fort Naxouat if they were to reach Hudson Bay that year. This part of the original plan was accordingly abandoned and the final preparations for the voyage were rushed through as quickly as possible. In place of the *Violent*, which was left behind for some reason or other, Iberville added to his fleet a thirty-ton brigantine called the *Esquimaux*. His brother, Bienville, who had served loyally in the recent campaign, joined him for what was to be his first adventure in Hudson Bay.

At last on July 8 the commander gave the order to weigh anchor. The ships set their sails to a favoring breeze and were soon on their way northward over the Atlantic, passing along the east coast of Newfoundland. For two weeks the going was fairly smooth, then as they neared Hudson Strait a northerly gale bore down on them, burying the decks and rigging under a coat of ice. When the weather cleared, they found themselves in the entrance to the strait just off Resolution Island, which lies twenty-five miles off mighty Baffin Land. This part of the strait seems to have been unfamiliar to the French, for La Potherie naïvely tells us of the great stress they laid on the discovery of some islands near by, naming one La Salle after an officer of the *Pelican*—probably the first one to sight it—and another La Potherie. After spending a day or two becalmed off La Salle Island, which La Potherie explored, the fleet emerged from the little archipelago through a strait to which the name of Iberville was given. Led by the *Pelican,* the ships managed to free themselves from the ice that had accumulated about them and work their way westward through the strait, gradually crossing over to the southern shore and coasting along it until they came, on August 2, to Cape Weggs. Passing this headland, they skirted the shores of Charles Island. August 4 saw them between Nottingham Island and Cape Digges, where they found themselves blocked by heavy, tightly packed masses of ice that held the ships in their grip for nearly three weeks, carrying them back and forth with the fluctuations of the current. During this time the ice took its toll: the little *Esquimaux* was crushed between two gigantic floes, and only the quick action of the crew in climbing out on the ice saved them from destruction. The *Palmier* suffered injury too when her rudder was broken, but the ship's carpenter speedily repaired the damage before she got into open water.

After three weeks of ice-bound inactivity an opening appeared, and the *Pelican* slipped her cable to join the other vessels in the offing; but scarcely was she under way when a fog spread like an opaque cloud over the waters, and the ships were carried back into the strait by the current, though Iberville, more lucky than the others, managed to steer his vessel into a small bay free from ice. Three days later he contrived to escape the floes and start for Port Nelson, leaving his consorts to follow as soon as they could.

When the fog suddenly lifted, those on board the *Profond* saw in the distance three ships bearing down on them with the current. Thinking they were part of the French fleet, Du Guay paid little attention to them; then as they drew nearer he recognized to his astonishment the English ensign fluttering at their mastheads. They were the Hudson's Bay Company's annual fleet, composed this time of the *Hampshire* (fifty-six guns, Captain John Fletcher), the *Dering* (thirty-six, Captain Michael Grimmington), and the *Hudson's Bay* (thirty-two, Captain Richard Smithsend). A fireship, the *Owner's Love*, had sailed with the fleet from England, but she did not appear with the other ships at this time and was probably lost somewhere with all on board. Du Guay at once headed for the ice, preferring to lose the *Profond* rather than surrender, for she carried on board all the munitions and supplies for the expedition. The English gave chase. Sérigny and Chartier with the *Palmier* and *Wesp* crowded on all sail in a vain attempt to come to the rescue, but the intervening ice barrier held them off. The following day—it was August 26—Du Guay opened fire on the *Dering* and *Hudson's Bay* at nine in the morning. The *Profond* fought under a severe disadvantage, for owing to her position she could bring only two guns to bear on the enemy, and no maneuvering was possible while the ice held her in its grip. All day long the ships battered away at each other, the *Hampshire* coming up in the evening to take part. Little was accomplished, however, by either side; it was a drawn battle; all eventually recovered from their wounds and in due time arrived at Port Nelson.

By September 4 Iberville had crossed Hudson Bay and anchored at the mouth of the Hayes River, about three leagues northeast of the fort. He immediately sent ashore twenty-two men under his cousin, Lemoyne de Martigny, with orders to secure, if possible, some Indians who could inform him regarding conditions at the fort and whether or not the English squadron had been there, for Iberville had no knowledge then of the action off Cape Digges. At dawn the following day he saw three ships to leeward tacking in toward the harbor. Raising his anchor, he set sail, determined to be ready for any emergency, and ran out in the direction of the oncoming vessels; but scarcely had he cleared the harbor when he saw through his spyglass that they were the English fleet that Du Guay had met in Hudson Strait.

The situation was indeed critical. Iberville had but one ship, albeit a powerful one, to oppose the *Hampshire*, quite the equal of his own, and the two others besides, which had between them sixty-eight guns. Moreover, the *Pelican* was handicapped because of the paucity of her crew. Twenty-two men had been put ashore the previous evening and were now prowling about the country-side, while forty more were down with scurvy. Twenty-seven sailors had been transferred to the undermanned *Profond* when the fleet was at Placentia, for no one then dreamed that the *Pelican* would be called upon to oppose the Hudson's Bay Company's fleet singlehanded. Then, too, she had never had her full comple-ment of fifty guns—forty-six were the most she had had when she left France, and of these two had been given to the *Profond*. Thus there were left for active service only about 150 men out of a regular quota of 250, while the Hampshire had a company of 230 all told. There was no question, however, on the part of the French commander as to what he should do. Great as were the odds against him, he must at all cost prevent the English fleet from entering the harbor and saving the fort. He immediately called a council of war, and to his intense joy he found his officers unani-mous in their decision to fight. Orders were given at once. Every able man was assigned to a post; the decks were cleared, the ham-mocks were stowed, ammunition was served out, and the matches were lighted, as the crew prepared to get every last bit of fighting power out of their ship's forty-four guns. The ship's company was divided into three groups, each under the command of com-petent officers. La Salle and Grandville commanded the lower battery, Bienville and the Chevalier de Ligondez the upper, and the men on the forecastle were placed under La Potherie. Iber-ville, of course, took his post on the quarter-deck.

The enemy advanced in battle formation, the mighty *Hamp-shire* in the lead, followed by the *Dering* and *Hudson's Bay*. The *Pelican*, with her topsails set, heeled over in a steady breeze so that Iberville had difficulty in bringing his lee battery into play. Battle was joined shortly after the noon hour (9:30 A.M., according to La Potherie). The French vessel bore down on the *Hampshire*, whose commander, thinking his ship was about to be boarded, set his main course, filled his fore-topsail, and slid out of range. Iberville then headed for the *Dering*, giving her a broadside that carried away the tackle of her main course. While the *Pelican* was thus engaged, the *Hudson's Bay* came up to assist the *Dering* and received for her pains a terrific volley that tore her rigging to pieces. At this point the *Hampshire* came about and brought her heavy guns to bear on the gallant *Pelican* already struggling bravely with the other two ships. Her first attack was deadly. She sent a volley of musketry that swept the forecastle, while her artillery lodged two shots on the water line, carried away the spritsail, and did considerable damage to the fore-rigging. For three hours the English ships hammered away at the *Pelican*, and the *Pelican* replied in kind. Her gunners, stripped to the waist, served the heated cannon, while the soldiers on the upper deck poured their musketry-fire into the enemy, picking off such as showed their heads above the bulwarks.

As the afternoon wore on, Captain Fletcher of the *Hampshire*, more and more exasperated at the failure of his fleet to get a decision, determined to end the conflict by sinking the pestiferous Frenchman. For this purpose he attempted to gain a windward position, a maneuver which Iberville succeeded in partially thwarting; then he bore down as best he could on the devoted *Pelican*. At this point there took place a curious incident that seems somewhat ludicrous to us today, though it was not entirely out of place in the naval etiquette of those times. As the two ships drew together Captain Fletcher called on Iberville to strike his colors, a command which he, of course, refused to obey. In admiration of his foe's courage the Englishman then took a glass of wine and drank his health, at the same time inviting him to dine on board the Hampshire at the end of the battle, if he should survive. Iberville replied in kind, drinking a toast to his gallant enemy.[3] These amenities over, Fletcher got down to business.

[3] Deposition of Thomas Morriss and Samuell Clarke, who witnessed the incident (*ibid.*, 1934, p. 7).

Loading his guns with grapeshot, he fired a broadside that tore away the *Pelican*'s rigging and strewed her upper deck with wounded men. Iberville made one last effort to stop the fast-approaching ship, which could have dropped enough men on his deck to overwhelm the crew. As he turned to receive her yardarm to yardarm he let loose from his battery a terrific broadside into her hull close to the water line. At this short distance every shot told. The *Hampshire* broached to, water poured into her hold, and before she had gone three lengths she sank into the Bay carrying the gallant Fletcher with her.[4]

The suddenness with which possible defeat was turned into certain victory stunned the French. Their own ship was in a sad condition with her crew badly decimated, and only such a complete annihilation of the enemy could have saved them. The lower battery alone had fourteen men wounded by the last volley, while seven cannon balls had pierced the hull at the water line, to say nothing of several others that had passed through the ship from side to side. La Potherie's men on the forecastle, the most exposed portion of the ship, had taken a terrible beating from the musketry and grapeshot, fired often at pistol range. The foremast was drilled with musket balls for a distance of ten or twelve feet above the deck. Only by taking cover when they saw the matches applied to the guns were they able to escape being killed to a man.

With the *Hampshire* sunk, the *Pelican* headed for the *Hudson's Bay*, as she was nearest the river's mouth; but Captain Smithsend struck his colors at once, evidently terrified by what had happened to the flagship, and Iberville started off in pursuit of the *Dering*, now retreating out of gunshot range. The chase, how-

[4] Such is the account given by Iberville, La Potherie, and Nicolas Jérémie. It is doubtful, however, as some commentators point out, if a ship of this size could have been sunk by one broadside however accurately it was delivered. It is more likely that a sudden squall struck her at the moment and overturned her. This is suggested in the deposition of Morriss and Clarke mentioned above.

ever, did not last long, as the *Pelican* was hampered by a broken mainyard—broken several days before—and a badly leaking hull into which the water was pouring faster than the pumps could expel it. Iberville was therefore only too glad to put about and warp his ship alongside the *Hudson's Bay* while he made temporary repairs. He sent fifteen men to the prize, then steered seaward toward the spot where the *Hampshire* had sunk, hoping to rescue some of her crew; but although he found the ship grounded on a shoal—it had evidently gone down in shallow water—high winds prevented him from lowering his boats.

During the night the wind which had been blowing hard from the northeast increased to a gale. A flurry of snow swept over the Bay and the temperature dropped below freezing, making it extremely difficult to handle the ice-encrusted running-rigging of the ship. In the morning, though the weather showed no sign of improvement, Iberville determined to learn, if possible, the fate of Martigny's reconnaissance party. He entered the Hayes River and there had the good fortune to find the boat which for two days had been anxiously awaiting his return, fearful lest the *Pelican* had suffered in the battle. The news which Martigny and his two or three captive Indians brought in was reassuring, for they informed Iberville that the fort was held by only thirty-five men. Here then was the opportunity. A mortar and some fifty bombs were hurriedly transferred from the *Pelican* to the *Hudson's Bay*, and Iberville ordered the latter to proceed farther up the river to a place near the fort, there to await the arrival of Sérigny with the rest of the fleet, when preparations would be begun for the siege. Iberville slipped his cable and beat hastily to windward hoping to gain an offshore position, for the violence of the wind was continually increasing; but he could make no progress and was finally forced to anchor in nine fathoms off a lee shore, a position dreaded by all mariners. Everything held until eight o'clock in the evening, when the kedge anchor's cable parted, leaving the vessel riding to a small bow anchor. In a raging storm this was little help; sail was made at once, the cable cut, and the *Pelican* stood out to sea.

The night which now came on was one of horror. On deck the crew were vainly trying to keep a footing on the icy planking as they hauled and belayed the ice-coated ropes, while below in the hold lay the wounded, many of them delirious, tossed about from side to side by the rolling ship. In the dim light of a few sickly lanterns the officers made their way among the stricken men, attempting to quiet them by expressing a confidence they themselves did not feel. At ten o'clock the blow came: the *Pelican* lost her rudder. As the tide rose she was dragged toward the shore along the southern side of the Nelson River, and here she lingered until dawn, when Iberville decided to make some attempt to save his crew. He assigned to La Potherie the task of finding a spot where a landing could be effected, lowered a boat, and sent him away with a handful of men. La Potherie rowed toward the shore, distant, so he tells us, some two leagues; when the water became shoal he was obliged to leap in up to his armpits and work his way ashore followed by his men. The experience was, to put it mildly, a trying one; the biting wind, the water just above freezing, the muddy bottom into which their feet sank at every step, the hunger and fatigue of the preceding night, all combined to make the landing almost impossible. When at last the exhausted men managed to scramble up on a snowbank, La Potherie collapsed.

After a short rest the party made their way inland to a more sheltered spot, La Potherie being helped there by one of his men. Here a huge fire was lighted at which the sailors warmed their half-frozen bodies. Meanwhile, the boat had returned to the *Pelican* with the news that a landing could be effected. Boats were launched and a raft of rather crude workmanship was constructed for the transportation of the wounded. With incredible effort the entire ship's company were finally landed on the shore, but so terrible was the short journey from the vessel that no less than eighteen perished in the attempt. The night was spent around the fire, and the next day, somewhat refreshed by sleep and food, they started across the peninsula for the fort.

During this time those in the fort had not been idle. On the morning of September 4 several men who had been down at the river saw the *Pelican* in the offing and hurried back with the news. Governor Henry Bailey, commander of the post, at once sent out a reconnoitering party, headed by his deputy, Henry Kelsey, who has left us a brief account of the events in which he took part. The following day two pinnaces were sent to investigate this strange vessel which might be either English or French; but before they could get close enough to learn her nationality, the French fleet came up ready for battle, and Kelsey was obliged to return to the fort. On the way back he saw the *Pelican*'s boat, dispatched the day before under Martigny, coming from the direction of French Creek. He gave chase but it escaped him. When Kelsey made his report, Bailey saw clearly the problem before him and gave orders for a sharp lookout to be kept for the attack he expected any day. If he had any doubts as to what was about to happen they were set at rest by the appearance, four days later, of the three French vessels, *Profond*, *Palmier*, and *Wesp*, which came suddenly into the river at this critical juncture. Iberville saw them too and immediately began preparations for the siege.

When Iberville approached the shore of the Hayes River after a short march across the peninsula separating it from the Nelson River and saw his fleet riding at anchor, he knew that the time had come to strike. His first step was to see that the ships were placed in a more sheltered spot and one where they would be more accessible to those on land. The anchorage he selected was known as the Trou, where at low tide there was as much as fifteen feet of water. Though not protected from the northeast blasts that bore down across Hudson Bay, it was the only place where he could unload with any degree of facility; so lacking anything better he decided to use it. Once the ships were in position, the work of preparing for the siege was carried on with alacrity: a mortar was landed, dragged over the rough ground to a place within gunshot of the fort, and erected in a battery, while the sick and wounded from the *Pelican* were ferried across the river and lodged in tents out of harm's way.

On September 11 Iberville led his men to a spot within range of the fort where he established a camp, naming it Fort Bourbon (as he had renamed Port Nelson when he last attacked it). That night fires were lighted to draw the attention of the defenders while the French reconnoitered along the river. The fort, they presently found, was well manned and plentifully supplied with artillery. To the regular garrison had been added seventeen men from the *Hudson's Bay*—she had been wrecked the same night as the *Pelican*—and the number of guns, which had been greatly increased since the siege three years before, comprised all told two mortars, thirty-four cannon, seven small pieces, and several swivel guns. La Potherie thus describes the place: "It has the form of a trapezium, flanked by three and a half bastions. One is in the north, the second east-southeast, the third south-southwest. The one on the north and the demi-bastion are joined by a covered way."

Governor Bailey attempted to inspire the garrison to put up a stiff resistance by offering forty pounds to the widow of any man killed in action, not an appeal to glory, it is true, yet it did produce some results. Shortly after pitching camp, Iberville dispatched a messenger under a flag of truce to demand surrender, as was the invariable custom in Hudson Bay military engagements. When the envoy, Lemoyne de Martigny, arrived at the palisade gate, his eyes were bandaged and he was solemnly admitted, a great show of mystery being made to impress him. A council of war was at once called to discuss the situation, for an opportunity to surrender before fighting was never rashly thrust aside. Fortunately for the English, Captain Smithsend had found his way to the garrison after surrendering his ship to Iberville. He was a man of spirit and had no desire to haul down the flag again, at least without a struggle. Perhaps his former capitulation rankled within him, and he hoped to redeem himself by putting up a stout resistance. By dint of argument and by force of personality he managed to dominate the meeting, telling his fellow officers that he knew Iberville had been killed in the recent naval engagement—possibly he believed it—and that the French forces had been greatly weakened by the taking of a prize crew from the *Pelican* to man the *Hudson's Bay*. He also said that many had been killed in battle and that the attack on the fort was the last resort of desperate men; in short, the demand for surrender was pure bluff. Smithsend carried his point, Martigny was dismissed, and preparations were begun to defend the fort.

When Martigny returned to camp, the mortar was erected at a place two hundred paces from the fort and well concealed by the surrounding woods. Scarcely was the work finished when the English opened fire. The French spent the afternoon landing supplies—including another mortar from the *Wesp*—within range of the English guns. That night the French cut off the approach by which the defenders were getting reinforcements from those of the *Hudson's Bay*'s crew who had managed to escape after this vessel was wrecked. Next morning the bombardment began in earnest, and after two or three volleys Sérigny summoned Governor Bailey to surrender. To Bailey's credit, he replied with considerable force that he would rather have his post burned to the ground than haul down his flag. His offer thus rejected, Iberville renewed his attack; but Bailey was equal to the occasion and served his pieces with great precision, though he had only the sound of the French mortars as a target, since they were completely hidden among the trees. At four in the afternoon Sérigny sent a third summons to the fort promising that this would be the last opportunity for the defenders to negotiate terms of capitulation, as the French were planning an assault.

This time Governor Bailey was open to reason, and he replied that he would give an answer in the evening. One is inclined to wonder why the governor was willing even to consider surrender at this point, since he was enormously superior to his foe in number and caliber of guns and was entrenched behind a stout palisade. But an assault by the French would be vastly more serious than bombardments. In an assault the great superiorty of Iberville's manpower would be the deciding factor. Then, too, the garrison, as was usual, were beginning to lose heart. Moreover, once Iberville had taken the place by assault, he would be in a position to dictate terms, and these were bound to be harsher than those he would exact if the place were peacefully surrendered. After considering all this, Governor Bailey sent a representative to Camp Bourbon at six o'clock that evening offering to surrender the place if he could retain all the beaver belonging to the company. This request was, of course, refused, for Iberville had his own expenses to meet and needed the booty to take the place of the plunder he had left in storage at Placentia. The following day (September 13), Governor Bailey decided to give up the fort if he were allowed to evacuate with the honors of war, a suggestion which, as it cost nothing, was promptly granted. Before making this request, Governor Bailey had attempted to infuse some fighting spirit into his men by offering them a year's pay if they would hold out. Some agreed, but most of them declined to risk their lives for so little money. The terms granted by the French were easy enough. The governor was allowed to keep the company's papers, officers and men were allowed to keep personal property, and all were to be fed as well as the French and were to be sent back to England. These terms were not unlike those of three years before.

At one o'clock in the afternoon, the hour set for the ceremony, Bailey marched out of the fort with drums beating, flags flying, muskets loaded, matches lighted, and his men carrying their arms and possessions and made his surrender to Ensign du Guay.

With the fort captured, Iberville turned his attention to the business of returning home; the season was getting late and he must be back in France. The *Palmier* was in no condition to sail that year as her rudder had been carried away. She was therefore moved in close to the fort for the coming winter. By good luck he found a small forty-ton craft, the *Albermarle*, which served to transport the furs and miscellaneous plunder to the *Profond*. The sick were placed on board the *Profond* and *Wesp*—there were about three hundred of them—and made as comfortable as possible. To Lemoyne de Martigny was given command of the post. Sérigny also stayed behind, but the following year he returned to France, where we shall find him making ready to follow his brother to Louisiana.

At this point the reader may well ask why Iberville made no attempt to recapture the post on the Albany River. His forces and his ships had taken a terrific beating before Port Nelson. The *Pelican* had been wrecked, the *Palmier* had lost her rudder, and of that gallant little fleet which had sailed so confidently into the port only the *Profond* and *Wesp* were fit for service. Nor was there any possibility of keeping such a large force through the winter and making an attempt the following spring when the *Palmier* might be in commission, for there would not be enough food for all these men, and besides, there were, as we have said, some three hundred on the sick list. It was necessary to leave, and to leave quickly while there was yet time, for ice was beginning to form in the river.

September 24 at one o'clock in the afternoon, Iberville ordered the *Profond*'s anchor to be raised, and accompanied by the *Wesp* he headed out to sea under a southwesterly breeze. The voyage home was a nightmare. As many as possible had been crowded on board the ships, French sailors from the *Pelican*, English sailors from the *Hudson's Bay*, and members of the garrison who wished to go back to England, since it would not do to leave too many in the fort during the long winter. Scurvy soon broke out among those who did not have it when they came on board, and there was some indecision as to whether or not the long voyage to France should be attempted that year, for there was the alternative of stopping in Newfoundland or possibly at Quebec. At last after six weeks of tossing about on the Atlantic, the weary men sighted the coast of France and the vessels stopped long enough at Port Louis to land their sick. The condition of these men was dreadful; twenty-five died soon after landing, and it was feared that a hundred more might follow them. The ships then proceeded to Rochefort, where those still capable of getting about were discharged.

The capture of Port Nelson in 1697 brought to an end Iberville's activities in Hudson Bay. His action off the Hayes River earned him unending applause, for it was indeed a great feat of seamanship. With one ship he had sunk an English man-of-war, captured another, and put to flight a third, an achievement perhaps unparalleled in the long history of Anglo-French naval warfare. The Treaty of Ryswick, signed between England and France while Iberville was still in the Bay, now put an end to the eight-year-old struggle between the two powers and guaranteed Port Nelson to France, a situation that remained unchanged during Iberville's lifetime. The expedition of 1697 was his last to the Bay and his most glorious one; it placed him on a footing with the great naval captains of France. Now that peace was restored, King Louis, no longer able to launch open attacks on his erstwhile enemy, had to content himself, for a short time at least, with extending his colonial possessions in America in a peaceful manner. With this end in view he undertook the establishment of a colony in Louisiana, and no one could be found more fitting to lead the first expedition than Pierre d'Iberville.[5]

---

[5] For data concerning this expedition see La Potherie's letter in Tyrrell, *op. cit.*, pp. 205–222; *Kelsey Papers*, pp. 97–100; Jérémie, *op. cit.*, pp. 29–30; Charlevoix, *op. cit.*, V, 54–59; Iberville to Pontchartrain, Nov. 8, 1697, *Bulletin des recherches historiques*, XXXI (1925), 469–476.

CHAPTER VIII

Louisiana Adventure

WITH the expedition of 1697 Pierre d'Iberville ended his career in his native Canada. From now on we shall follow him to a region far remote from the ice-laden waters of Hudson Bay, where he appears not as a warrior but as a colonizer intent on reclaiming the wilderness for France by peaceful means. Here on the shores of the Gulf of Mexico, in the intense tropical heat so different from the frigid temperatures he was accustomed to, we find him laboring with his customary ardor to lay the foundation of that great French colony, Louisiana. It is his most memorable achievement. And here, as in the North, we find him actuated by the same impulse that runs like a thread throughout his entire career—hatred of England and a determination to drive her, if possible, from the American continent.

In transferring his activities from Canada to Louisiana, Iberville was followed by four of his brothers; only Charles de Longueuil, presently to be raised to baronial rank, and Paul de Maricourt remained in the northern colony. Jacques de Sainte-Helène, François de Bienville, François-Marie, and Louis de Châteauguay had either died or been killed on the field of battle; the others, Joseph de Sérigny, Jean-Baptiste de Bienville, Gabriel d'Assigny, and Antoine de Châteauguay, left the land of their birth to follow the

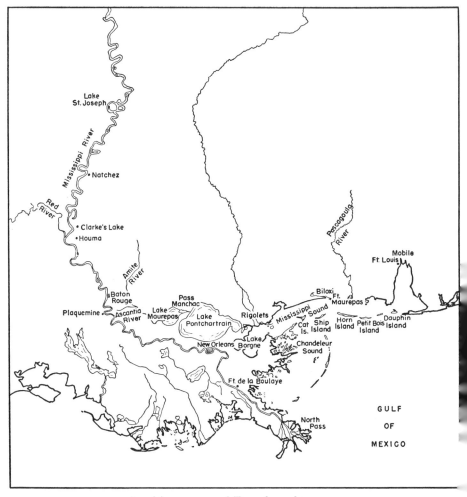

Louisiana area and French settlements.

fortunes of their distinguished brother. At this time Pierre d'Iberville was the ablest, certainly the most famous, and probably the wealthiest of the Lemoynes, a man as well known in Versailles as in Quebec. One can well understand, then, how his brothers, young men and adventurous, were only too eager to follow him.

Of these four men, all save Assigny, who died quite young, played important parts in French colonial history. Sérigny, oldest of the group, who had been the closest to Iberville after the death of Sainte-Helène in 1690, enjoyed a distinguished naval career and was awarded the rank of captain in 1720. He had followed his brother to Port Nelson in 1694 and had attempted, unsuccessfully, to take this post two years later. It was he, the reader will recall, who brought the fleet from France to Newfoundland and had then accompanied Iberville to Hudson Bay for the second time, where he was left in command of Port Nelson. Now we find him ready to follow his brother to Louisiana. He served in that colony in a secondary capacity, and when Iberville left Louisiana, Sérigny returned to France. He was back again in 1718 to fight by the side of Bienville and Châteauguay in the war with Spain. Later he was recalled and appointed governor of Rochefort, where he died in 1734.

Jean-Baptiste de Bienville outlived them all and, with the exception of Iberville, enjoyed the greatest distinction. When Iberville left Louisiana Bienville was made governor of the fledgling colony, holding the post until 1712. Then, when Antoine Crozat became proprietor and appointed La Mothe Cadillac as ruler, he remained as second in command, aiding the colony by his experience and advice. Six years later Crozat ceded his rights to the Company of the West, and Bienville again resumed the post of governor, to hold it until 1725. No sooner had he assumed office than he took the step for which he is perhaps best remembered— the founding of New Orleans. In the year 1733 he was appointed governor for the third time. Ten years later he went back to France never to return. After living quietly for twenty years the now aged man once more stepped forward as the champion of Louisiana when he made a vain attempt to persuade the government not to cede the colony to Spain. He died in Paris at the advanced age of eighty-eight in 1768. He may be truly called the father of Louisiana.

Antoine de Châteauguay also lived a long and useful life. Like Sérigny, he began his career as a naval officer. After varied experiences, among which are fights against the Indians and the Spaniards—at one time he was held prisoner of war in Havana—he was appointed second lieutenant of Martinique in 1727 and ten years later governor of Guiana. His administration of this colony was so successful that he was given the important post of Cape Breton, but he died at Rochefort in 1747, at the age of sixty-four, before he could reach his new command.

With the end of the war King Louis again turned his attention to the great territory along the banks of the Mississippi. Robert Cavelier de la Salle, following in the footsteps of Father Jacques Marquette, had descended the Father of Waters to its mouth in 1682, and two years later had started from France by sea with a party of settlers to establish a colony there. Sailing by the huge delta of the Mississippi that spreads fanwise into the gulf, he landed at Matagorda Bay in Texas and there disembarked his followers. The colony languished; nothing seemed to prosper; and after two years of struggling against insurmountable obstacles La Salle and a small detachment decided to proceed overland to Canada for help. Yet even this attempt brought no succor for the wretched settlers, for La Salle was murdered on the way by his mutinous companions. The little settlement thus thrown on its own resources was left to perish, since the King felt that he had neither money nor men to spare for an expedition to search for a handful of men lost somewhere on the shores of the Gulf of Mexico.

Yet during this time the possibilities of colonization in Louisiana were kept alive by a few interested men who set their views on paper for the benefit of the government. Henri de Tonty, one of La Salle's lieutenants who had been with him in the West, wrote from Montreal earnestly requesting the government to finish the work begun by his illustrious companion. Grouping his reasons under three headings, he pointed out the advantages the King would gain by establishing a post on the Gulf, which would inconvenience the Spaniards to the westward, serve as an outlet down the Mississippi for the furs collected in the North, and last, but not least, cut off the English who were beginning to work their way westward along the Ohio.[1]

Late in 1697, while Iberville was transporting the scurvy-ridden remnants of his Hudson Bay expedition back to France, Louis de la Porte de Louvigny, an authority on the western situation, was drawing up a memorandum in which he guaranteed to spread the terror of the King's name along the Mexican border without further cost to His Majesty than furnishing a mere one hundred men. Together with D'Ailleboust de Mantet, leader of the expedition against Schenectady, he had labored for five years to find some way of carrying on the work of La Salle. He had consulted Indians of various nations regarding the lands to the southwest, he had read the journals of La Salle's companions and of others who had visited this country since his time, and he gave it as his considered opinion that present circumstances now favored a successful project of colonization. Such an undertaking he proposed to finance by persuading various persons to underwrite it for the sake of a generous profit.[2] This report Louvigny sent to France, where it was immediately placed in the hands of Jerome Phélypeaux, Comte de Maurepas (son of Louis, Comte de Pontchartrain), who for the past four years had been assisting his father in the Ministry of Marine and had much to do with organizing the expedition to Louisiana.[3]

[1] Margry, *op. cit.*, IV, 3–5.
[2] *Ibid.*, pp. 9–18.
[3] As Jerome also took the title of Pontchartrain in 1699, it is sometimes

At the same time Maurepas also received a communication from the Sieur d'Argoud, a man who held the position of *Procureur des Prises,* and had once lived for some time in Lisbon. He was a friend of that learned cleric, the Abbé Eusèbe Renaudot, and of the Abbé Claude Bernou, both of whom had been well acquainted with La Salle and were anxious to see his work continued. It was from them that Argoud got his enthusiasm for the Louisiana project. It is evident from his letter to Maurepas, written at Paris in December, that he had already been in correspondence with the Minister, for he tells him that for the past eight months he has been hard at work gathering all the information he could, reading every account he could lay his hands on, and interviewing persons well posted on the subject. The most reliable information he was able to obtain was, in his opinion, that given him by the Sieur Remonville, an erstwhile friend of La Salle who had traveled much in the Illinois country. The substance of this he embodied in his letter. It contains a prospectus of Louisiana describing the richness of its land, with its lead mines, peltries, timber, and vegetation. The dangers of English opposition are also vividly set forth as an additional reason why a post of considerable strength should be established near the mouth of the Mississippi.

Remonville seems to have had two different plans in mind which could be put into effect either conjointly or separately. One was to strike westward through Canada and follow La Salle's route down the Mississippi; the other was to proceed by sea to the river's mouth, there to erect a fort which would serve as evidence of occupation and suzerainty over the great territory. Argoud warned, however, that the English would be on the alert to wreck these schemes. He speaks of an acquaintance of his, a young merchant trading with England named Fouessin, who was kept in-

difficult to distinguish between father and son. Margry, however (*ibid.,* p. xx) tells us that Jerome handled most of the work connected with Iberville's expeditions.

formed of English colonial designs by his two brothers, one of whom was in Virginia, the other in Florida. From them he learned that the English would find some way of thwarting the expedition through Canada—a somewhat doubtful possibility—and would use buccaneers and pirates to destroy any expeditions venturing into the Gulf of Mexico by sea. This latter method, he pointed out, had decided advantages since the British government could later disavow any responsibility for outrages committed by such persons. Argoud also informed the Minister of a rumor he had picked up that the famous William Penn was sending a colony of fifty men to the Ohio River, and this might eventually cause trouble in the Mississippi Valley. In gathering this information Argoud and Fouessin had in mind the formation of a company similar to the West India Company, backed by the government, of course, to exploit the Louisiana territory; and for this purpose they drew up a detailed and elaborate plan.[4]

In glancing over the various projects for the founding of a new colony Count Maurepas decided that at least one previous mistake should not be repeated: La Salle in sailing for the Mississippi had overshot his mark and landed on the coast of Texas. Since this error might be attributed to the commander's ignorance of seamanship, the next expedition should be headed by an experienced navigator who could be relied on to find his objective; and who could be more fitted for the task than the naval captain fresh from his expedition to Hudson Bay? Pierre d'Iberville was accordingly appointed commander of the expedition to Louisiana in recognition of his services in Hudson Bay, Newfoundland, and Pemaquid. There were, perhaps, other reasons than his skill as navigator that led to his selection. For some time past, as we have shown, he had been interested in various schemes to confound the English in North America; but when he arrived in France where he could offer his plans verbally to the government the war was over and the authorities were obliged perforce to set aside any

[4] *Ibid.*, pp. 19–43.

idea of attacking their former antagonists. Yet, Iberville, sworn
enemy of England, never put the matter entirely out of his mind,
for he well knew, as did every well-informed Frenchman, that
the peace ushered in at Ryswick was merely a lull in the storm,
and it was only a question of time before the age-long struggle
would break out again. Meanwhile, the present plan for colonizing
Louisiana appealed to him as the best way, perhaps the only way,
of circumventing the English in time of peace.

The danger of British aggression in North America was, of
course, well known to the government, and the King had been
wide awake to the seriousness of the Louisiana situation during
the preliminaries of the Treaty of Ryswick. At this conference
he had repeatedly warned his representatives not to cede to England any territory south of the Illinois country, as he was already
planning to seize the Mississippi Delta, the natural outlet of Louisiana, thus assuring for France control of this vast region.[5] To
make matters worse, that curious and unreliable character, Father
Louis Hennepin, whose false claims of having descended the
Mississippi to its mouth had been exposed by La Salle, had just
published a new edition of his voyages which he dedicated to
William III, inviting him to take possession of the Mississippi
Basin. Moreover, England had in some of her charters to the
American colonists asserted a theoretical claim to this territory by
extending the grants indefinitely westward; and now one Daniel
Coxe was organizing a company in London to found a settlement
in the delta.

The winter of 1698 was spent discussing the coming expedition
to Louisiana; but it was not until late spring that the ships were
selected and the officers chosen. Meanwhile, Iberville spent his
time refreshing his memory. He was well read on the subject; and
while in Canada he had met La Salle when the latter returned from
his journey down the Mississippi and had obtained from him some
useful hints about soundings in the delta. Armed with this knowl-

[5] *Ibid.*, p. iv.

edge, he now voiced his opinions in a letter to Maurepas, telling him how he thought the expedition should be conducted. He requested a ship of from forty to fifty guns with a crew of 250 men, a frigate of twenty guns, a corvette of ten, and a flute of three hundred tons. Provisions for eight months should be placed on board.

Iberville would go first to Santo Domingo, for at this time the western part of the island, known today as Haiti, was held by the French and governed by Jean du Casse, one of the most celebrated buccaneer leaders of his day, whose experience in the West Indies was long and varied. Here the commander would obtain some soldiers from the local garrison, or perhaps some buccaneers, if, as he naïvely puts it, they are "gentle, peaceful, and obedient." He would also pick up some pirogues or small boats, good for navigating the river, and, of course, some additional provisions. On leaving Santo Domingo he would sail to Florida, ascend its western coast, and eventually reach Mobile Bay (known on early maps as St. Esprit), which was to be the rendezvous of his flotilla. While exploring this bay carefully he would send the corvette with a pirogue and a light boat called a *biscayenne*, a popular fishing boat from the Bay of Biscay, to the westward to search for the river's mouth. This they could hardly fail to find, since it discharged a current of whitish roiled water well out to sea. Of this he felt certain, for La Salle had assured him that there was ample water at the river's mouth for any ship, as he had himself tried soundings at three leagues from the coast and found no bottom at thirty fathoms, while at a gunshot from the shore, as one went eastward, the lead registered twelve fathoms. However, if Iberville found a good harbor at Mobile Bay where he could lay up his ships, he had decided that he would retain the corvette for a few days, then take it to go in person to discover the mouth of the river; he would even go beyond it to Matagorda Bay to see if anything remained of La Salle's colony. With headquarters at Mobile, he would keep with him two hundred men selected from his crews, half of whom would settle there while the other half might be used to form a colony at Matagorda Bay. He would then send the ships back to France, retaining only the corvette and some small boats for transportation purposes. He also wanted to send a vessel to Quebec to obtain fifty or sixty Canadians who would join him the following August. As for the cost of the equipment and supplies for the establishments, he estimated it at 20,000 francs, half of which he thought should be furnished by the King's warehouses.[6]

At the same time, Iberville informed the Minister of reports he had received from London of the formation of a company under Daniel Coxe, owner of the Carolana Patent. Coxe did in fact send out an expedition, but fortunately for the French, it got no farther than Charleston, though one of its vessels did, as we shall see later, enter the mouth of the Mississippi. The presence of an English settlement in the delta would, of course, mean trouble, and it was for this that Iberville wanted the ten-gun corvette to remain with his colony. He closed his communication with a request for the wherewithal to pay the wages of a detachment of Canadians, remnants of the previous year's expedition, which he expected to take with him.[7]

Count Maurepas turned over the actual business of equipping the expedition to Michel Bégon, who threw himself heartily into the work. The ships selected were the frigates *Badine*, thirty guns (to be altered to hold more cargo) and the *Cheval-Marin*, known simply as the *Marin*, also thirty guns. Iberville was to take personal command of the former with his brother, Jean-Baptiste de Bienville, future governor of Louisiana, as one of his companions, while the latter vessel was to be under the Chevalier Grange de Surgères, who was to have among his officers the Sieur Sauvole de la Villantray, a man destined to play a leading part in the foundation of Louisiana. This Sauvole was a wealthy man who

[6] *Ibid.*, pp. 51–57.   [7] *Ibid.*, pp. 58–62.

had made a reputation for himself as poet and soldier but preferred, as such men occasionally do, a life of adventure and excitement. The Minister detailed the Sieur Le Vasseur de Boussouelle
to accompany the expedition—also two Canadians, who through
some misunderstanding sailed away to Canada much to Maurepas'
chagrin.[8] The rest of the officers are all newcomers in our story:
the old familiar names such as Denys de Bonaventure do not appear on the expedition's roster.[9] Among the crews was to be found
a youth of eighteen, André Pénicaut by name, a ship's carpenter,
who left for posterity an account, written from personal knowledge, of the first voyages to Louisiana and the early years of the
colony.[10] The ships were well manned. The *Badine*, then being
equipped at Rochefort, was to have a crew of 150 men; the *Marin*,
then at Port Louis, a port near the city of Lorient, would have a
company of 130.[11] In order to facilitate matters at the other end
of the voyage, the Minister sent instructions to Governor du
Casse ordering him to give all possible assistance to the expedition
when it touched at Santo Domingo.

Every effort was put forth to make the venture a success. Reports were drawn up from the information given by La Salle's
companions, and Bégon was instructed to secure, if possible, some
Spanish-speaking sailors, who would be useful as interpreters
should the French come in contact with the colonists of Mexico.[12]

[8] *Ibid.*, p. 64.
[9] This list of officers given by Margry (*ibid.*, pp. 50–51) differs somewhat from that given in B. F. French, *Historical Collections of Louisiana
and Florida*, 2nd ser. (New York, 1875), p. 30. This latter is taken from a
document published after the expedition took place, while Margry quotes
from a document of June, 1698. The former would appear more reliable,
since changes could have been made before the ships sailed. In the main,
however, the lists agree.
[10] André Pénicaut, "Relation," in Margry, *op. cit.*, V, 375–415. For an
English translation see *Fleur de lys and Calumet*, ed. by R. G. McWilliams
(Baton Rouge, 1953).
[11] Margry, *op. cit.*, IV, 66. [12] *Ibid.*, p. 72.

The *Marin* was now ordered to La Rochelle, where she was to receive the same amount of provisions in proportion to her needs as the *Badine*. Bégon was instructed to provide a chaplain for her, this having been inadvertently overlooked at Port Louis, and he appointed Father de Bordenac, while Father Anastase Douay was named for the *Marin*.

On July 23 the Minister sent the King's instructions to Iberville. Louis, with a confidence in his officials not warranted by the results, assumed that everything was ready for the voyage and that the commander would sail on receipt of his orders. Yet delay after delay occurred, and it was not until late October that Iberville was able to leave. The King's orders were very elastic in regard to navigation, complete discretion being given the commander as to how he should reach his destination. After stopping at Santo Domingo, where he was to receive assistance, he was to proceed to the Mississippi by whatever route he deemed advisable. On arriving there he was to select for his fort the site best suited to guard the mouth of the river against other nations. There he was to build the fort and supply it with the necessary artillery and ammunition, leaving as garrison the Canadians, who were to accompany him, and a portion of his crews. Detailed instructions were to be given the officer in charge of the post as to what he should do until the arrival of the vessels sent out the following year, particular emphasis being laid on the necessity of preventing any other nationals from acquiring a foothold there, even if such encroachments had to be resisted by force of arms. Care should be taken to make a geographical survey of the territory, with particular reference to taking soundings in the Mississippi River. It is hardly possible, so ran the instructions, that any nation had already seized this river, but if Iberville should find it occupied by a superior force he should make a detailed survey of the coast and then return at once with his data to France.[13]

In addition to all these instructions and preparations, still further

[13] *Ibid.*, pp. 72–75.

assistance was planned for Iberville. The government at this time had occasion to send the Marquis Joubert de Châteaumorant to Santo Domingo in command of the *François,* a fifty-two-gun ship, with orders to convoy our old friend the *Wesp* and leave her there with a cargo of munitions for Governor du Casse. Châteaumorant was also ordered to proceed to the Gulf of Mexico, after cruising about the West Indian islands for a month, find the place where Iberville had settled, and remain there to protect it with his reinforcements; for it was considered well within the bounds of possibility that the English might attempt to found a post there. The marquis was to remain as long as Iberville believed he had need of his protection, but he must be careful not to attack the English unless they began hostilities, as the two nations were then officially at peace.[14] The marquis received his instructions late in August, but he did not sail until October 15, a few days before Iberville.[15]

The summer wore on and still the expedition did not sail. By this time the authorities were becoming impatient at what appeared to be an unnecessary delay, and the Minister felt called upon to write those in charge informing them of the King's displeasure.[16] The delay occurred because it had been found impossible to obtain in the neighboring ports auxiliaries for the frigates which Iberville considered suitable. Instead of the corvette and flute requested by the commander, two vessels known as *traversiers* [17] were finally purchased by the government after the possibilities of all other craft had been exhausted, and these had to undergo drastic alterations before they could meet Iberville's requirements. The *traversiers* were named the *Precieux* and *Biscayenne.* They were commanded by J. F. le Vasseur and F.

[14] *Ibid.,* pp. 78–81.

[15] French, *Historical Collections of Louisiana and Florida,* new ser. (New York, 1869), p. 21*n.*

[16] Margry, *op. cit.,* IV, 83.

[17] A small ship used in coastwise trade.

Guyon.[18] When this work was completed late in September, the fleet proceeded to Brest, arriving there sometime in October. It was perhaps just as well that they did not sail earlier, for they would have reached the Caribbean Sea during the hurricane season.

At last, on October 24, Iberville set sail from Brest in the *Badine*, with the *Marin* and the two *traversiers* to keep him company, and arrived at Cap François (known today as Cap Haitien) on the northern coast of Santo Domingo, on December 4. Little occurred during the crossing save that one of the *traversiers* became separated from the fleet in a storm off the Madeiras and did not reach the Cap until ten days later.[19]

On December 12 Châteaumorant arrived. When he informed the commander of his orders not to join the expedition until he had cruised the islands for a month the latter pointed out that his assistance might then be of little value, since by that time some foreign power might have established a post near the Mississippi. Châteaumorant saw the wisdom of this, but he was unwilling to go against his orders without first consulting Governor du Casse. At this time the governor was at Port aux Paix. He was in poor health, and when Iberville sent Sauvole, Lescalette, and Surgères in the *Marin* to wait on him, he persuaded them to carry him to Leogane in the southern part of the island. He did, however, what he could for the expedition, giving orders to the commander at Cap François to furnish the ships with everything they might require. As Iberville would need a pilot, he procured for him the services of one Laurent de Graff, a buccaneer of Dutch origin who had sailed the West Indian waters for many years. He also informed the French commander that four English ships had been

[18] French, *Hist. Coll. of La. and Fla.*, 2nd ser. (New York, 1875), p. 30.
[19] The sources for this voyage are the various journals published in Margry, *op. cit.*, IV, 95–289; Pénicaut, *op. cit.;* "Historical Journal," in French, *Hist. Coll. of La. and Fla.*, 2nd ser. (New York, 1875), pp. 31–142; Iberville to Minister, July 3, 1699, *ibid.*, new ser., VI, 19–31.

sighted off the island, destination unknown. This decided Château-morant, and he at once agreed to join Iberville without first mak-ing his month's cruise among the islands. The two men now proceeded to Leogane for an interview with the governor. The conference was a brief one. Iberville managed to obtain from Du Casse 1,666 *livres* with which to pay the "gentle, peaceful, and obedient" buccaneers, of whom he selected about a dozen; but he could get no information concerning the exact location of the Mississippi Delta; no one in Santo Domingo had been there or had any knowledge of its whereabouts.[20]

At last refreshed and revictualed, the expedition, consisting of the *Badine, Marin, François,* and the two *traversiers* (the *Wesp* was left behind), left Leogane on the last day of December and rounded the western tip of Cuba two weeks later. On leaving the island the fleet was at first favored by easterly winds, but later on as it headed for Florida it was obliged to beat against heavy blows under double-reefed topsails. Iberville and Surgères navigated carefully, keeping constant check on their position and entering the results of their observations in their journals. It is unnecessary to weary the reader with a day-by-day account of what took place during the crossing; suffice it to say that after an uneventful voyage the ships anchored on January 26, 1699, in Pensacola Bay, having touched at the mouth of the Apalachicola River in north-ern Florida where the coast takes on its westward trend. Here they found two Spanish vessels riding at their moorings. Next morning Iberville sent Lieutenant Lescalette to get some informa-tion regarding these craft and to see if he could obtain wood and water from the local commander. Lescalette did his work well. He returned presently, after having been received with honors by the commander, with the news that the ships in question were Spanish frigates of eighteen and twenty guns. On shore he found a colony of some three hundred men, chiefly slaves and convicts, who had been recently brought from Vera Cruz and were now

[20] Margry, *op. cit.,* IV, 90–91.

busily engaged in building a stone fort. The post was called Santa
Maria de Galve. The governor informed him that he had been
forbidden to allow strangers to enter the harbor, but they might,
he conceded, anchor in the outer bay, where they would find
suitable shelter.

This, then, was a Spanish settlement—no sign as yet of the
English. From this point on the expedition was entering unfamiliar
waters, and Iberville proceeded carefully, taking frequent soundings and never losing sight of the shore, for he knew the mouth
of the Mississippi could not be far off. Then, on the last day of
January, just one month after leaving Santo Domingo, he anchored off Mobile Bay.

The bay which Iberville now proceeded to explore extends
northward some twenty-five miles inland to a point where it re-
ceives the mingled waters of the Mobile and Tensaw Rivers. The
main entrance to it lies between Dauphin Island [21] on the west
and Mobile Point on the east. On entering the bay one finds to the
east a deep gulf called Bon Secour Bay, cut off from the sea by a
long, narrow peninsula ending at Mobile Point. Dauphin Island
is separated from Cedar Point on the mainland by a two-mile
stretch of water filled with little islets, sandbanks, and shoals,
through which lies a narrow channel now carefully marked by
buoys. Modern hydrographical charts give detailed information
as to depths of water, but these soundings, of course, are apt to
be quite different from those taken in Iberville's day. Westward
from the bay a geographical formation typical of the Gulf of
Mexico is to be found. A sand bar some fifty miles in length
emerges from the water at a distance ranging from five to ten
miles from the coast, cutting off Mississippi Sound from the Gulf.
This sand bar is broken at intervals by the sea, so that it forms a
series of long, narrow islands separated by shoal water and oc-

---

[21] Wherever possible we shall give the islands and other geographical
features their modern names, which are sometimes different from those
given them by the French.

casionally by fairly deep channels. These islands, beginning with Dauphin, are Petit Bois, Horn, and Ship; then to the west of the last named is Cat Island, a T-shaped formation with the crossbar running north and south on its eastern side. Beyond Cat Island we find an archipelago extending southward along the coast of Louisiana, a perfect labyrinth of islands and shallow bays, separating the waters of Lake Borgne from those of the Gulf. Running parallel to this archipelago at a few miles out to sea is another, a bow-shaped group some forty or fifty miles long, called Chandeleur. Its southern tip lies near the northernmost mouth of the Mississippi, called North Pass, the one used by Iberville and his men. The delta, we would remind the reader, is a group of channels extending into the Gulf like the fingers of an open hand. It is this peculiar formation that made it difficult for an explorer unfamiliar with the topography to locate the mouth of the great river.

Unwilling to risk his vessels in unknown waters, Iberville proceeded to take soundings. He sent Ensign Desjordy-Moreau with Bienville in the larger *traversier* and Ensign Villautreys in the smaller accompanied two feluccas [22] to examine the bay, while Lieutenant Lescalette was dispatched in the long boat to survey the mainland. Next day the feluccas and the long boat returned. Lescalette reported five fathoms at one league from land, but bad weather prevented further soundings. Iberville himself went ashore with Sauvole and Bienville to spend the night. Next morning after a heavy rain the sky cleared, enabling the explorers to obtain a more accurate picture of the bay, but in the afternoon the rain came down in torrents, forcing them to seek refuge on Dauphin Island, called Massacre Island by Iberville because some sixty skeletons were discovered there. That night a strong wind sprang up, putting a stop to all further work in the bay. When

[22] The felucca was a small sailing vessel. As we find no mention of such a craft in Iberville's armada, it is possible that they were under Châteaumorant's command.

daylight came the party set out to amuse themselves by hunting the bustards and ducks with which the island abounded, while the Lemoyne brothers crossed over to the mainland northwest of the island, that is, to Cedar Point. After following the shore for four leagues up the bay the commander landed and climbed a tall oak, from which point of vantage he could survey the extent and nature of the land to the north of him. He saw, indeed, the mouth of a river tumbling its muddy waters into the bay, but nothing in the contour of the coastline that would lead him to seek the Mississippi in this direction. The land roundabout appeared fertile enough, with its forests of oaks, elms, pines, and nut trees and its carpet of flowers similar to those he had left in Santo Domingo; yet despite its alluring aspect it did not offer the key to the problem. When the weather cleared the following morning, Iberville finished the work of sounding, but to his great disappointment he found too little depth to permit his ships to take shelter under the lee of Dauphin Island.

He now sailed westward along the southern shore of Dauphin. Off his starboard bow he saw Petit Bois and beyond it Horn Island. At noon the wind hauled to the south, forcing him to change his course to a more northerly one and driving him toward these islands, where he came to anchor that night in nine and one-half fathoms of water. Early next morning Bienville was sent around the western end of Horn to search for a channel deep enough for the ships to pass through to the shelter on its northern side. For several days the fleet had been in a precarious position, unable to face a storm arising in the south, and Iberville was determined to find some spot where they could ride in safety. To make a complete survey of the neighboring waters, Surgères and Sauvole were ordered to accompany Bienville and to take the *traversiers* and two boats. In the evening Bienville returned with the welcome news that, although the passage between Horn and Ship Islands was too shallow, he had found a depth of twenty-four feet between Cat and Ship Islands. The following morning

Iberville hoisted sail and drove the *Badine* through the passage closely followed by the other two ships, and at last all were safely anchored in the lee of Ship Island within cannon shot of its shores.

With his fleet now secure Iberville determined to examine, if not to explore, the mainland to the north of him. Taking a *traversier*, he embarked with Father Douay and a small group of men and proceeded across Mississippi Sound to a place where he had seen a column of smoke the day before. On landing here he saw the tracks of Indians. The French quickly built a hut and spent the night on the spot, and when they quit this temporary encampment the following morning, they left behind two axes, two pipes, and some odds and ends as gifts to show their friendly intentions should the savages show up during their absence. Then they started off on the trail of the Indians, hoping to overtake them. Iberville presently came to the shore of a small bay; on the other side he saw several canoes manned by Indians who were paddling desperately toward the shore. Climbing hastily into the canoe he had brought with him, he started off in pursuit and caught up with the savages just as they drove their boats up on the beach. Alarmed at the sight of their pursuers, the Indians rushed into the forest, abandoning their canoes and property in their haste to escape from those they believed to be Spaniards. But in their eagerness they had been obliged to leave behind an elderly chief stricken ill with a disease that was beyond cure. Iberville treated the old man kindly, built him a hut, brought him food, and did everything to win his confidence, while Bienville and two Canadians set out in pursuit of the others.

In the morning several Indians were rounded up, brought to the camp, and given presents. They proved amenable to this kindly treatment, and Iberville was able to persuade three of these braves to come on board the *Badine*, after he had left on shore Bienville and two Canadians as hostages. Here they were entertained royally; guns were fired for their edification and amusement, and an opportunity to examine the mechanics of the ship was given them. The noise of these salutes attracted some members of the Bayogoula and Mougoulacha tribes who happened to be hunting in the neighborhood. These two tribes shared the same settlement on the banks of the Mississippi. The braves proved friendly, and when Iberville returned to the shore they received him with their usual forms of salutation, rubbing their hands on their heads and bellies and on those of their guests, then raising them to heaven, a greeting to which the French commander and his followers replied in kind, hoping to seal a pact of friendship. All then adjourned to Bienville's tent, where they smoked the pipe of peace, while presents were given out by the French: axes, blankets, shirts, knives, and numerous other things that struck the Indians' fancy. At the evening meal wine and whisky were served, to the intense delight of the savages, who, strange to say, showed no desire to imbibe too freely as their northern brothers were inclined to do. The alliance thus made by the French was held binding on the six or eight tribes in the neighborhood.

Iberville was now within striking distance of the Mississippi. With his vessels safely at anchor he could leave them and begin the second phase of his expedition, namely, finding the actual mouth of the river and ascending the stream to a spot where he thought a settlement could be suitably located. It was therefore unnecessary to keep Châteaumorant and his *François* any longer. On February 20 he invited the marquis to dinner on board the *Badine* and put the situation before him, explaining his intention of leaving the vessels under Surgères and pushing on himself with the boats to find the Mississippi River. As a parting request he asked his colleague to furnish him with some flour and wine which had been obtained at Leogane, tendering an order on Governor du Casse in payment for them. After a brief demur, for he was not overstocked with provisions himself, Châteaumorant agreed to oblige; and having transferred the supplies to the *Badine*, he set sail the following day for Leogane, arriving there April 1. Ten days later he sailed for the Cap. Here he was delayed for some time making extensive repairs to his rather leaky ship, then on May 10 he finally set forth, reaching France in about six weeks. His first act on landing was to send a long letter to the Minister telling of his voyage with Iberville from the time they left Leogane together until he arrived off the French coast. His account of the Spanish settlement at Pensacola was particularly interesting to the authorities.

During his brief intercourse with the savages Iberville had so impressed them with his friendly intentions that they had arranged a feast in his honor, and now they dispersed into the woods for the necessary hunting, promising to announce their return by lighting a fire on the shore. Shortly after the departure of Châteaumorant a column of smoke was seen, and Iberville at once embarked in his boats, taking on board his lieutenant, Lescalette, and Surgères, Sauvole, and the Canadian members of the expedition, for the latter were better fitted by training to deal with the natives than the French sailors. Guns were fired to apprise the braves of their coming, and the party set forth for the celebration. We can imagine their disappointment when they reached shore only to find that the smoke was caused by burning grass and that the Indians were nowhere to be seen. The feast itself had little attraction for Iberville—he had attended too many in his day— but he was extremely anxious to continue his friendly relations with his savage friends. Bienville was therefore dispatched in a canoe to find them, but they had completely disappeared, and he only succeeded in bringing back a squaw, who informed the commander that the Bayogoulas had left for the Mississippi as they had run short of provisions.

Returning immediately on board the *Badine*, Iberville began his preparations for the discovery of the river. After sending two ensigns to explore the Pascagoula River, which flows into the Gulf a short distance east of his anchorage, he set to work organizing the main expedition. To one of the *traversiers* he assigned Sauvole, Father Douay, the pilot (a man named Cateau) and twenty men, while he took personal command of the other with his brother and a like number of the rank and file. Provisions for twenty days were stored in the little craft with the usual supply of arms and ammunition. Two small cannon were taken on board to be used chiefly for firing salutes, and to complete the equipment each boat took a canoe in tow. The men chosen for the venture were drawn almost entirely from the Canadian contingent, plus the buccaneers enlisted in Santo Domingo, who were to remain as settlers should a suitable site be found for a colony.

The expedition started on February 27. The sky was overcast, rain was falling. The route taken by Iberville lay to the westward along the shore of Ship Island; then passing Cat Island, he turned southward through the archipelago that covers the sea just south of the entrance to Lake Borgne. For several days the little vessels threaded their way through this maze, beating against head winds or bowled along by following breezes, anchoring at sunset off some island to pass the night. It is impossible to identify each islet Iberville passed, even if it were desirable to do so, or even to name those at which he stopped as he journeyed through the labyrinth always keeping a sharp lookout for the presence of an opening in the shore line that would indicate the mouth of the river. The weather was bad; high winds, torrential rains, thunder, and lightning made progress difficult.

At last on the second day of March there came a sudden change. All day the little ships had been buffeting their way along the shore, scudding before a northerly gale with gunwales awash, the water kept back by tarpaulins stretched above the railings. It was necessary, of course, to keep fairly close to shore lest the river be passed, but the low-lying land betokening shallow water warned Iberville to keep well off, though a heavy sea made the going dangerous in deep water. After taking careful soundings he chose the lesser of the two evils and headed for the open sea. As he raced along under a quartering wind he saw lying ahead of him to the southeast a line of rocks projecting from the coast. It was almost dark when he reached them, and gazing intently through the fading light, he saw a rift in the line stretching across his course. It was a chance and he took it. Putting his helm over, he swung the boat so as to bring the wind dead astern and slid through the passage into water twelve feet deep to find himself riding easily on a quiet stream. He had entered the Mississippi by the branch of the delta known as North Pass.

Once within the river he found many evidences to show that he had reached his objective. The water was fresh; it presented a thick, whitish appearance and did not mix readily with the salt water of the ocean, just as La Salle had described the mouth of the Mississippi. Moreover, the rocks that had loomed so threateningly across the course proved on closer inspection to be masses of petrified logs and driftwood piled up by the current for generations until, blackened by age and cemented together by fluvial sediment, they resembled a rocky palisade. In his narrative Iberville gives a description of the mouth he had entered in considerable detail, telling of the various depths he had noted at the several entrances between the "rocks," describing how the mighty current of fresh water was felt for three-quarters of a league out to sea. He took the latitude of the entrance and made it 28° 50′ N. From all indications this, then, must be the mouth of the Mississippi. But could he be sure? This was a question that was to vex him for some time to come.

On the following day, Shrove Tuesday, the pioneers began the ascent of the river. Two and one-half leagues above the entrance to North Pass they found that the main stream separated into three branches, the middle one being as large as the one they had ascended, that is, from 750 to 850 yards in width. They had come to the junction of the principal mouths of the river: South Pass, Southwest Pass, and North Pass or, as it is called at this point, Pass à l'Outre. Above this junction the stream broadens out to well over one thousand yards; and then as they proceeded the banks drew gradually together until the width was reduced to about one-half that distance. As they proceeded northward, the rushes and reeds growing along the shores gave way to trees, and the river changed its course from a fairly straight line to the meandering curves that form such a distinctive feature of its channel. Climbing to the top of a stout tree, Iberville saw unfolding before him a vast tract of canes and rushes stretching northward as far as the eye could see. Salutes were fired by the cannon to attract the attention of any savages who might be lurking in the neighborhood, but when this failed to bring forth any sign of life he decided to continue on his way until he met the Bayogoulas, who might be able to give him news about the Quinipissas, a tribe which reports had placed on the river some twenty-five leagues from the sea.[23]

For several days the expedition continued on its way upstream, always keeping a sharp lookout for stray Indians who might be found wandering along the banks of the river. Progress was slow, for lack of wind compelled the sailors to resort to their oars, and it was difficult to make headway against the current with this form of locomotion. Peering across the flat terrain, they saw to the north of them the waters of Lake Borgne, that huge bay whose entrance they had passed on their way down the coast, but as yet no trace of Indians. Provisions were now getting low; no fruits, save blackberries, and no vegetables could be found growing along the banks to replenish the fast-shrinking larder. Game was also scarce, though the hunters were occasionally able to bring down a wild steer.

At last, on March 7, came a break in the monotony, and for the first time the explorers met with the long-sought Indians. Early

[23] The Quinipissas appear to have had various names such as Colapissa and Queripasa, names which in the Choctaw language mean guardians or sentinels. These Indians served as watchers for hostile parties about Lake Pontchartrain and the coastal lagoons. Quinipissa was considered, therefore, more of a generic term than the name of a particular tribe (A. S. Gatschet, *A Migration Legend of the Creek Indians* [Philadelphia, 1884], p. 112).

in the forenoon the explorers saw a canoe vigorously driven toward the riverbank by two savages who fled into the woods as soon as they touched the shore. Farther on they came across five others who also took to their heels, but one whose curiosity overcame his fear remained to be captured by the French, who showered him with presents in exchange for his supply of beef and dried bear meat. He proved to be an Annochy, friend of the Bayogoulas. Reassured by this kindly treatment, the brave induced his companions to join him, and they approached the French, showing their friendship in the customary manner of head and stomach rubbing. Iberville, anxious to learn of the tribes farther up the river, inquired if they knew the whereabouts of those Indians who had disappointed him in their rendezvous at the feast and was told that they had been seen a few days before coming to the Mississippi by a short cut from the sea, and were now back in the Bayogoula village. Questioned as to the location of this place, they replied that it was a five days' journey distant, a bit of information that somewhat staggered the French, for they were now weary and in need of food. In response to a request for guides to take them thither the savages answered that they were too busy with their hunting to spare the time to lead a tour up the river, but after a little persuasion and much cajoling by means of gifts, a brave was induced to drop his pressing business and lead the way. That night they pitched camp forty-four leagues from the river's mouth.

The following morning the expedition got under way to an early start. The weather was warm and the current flowed more rapidly than before, causing the men to grumble at the extra labor; but by strenuous rowing and occasional assistance from the sails they managed to proceed at a fair pace for several days, stopping at night to sleep on land beside the river's edge. The aspect of the ground now began to change, the banks became higher, high enough to prevent the river from overflowing, while the trees increased in size. Near the site of modern New Orleans the guide pointed out a portage trail leading to Lake Pontchartrain, which, so he told Iberville, gave a short cut to the sound where the ships had been left, and to prove his point he took a package and made the trip to the lake and back.

One day two Breton sailors ventured into the wood on a hunting expedition. In the evening when they did not appear guns were fired to attract their attention, but the night passed without any sign of them. In the morning Iberville took charge of the search. Parties were sent out to scour the countryside in all directions, with orders not to return until a cannon-shot gave the signal. Two boats were also dispatched along the shore. Late in the afternoon Iberville caused the gun to be fired, and toward evening the search parties returned without the sailors. Heartless as it may seem to us, the commander decided to abandon all further effort and to push on up the river. Food was running short, making it necessary to reach the Indian village as soon as possible, and perhaps these men would turn up later.

On March 13 the party passed the Bayou Plaquemine and the next day reached the Bayogoula village. This village, which the Bayogoulas shared with the Mougoulachas, each tribe under its own chief, was situated on the western side of the river sixty-four leagues above its mouth and thirty-five below the Houma settlement, the next tribe beyond them.[24] At two o'clock in the afternoon the French met a canoe containing four Mougoulachas. One of these, an aged warrior whose scalp had been removed in a recent battle, held a calumet pipe three feet long, embellished with multicolored feathers. Clad in a bearskin, his face smeared with mud to enhance his appearance, he came as the ambassador of his people to welcome the white men. The pipe of peace was passed to the French leaders, who smoked it to show their good will. A savage then seated himself in Iberville's boat and led the way to the landing place where the braves had assembled to give the French a proper welcome. The Indians to the number of sixty,

[24] *Ibid.*, p. 113.

comprising a few squaws, were gathered on an eminence some six feet above the water's edge where they had made a clearing in the canebrake.

As Iberville stepped ashore he was greeted with the customary abdominal caress, which he returned in kind. In the middle of the clearing he saw, much to his surprise, a large pipe which he had given the Indians when he met them on Mississippi Sound. It was mounted on two forked sticks and an Indian stood guard over it. Food was brought, a rather unpalatable concoction of sagamite, beans, and Indian corn, cooked in bear grease, but it was not unwelcome to the hungry Frenchmen. Iberville for his part brought out a supply of whisky, added a portion of water to it, then passed it to the braves, who found it rather strong for their undeveloped tastes. He also gave out as presents the usual assortment of needles, mirrors, and knives. An exhibition of dancing was then staged by the youth of the village, who kept time to the rhythmic sound of pebbles rattling in gourds and ended their gyrations by frightful yells that could be heard a mile away. In this manner the afternoon drew to a close and the weary braves left off and betook themselves to their village.

While the singing and dancing were going on Iberville got the ear of a chief, who was strutting about superbly clad in a blue French coat given him by Henri de Tonty, and was able to obtain from him considerable information regarding the tribes scattered along the lower Mississippi. Bienville, too, helped out in the search for knowledge, as he had managed to pick up some words of the local dialect; thus the French learned, partly by word of mouth, partly by signs, that the Quinipissas were living in a settlement an eight days' overland journey to the northeast. Iberville also seized the occasion to make inquiries about a point of geography that was causing him considerable anxiety. He had read in the accounts of La Salle's expedition that the Mississippi somewhere in its course was divided into two channels, both of which led to the sea. Anxious to find this fork, the French commander put the Indians to an exhaustive examination, only to be assured by them that the great river had but one channel, and that Tonty on his voyage both to and from the delta had passed by their village, evidence that he had not found any branch in the stream higher up. The savages drew rough sketches of the river above their settlement to prove their contention.

All this was extremely annoying to Iberville; the absence of such a fork which all narratives, including the fictitious account of Father Hennepin, insisted did exist, might mean that the river before him was not the Mississippi after all, a most distressing possibility, since he was now ninety leagues from the harbor where the *Marin* lay at anchor, with her commander holding an order to sail for France if the boat expedition was not back within six weeks. The positiveness with which the narratives spoke of the fork might cause the authorities at home to question the validity of his discovery if he did not find it or did not explore northward far enough to prove its nonexistence. Such being the case, he decided to continue up the river to the Houma settlement. From this tribe he might obtain more accurate information, as he had noted a strong dislike on the part of his savage friends for the Houmas, and it might be possible that they had lied to him about the fork to prevent his visiting their rivals.

During the night the French encamped on the river bank. The following day, by special invitation, Iberville, Bienville, Sauvole, Father Douay, and two Canadians were escorted to the village, situated a quarter-league from the camp. Because it was Sunday, Father Douay first celebrated Mass; then the party led by the reception committee made its way inland. The village was a collection of huts surrounded by a ten-foot wall of canes, just a palisade with an open gateway. This enclosure contained a hundred-odd cabins inhabited by 250 men and a few women,[25] many of whom were afflicted with smallpox. The usual presents were given by the French, the chief being especially honored with a bright

[25] The *Marin* narrative gives the number as four to five hundred.

scarlet jacket trimmed with imitation gold facings, red stockings, two shirts, and various other gifts, while a generous supply of trinkets was distributed among his followers. In exchange for all this the French received a number of buckskins, which they used for patching their shoes, and a dinner of dried meat, of which they ate sparingly.

When the repast was over, the chief took Iberville on a tour of the village. The first point of interest was the temple. It was a curiously constructed building entered by way of a lean-to eight feet by twelve, upheld by two posts supporting a large beam. Near the door were replicas of various animals, such as wolves, bears, and birds; an opossum in particular attracted Iberville's attention. The door was eight feet high, and on passing through it the visitors found themselves in a cabin some thirty feet in circumference, built very much like the other cabins. At the farther end was a scaffold displaying skins of various animals placed there as offerings to the local god. As a place of worship it was most unimpressive. The cabins, Iberville notes, were crude affairs. They had no windows, only a small hole at the top to let in light and air. They did, however, contain beds. These consisted of four posts supporting a wooden frame about two feet from the ground. On the whole, the commander had a rather low opinion of these people, whom he describes as the most primitive he had ever seen. They lacked almost everything in the way of furniture and equipment and did not appear to have enough ambition to improve their lot. The men, though well built and strong, were not warlike in appearance, while the women were deplorably lacking in good looks, not to say beauty. Before leaving Iberville took an observation and computed his latitude as 31° 02′ N. Bayou Plaquemine is in latitude 30° 18′ N., so that the village was about 30° 20′ N.; thus his calculations placed him about forty-two geographical miles north of his true position.

Early next morning (March 16) the explorers embarked in their boats and again took up the dreary task of rowing upstream, taking with them a canoeload of Indians as guides. A short distance from the landing place they passed a small stream on the eastern side of the river which offered a short cut to Mobile Bay. It is called Bayou Manchac today but was known to the French as Ascantia. Its source lies nine miles south of the city of Baton Rouge in a straight line, or about twice that distance by water, for here the Mississippi takes a long S-shaped curve. Bayou Manchac flows into the Amite River, which empties into Lake Maurepas, the distance between the lake and the Mississippi being thirty-five miles as the crow flies. Lake Maurepas in turn empties at its northern end into the much larger Lake Pontchartrain by a five-mile channel called Pass Manchac, and from Pontchartrain a passage leads into the Gulf. Here, then, was another short cut leading to Mississippi Sound, where the ships lay at anchor.

Iberville continued on his journey up the river until he saw on the east bank a pole, called by him a maypole, stained with some red substance and adorned with the heads of fish and bears attached thereto as a sort of sacrificial offering. It marked the dividing line between the Bayogoula and Houma tribes. These nations, according to Pénicaut, were so jealous of each other that they shot at sight any member of a tribe hunting on the wrong side of the boundary. The Indians called the marker "Istrouma," which in French means "Baton Rouge," the name of the present capital of Louisiana. The pole is believed to have been planted on Scotts Bluff.[26] This fixes the party's position on March 17.

The next day the explorers sailed past an island about a league in length, known today as Profit Island, the first they had encountered thus far; then they came to one of those topographical peculiarities of the Mississippi formed by the river swinging around in a loop, almost in a circle, in such a way as to bring the banks close together. In course of time erosion eats away the

[26] A. C. Albrecht, "The Origin and Settlement of Baton Rouge, Louisiana," *Louisiana Historical Quarterly*, XXVIII (1945), 5–68.

banks and the river takes a short cut, forming a new channel, and the erstwhile loop remains by itself separated from the waters of the river in what is known as an ox-bow cut-off. The French had now arrived at the Fausse River Cut-off, where the channel made an enormous sweep to the westward. Here, the Indians said, a day's journey could be saved if they could manage to drag their boats across the intervening neck of land. The job was no easy one; a pile of wood and debris thirty feet high, thrown there by the current, blocked the way to a little bayou that led to the upper channel; but the French went to work with a will and in a few hours had cleared a path 350 feet long over which they managed to drag the boats and launch them safely on the other side of the portage.

Two days later they reached the landing place where they were to pick up the trail to the Houma village. Gathered on the shore to meet them was a delegation from the settlement bearing the pipe of peace. The Houmas were a branch of the Choctaw nation and dwelt in a village on the eastern side of the river. The information which Iberville gives us about its location is meager, and the observations he took on his second voyage to establish its site are no more accurate than those he took at the Bayogoula village on his first. But by piecing together the data given by him and by Pénicaut we are inclined to believe that the landing place was somewhere just north of Tunica Island, say in latitude 30° 54' N., while the village itself was a league to a league and a half southeast of Clarke's Lake, which is so close to the river that it may well have been a bay in Iberville's time. Its latitude was probably close to the thirty-first parallel. In his report of his second voyage the commander gives some additional information, telling us about a second landing place farther up the river. We shall discuss this more fully in the following chapter.

Iberville with a few companions and the Bayogoulas who had accompanied him was now escorted to this village by his hosts, leaving the bulk of the party at the landing place. A short distance from the settlement they were met by a delegation who presented their guests with the usual pipe of peace, much to the discomfort of the commander, who tells us, with tongue in cheek, that he had never smoked before. It was now noon; the heat had been intense, the rate of travel slow; and the weary Frenchmen were glad to throw themselves down for a little rest. But it was not for long, as their guides soon urged them on to complete the journey. At the entrance to the town they were met by the chiefs, each one of whom bore a little white cross in his hands and saluted the commander after their fashion. Then taking him by the arm they led him to a square where the customary amenities were exchanged. In the afternoon a dance was staged by a group of young men and women scantily clad in skins and feathers, their bodies painted in different colors, who for three hours favored their guests with a complete, if somewhat tiring, exhibition of Indian terpsichorean art. After a dinner, which consisted solely of saga-mite, a huge torch was planted in the middle of the square and the young people renewed their dance until midnight. By this time the white men had had enough.

The French spent the following day with their hosts. As the welcome had been most cordial, Iberville gave presents of knives, hatchets, clothing, and trinkets, for which he received a plentiful supply of grain in return.

Yet there was still the question of the fork in the river: was there a branch west of the stream he was on, or was there one to the east? Perhaps it was the one flowing into Mobile Bay. He could learn nothing from his hosts, although they assured him that Tonty had stayed with them for five days. Still determined to solve the puzzle, Iberville decided to push on with a few companions to the village of the Coroas on the Yazoo River, for Father Zenobe Membré had stated that the fork would be found fifteen leagues below that settlement.

On the twenty-second, therefore, Iberville started on his journey with two boats. To his own party he added six Houmas and also a chief of the Taensas, a tribe living in what is now Taensa County, Louisiana, whom he ordered to make a map of the river, for he wished to see if this brave would give information different from that of his colleagues when separated from them. The man complied, but the drawing had no fork in the Mississippi. It did show, however, a large river coming in from the west which divided into two channels. The chief went on to give a list of the various tribes to be found in this region and the distances separating them. At noon the party halted for refreshments and Iberville seized the occasion to make a careful analysis of the information thus acquired. He made a tabulated list of the tribes and the distances and set it down opposite a similar list compiled from the data in Father Christian Le Clercq's *Establissement de la foi,* which in turn had been taken from Father Membré's journal. The two lists showed a wide discrepancy. According to the Indians, the Arkansas tribe, northernmost of the group, was situated 263 ½ leagues from the sea, while Le Clercq placed it at 190½ leagues. This difference of seventy-three leagues bothered Iberville. Evidently the narratives upon which he had been relying could not be accurate. Certainly they could not be more reliable than the consensus of Indian opinion. And if they were inaccurate in this respect, they might likewise be erroneous in regard to the fork; for the savages were unanimous in assuring him that it did not exist. Furthermore, the Indians had provided him with many facts to prove that the river before him was indeed the Mississippi.

At this point a chief of the Bayogoulas remembered that Tonty had left with the Mougoulachas a written document which was to be given to a man who should come there from the sea. Obviously the letter was intended for La Salle, and obviously too this was the Mississippi down which he had traveled to the Gulf. Yet, could it be a western branch connected to an eastern branch at a fork farther up the river? If so, then at what point along the coast did the eastern channel flow into the Gulf of Mexico? Recalling his coastal journey, Iberville remembered that there was no river east of the delta corresponding to the descriptions of the Mississippi furnished him by the original explorers. The Mobile River he believed to be large enough, but it debouched into a large bay and the surrounding topography bore no resemblance to Father Membré's description of the river's mouth. Neither did the river flowing into Pensacola Bay seem any more satisfactory. In the end he branded Membré as a liar and decided, fork or no fork, to accept the river before him as the main stream, the channel down which La Salle had sailed on his journey to the sea.

Having reached this conclusion, he determined to retrace his steps to the coast. The boats were headed downstream, and at half after six o'clock the party reached the landing place they had left in the morning. To his surprise he found the place deserted, so he sent Bienville with two Canadians to the village to gather up the Bayogoula braves in order to make an early start the next morning. Bienville found his men easily enough, but they proved reluctant to go, for they had improved their time during the commander's absence by enjoying themselves with the Houma squaws. Unable to do anything with them, Bienville returned to the landing place. An hour later Iberville was startled by the sudden appearance of three Bayogoulas and six Houmas bearing the pipe of peace. They said that Bienville's departure from the village had caused an uproar, for the savages assumed that the white chief was angry; hence this delegation was sent to appease him. The commander promptly seized the opportunity to send these men back with a request for provisions, and early the following morning the Houma chief appeared with a band of eighty braves and their squaws bearing a generous supply of pumpkins and fowls as gifts for the departing strangers. They were accompanied by the Bayogoulas, now ready to obey orders. Out of deference to their guests the Houmas carried a little cross, and forming in procession marched around the large cross planted by Iberville on the river-bank, tossing handfuls of tobacco on it as a sign of veneration. Not to be outdone, the French gave them the usual presents of trifles in return for the much-needed provisions they had brought. At ten o'clock in the morning of March 23 the French embarked, gave a rousing cheer for their hosts, and disappeared around a bend in the river, taking with them a chief of the Bayogoulas to act as guide.

Traveling with the current, they were able to make better time than on the outward journey, and the following afternoon at three o'clock they came to the Bayou Manchac, the little stream leading to Lake Pontchartrain. As this offered a short cut to where the ship lay, Iberville decided to take it. The stream, however, was too shallow for the boats, only three or four feet at low water, so the party separated. Sauvole and Bienville took the boats down the Mississippi, while Iberville, accompanied by four of his men and a Mougoulacha for guide, packed his belongings in two birchbark canoes and launched them on the bayou. The going proved no easy task. In the first two leagues they crossed ten portages varying in length from a biscuit toss to upward of four hundred paces. The following day the going proved no better, with fifty portages over masses of fallen trees, brushwood, and all the obstacles a wilderness can throw across a traveler's path. The second day out the Mougoulacha deserted, leaving Iberville with the choice of either pursuing the journey or returning to the Mississippi and attempting to overtake the main body under Sauvole. There was no hesitation on his part as to which course he should follow. It was doubtful if he could overtake Sauvole, while, on the other hand, it would be a good lesson to the savages to learn that the French could find their way home unassisted.

As Iberville proceeded, the river grew wider and deeper, thanks to the numerous tributaries that fed its stream. By this time he had passed from the Bayou Manchac to the larger Amite River. The surrounding country was low and marshy, usually flooded at high water. Game was plentiful: the guinea fowl gave utterance to their raucous cries, while a herd of wild cattle was seen in the distance—too far off, unfortunately, to be brought down by a musket shot, despite valiant attempts to do so. Once the explorers noticed a number of alligators. The commander tells us that he killed one, which he found good eating, though it was found advisable to let it air for a while until it lost its strong odor of musk.

Three days after embarking on the Manchac the party entered Lake Maurepas, which is described as oval in shape, its main axis six leagues long, its width four. It was shallow, only a scant ten feet deep. Crossing it hurriedly, Iberville found its outlet, a short stream called the Pass Manchac that led him to Lake Pontchartrain. This lake, much larger than Maurepas, is connected with the Gulf of Mexico by a channel of considerable depth called the Rigolets. Its waters are brackish, not fresh like those of a river-fed lake. The commander made his way along its southern shore and arrived on the second day at the Rigolets, which he describes as a passage through a group of islands, a description certainly not in keeping with modern maps. Its mouth, he says, was eight or ten leagues from the ships. The evening of the thirtieth, after covering seven leagues, he encamped on a point where he lighted a blazing fire in order to attract the attention of those on board the *Badine*, riding beside her consort four leagues away. Next day as he headed out to the ships, he was met halfway by two boats coming out to investigate the fire. By noon he was again on board his flagship, and two hours later Sauvole arrived with the boats from North Pass. The short cut down the bayou and across Lake Pontchartrain had proved short in distance only, not in time; the many portages had offset the advantage in mileage.

Once aboard the *Badine*, Sauvole gave an account of his adventures. After leaving his commander he had led his men down the Mississippi, arriving at the Bayogoula village at seven in the evening, where he found to his intense joy the two sailors who had strayed off from the main party into the woods two weeks before. They were apparently none the worse for their experience. While Sauvole's party was resting at this village, an unfortunate incident occurred that caused a break in the friendly relations which had thus far prevailed between the French and the Indians. Father Douay suddenly raised a cry that he had been robbed of a wallet containing his breviary and a journal he had been keeping of the expedition. His suspicions fell on an Indian who had traveled in the same boat with him and was continually gazing at him while he was reading. In despair at the loss of his treasures he laid his complaint before the chief, who called his people together and asked them if the package had been found. As this failed to produce the missing articles Father Douay indulged in the somewhat undignified proceeding of weeping and bewailing his loss, finally ending up with a search of the cabins, to the great indignation of the Bayogoula chief, who now refused to furnish the French with provisions because of the slight put upon his people. In the end, however, Sauvole managed to calm the irate Indians and secure a few supplies in exchange for some trinkets.

Bienville then discovered an important document—the letter, dated April 20, 1685, which Tonty had left with the tribe when he came to the delta in his search for La Salle's expedition. It was addressed to La Salle as governor-general of Louisiana. From the contents we learn that Tonty had heard of La Salle's difficulties and had hastened down the river to bring help. After coasting along the shore both east and west of the delta for some distance he had been obliged to give up the search and return to the Illinois country. He had found the post on which La Salle had nailed the coat-of-arms of France when he discovered the river's mouth in 1682 and took possession of the vast Louisiana territory in the King's name. The post had been overturned, and in its place Tonty had erected another some seven leagues from the sea. There was no longer any doubt that the river was indeed the Mississippi.

Provisions were now running low, and it was high time to select a place where the colonists might reside while the ships returned home. There were two bays in the neighborhood that offered suitable shelter: Pascagoula just north of Horn Island and Biloxi ten miles west of it. Soundings of the former had been taken during the commander's absence on Surgères' orders, with unfavorable results. On hearing this report Iberville sent a boat to investigate the possibilities of Biloxi. It was to all appearances a favorable spot, well sheltered from the winds, near enough the neighboring Indian villages for the settlers to obtain assistance in case of need; in fact, it was the ideal place for a fort. Next day the exploring party returned to say that unfortunately the entrance yielded but a scant five feet of water, too little to accommodate the *traversiers* when loaded down. Blocked in this direction, Iberville decided to go back to the Rigolets, since he had noticed that there was considerable depth in its channel. Upon taking soundings there he found bottom at thirty-six feet, ample for the largest ships afloat; but the distance from this anchorage to a suitable place on Lake Pontchartrain where a fort could be erected was too great to permit the transportation of men and supplies there in time to build the fort before the fleet sailed for France. He returned to the *Badine* and was informed by an officer of the *Marin* that a channel had been found in Pascagoula of sufficient depth to permit of ready access. Relying on this information, Iberville took a detachment of forty-five men from the flagship and thirty from her consort and began to take soundings. The result, however, was unsatisfactory. For two hours he hove the lead, vainly trying to find a channel, but his only discovery was an oyster bank lying across the entrance cut by a passage three feet deep.

With both Biloxi and Pascagoula now eliminated there was nothing to do but to select a site on Lake Pontchartrain despite its obvious disadvantages. The *traversiers* were therefore sent back to the ships to await further orders while Iberville pursued his way westward along the coast. On the way he decided to have a look at Biloxi, as he had not yet surveyed it in person. The boat was headed toward the bay and the lead tossed overboard. In a short while the leadsman announced a depth of seven feet in a channel which the commander had unexpectedly discovered.

Cheered by this good fortune, Iberville summoned the *traversiers*, while the pioneers scrambled ashore to select a location for a temporary fort.

The spot chosen was one commanding the entrance to Biloxi Bay—that is, just inside the seven-foot channel. Biloxi Bay is formed by a long peninsula lying parallel to the shore and connected to it at its western extremity by a short isthmus. Here, on the eastern side of its entrance, on a bluff behind a bridge erected in modern times by the Louisville and Nashville Railroad, Fort Maurepas was built,[27] a regulation affair, square in shape with four bastions, made of oak, with which the region abounded.[28] Its armament consisted of twelve guns. Work was begun April 8, but progress was slow and it took longer to finish the structure than the commander had expected, for his men were not skilled woodsmen and the toughness of the wood worked havoc with the axes. Supplies were now brought ashore, including assorted livestock consisting of a few cows, some pigs, and a bull. With an eye to future provisioning of the fort twenty-five men were set to work clearing the land and planting peas and beans.

While this work was going on, Iberville was fortunate enough to learn something about the plans of the Spaniards for this region, thanks to five Spanish deserters who had arrived from Pensacola

[27] There has been some confusion about the name of this fort; some authorities call it Maurepas, the others, Biloxi. H. Mortimer Favrot in "Colonial Forts of Louisiana," *Louisiana Historical Quarterly*, XXVI (1946), 725, says it was named after Jerome de Pontchartrain's son, Jean Frédéric, who later became Comte de Maurepas; but this is impossible as he was not born until 1701. In Iberville's own account (Margry, *op. cit.*, IV, 195) no name is given the fort and the same is true in the log of the *Badine* (*ibid.*, p. 284), while the ship's carpenter, André Pénicaut, writing much later, calls it Fort Biloxi (*ibid.*, V, 378). Guillaume de Lisle's *A New Map of North America* (1703) shows Fort des Bilocchi. (For reproduction see *Louisiana Historical Quarterly*, XIX [1936], 878.) Nevertheless, Iberville in his letter to the Minister of Aug. 11, 1699, speaks of it as Fort Maurepas (Margry, *op. cit.*, IV, 328), which should clinch the matter. It was obviously named after Jerome, Comte de Maurepas.

[28] P. J. Hamilton, *Colonial Mobile* (Boston, 1897), p. 31.

on their way to Mexico. They had been originally sent, so they said, from Vera Cruz to form an establishment on the Mississippi. Not knowing the exact location of the delta, they had settled at Pensacola with upward of three hundred men, of whom forty appear to have been criminals. As food soon ran low, the governor went to Havana to obtain a fresh supply, and during his absence the settlement broke up, the men dying or disappearing into the hinterland until the number was reduced to fifty. As the post at Pensacola was founded simply to prevent the French from settling on the coast—the Spaniards did not know that there was another bay on the Gulf where large vessels could find shelter—the deserters felt sure it would now be abandoned. Furthermore, they gave a picture of the Spanish situation along the Gulf that was calculated to encourage the French. The road to the mines of San Luis Potosi lay open, they said, and thither they would be willing to lead their hosts. The idea pleased Iberville, who noted in his journal that if war should break out between France and Spain five hundred Canadians could spread terror in Mexico. Putting this idea aside for future reference, he embarked the deserters in his ships.

The next few days were spent in making final preparations for leaving. Short excursions were made into the country round about to get the lay of the land; the fort was fully equipped with guns and munitions, enough to withstand hostile Indians should any appear or to put up a stiff resistance against possible Spanish aggression. An inventory of provisions did not reveal a happy state of affairs, for many articles had spoiled, and Iberville decided to send one of the *traversiers* to Santo Domingo to obtain supplies from Governor du Casse, though he felt certain that as soon as he reached France he could send over a shipload that would reach the fort in time. The Sieur de Sauvole was appointed commander of the fort with Bienville as his lieutenant. Under them was placed a garrison of seventy men and six boys with a six months' supply of provisions. Farewells were said, and on May 3 the *Badine* and

Marin raised their anchors and set sail for home. The voyage across the Atlantic was uneventful as far as Iberville's journal shows. When sailing through the Bahama Channel the ships were separated by wind and fog. Both continued on their courses independently; the *Badine* anchored in the port of Rochefort July 2, the *Marin* a few days later.

CHAPTER IX

Explorations up the Mississippi

IBERVILLE'S expedition, as originally planned, had been sent out more for the purpose of establishing a post to keep the westward-moving English from seizing a point of vantage on the Gulf of Mexico than with the idea of founding a permanent colony.[1] Governor du Casse was quite emphatic on the subject, expressing his disapproval of colonial activities on the lower Mississippi in a letter to the Minister of Marine. Châteaumorant, he wrote, had just gone to France, bringing the latest news of Iberville's achievements. As Du Casse had predicted, the Spaniards were found securely ensconced where he had said they would settle; but this could not be taken to mean that the country was worth colonizing; it merely showed the eagerness of Spain to forestall France. As a French colony, Louisiana, according to Du Casse, offered a sad prospect. It was separated from New Spain by a stretch of land four hundred leagues in length inhabited by millions of barbarians. Furthermore, the Spaniards could put a hundred thousand armed white men in the field, besides their own natives, who could easily destroy any settlement the French tried

[1] Margry, *op. cit.*, IV, 294.

to make. Where he got these fantastic figures he does not say. "It seems to me absolutely useless," he concluded, "to engage in the founding of a colony." [2] At the same time Louis de Callières, who had replaced Count Frontenac as the King's representative in Canada, transmitted to the government the information he had received from a former French resident of New York telling of the preparations which were being made in England and the Netherlands to send a group of colonists to seize the lower Mississippi. This proposed expedition appears to have been part of the general westward movement, for a rumor was abroad that the English settlers were already en route overland to the Illinois country.[3]

Whatever may have been the opinion of his subordinates, the King, at any rate, was determined not to abandon the enterprise before making further investigation. Thus it was that as soon as Iberville returned to France His Majesty issued orders to dispatch a forty-six-gun frigate, the *Renommée*, a newly built vessel fresh from the shipyards at Bayonne, with a cargo boat to carry supplies to Fort Maurepas and to transport there some Canadians whom Sérigny had brought from Hudson Bay—men who would, so the King thought, make the best material for colonists. The frigate and, of course, the entire expedition, were to be commanded by Iberville, since he was the one best qualified to pass judgment on the advisability of remaining at Biloxi.[4]

In issuing these orders Louis had the wholehearted backing of Count Maurepas, Minister of Marine, who in turn was prodded by that great military authority, the Marquis de Vauban,[5] himself an enthusiast for colonial expansion. Vauban first touched the young Minister's vanity by suggesting that he might well become known in history as the founder of one of the greatest realms of the world, as Louisiana might well become such; then coming down to the more practical side of the business, he pointed out

---

[2] *Ibid.*, pp. 294–296.   [3] *Ibid.*, pp. 303–304.

[4] *Ibid.*, pp. 305–306.   [5] Sebastien Leprestre, Marquis de Vauban.

that should war break out with England and the Netherlands, France might lose the colony never to regain it, unless it were colonized in sufficient force to make it impregnable.[6] Maurepas, greatly influenced and probably much flattered by advice coming from such a distinguished source, ordered Iberville to send a complete inventory of the men and supplies he had left at Biloxi to Ensign du Guay de Boisbriant, erstwhile commander of the *Profond*, who was then at Rochefort in charge of the preparations.[7] The reason for this interest in Fort Maurepas was the Minister's determination to make it a sort of headquarters for further exploratory work. Its garrison was now to be increased to one hundred men and supplied with a year's provisions in case they could not get a living from the surrounding country; but on second thought Iberville was told that he might, if he deemed it wise, move the post to another location and destroy Maurepas entirely.[8] Evidently the King wished to establish a permanent stronghold in Louisiana, the choice of site being left to Iberville.

Iberville's enthusiasm for pursuing the project was unbounded. In a long memoir he extolled the advantages to be obtained for France by the acquisition of Louisiana, discussed its geography in great detail, explained its relation to the Spanish settlements, both in Florida and Mexico, and ended up by warning the government that unless quick action were taken it might be lost to the English. A strong colony, he said, was therefore necessary, as the English colonies along the Atlantic coast were powerful and continually increasing in population, so that within a century the British might well be able to seize all America and drive out other nations. Unfortunately the number of French colonists in the West Indies was not growing in the same proportion as the English, for the English did not return to England, as the French did to France, once their fortunes were made, but remained as perma-

---

[6] Le Jeune, *op. cit.*, p. 195.   [7] Margry, *op. cit.*, IV, 307.
[8] *Ibid.*, pp. 308, 349–350.

nent colonists. This situation, Iberville believed, would not be duplicated on the mainland if France should establish a strong colony there, for the climate there was more healthy than that in the islands; thus in less than fifty years the French, with the help of the natives, could hold off all New England and even, perhaps, take it over.[9]

Iberville wished to delay his departure until October, but the King was anxious to have him leave as soon as possible, since Fort Maurepas had only six months' provisions. For this reason orders were issued to put the *Renommée* in commission with the least possible delay, together with her prospective consort, a seven-hundred-ton flute called the *Gironde*, and two feluccas requested by Iberville for use in navigating the Mississippi.[10] The Chevalier de Surgères was offered command of the flute, an offer which he magnanimously accepted, though his rank entitled him to a frigate.

Iberville now sent his plan of campaign to Maurepas. His purpose in making the voyage was to obtain a thorough knowledge of the country, and to succeed in this he considered it advisable to build another fort, to be situated on or near the Mississippi, as a sort of headquarters for extensive explorations. He proposed therefore to sail directly to Fort Maurepas without stopping at any of the West Indian islands, and on arriving there to begin operations by sending his brother, Bienville, with a force of fifty Canadians, the feluccas, and some birchbark canoes, up the Mississippi as far as the Red River, then up this latter stream to the Cadodaqui Indian settlements. This would take him into the heart of Louisiana. Here Bienville would send detachments up the various branches of the Red River to explore the territory as far as the country of the Cenis. Meanwhile, Iberville himself would go to the site of La Salle's ill-fated colony on Matagorda Bay, a place he would designate as a rendezvous with Bienville two

[9] This document does not bear Iberville's name, but it is obviously written by him (*ibid.*, pp. 308–323).

[10] *Ibid.*, pp. 324–325.

months after the latter had started on his exploratory expedition. This would give the commander ample time to survey by ship the coast as far west as the Panuco River, which flows into the Gulf not far from the nearest Spanish colony. At Matagorda Bay he would meet Bienville, obtain from him the details of his journey, embark his party in the ships, and send them back to Fort Maurepas, then proceed over his brother's route to the Cadodaquis, where he would pick up the feluccas, glide down the Mississippi, rejoin his fleet, and sail back to France.[11] It was an elaborate scheme, and one which was never carried out.

The King, however, approved the plan. Orders were given to hasten the work on the *Renommée* and the *Gironde*. Their hulls had to be protected against the marine worms that had caused such havoc with the planking of the *Badine* and *Marin*, and this work had to be done in time for the ships to leave in mid-September. Several officers who had served in the first expedition joined the afterguard, but there were many new names on the roster. Among the veterans were Ensigns Desjordy-Moreau and Villautreys. Pierre Charles Le Sueur, a native of Canada and well-known fur trader, who wished to reach some mines in the Sioux country by ascending the Mississippi, was given passage with eight or ten of his men, as were also one Louis Juchereau de Saint-Denis, a kinsman of Iberville's wife, and the youngest of the Lemoyne brothers, Antoine de Châteauguay, a young man who did yeoman service in the embryo colony and became adept in Indian dialects. The commander had as his chaplain the Jesuit father, Paul du Ru, whose journal throws much light on certain events in the expedition. He had been selected by his superiors to found a mission in the colony. At the last moment the Sieur de Remonville came on board the *Renommée* with his valet.[12] Plentiful provisions were taken on board the ships and enough ammunition to arm the fort against any possible attack. Sérigny's Canadians were rounded up and sent to Rochefort for embarka-

[11] *Ibid.*, pp. 328–332.   [12] *Ibid.*, pp. 340, 347.

tion, after a sufficient sum had been allotted them for their wages.

As a crowning mark of appreciation for past services and an incentive for future endeavors, the King was graciously pleased at this time to confer on Pierre d'Iberville—at Iberville's urgent request—the Order of St. Louis, and the same honor was also bestowed on M. de Surgères.

While these preparations were being made, Iberville had been keeping in touch with the situation in England. From his London correspondent he learned that certain English merchants were eagerly awaiting the return of two ships sent out the previous October under Captain Lewis Banks to explore the shores of the Gulf and found an establishment there, preferably at the mouth of the Mississippi. He had left London the previous October with three ships to convey an assorted group of English colonists and French refugees to America. The French who had left to escape religious persecution were still loyal Frenchmen at heart and hoped to settle in French territory if only they could enjoy freedom of conscience, a wish which King Louis did not see fit to grant. A second expedition was ready in the Thames to sail when the first returned; in any event it would sail in October. There was great interest in the Mississippi venture among the London merchants at this time, and a determination to see it through, the adventurers vowing they would occupy one bank of the river if the French settled on the other. Then there was also a group of Carolina settlers moving westward to the Chickasaw territory and even to the Mississippi, trading and selling arms to the savages. Iberville himself discounted much of this talk, though he held the firm belief that what the English really planned to do was to found a post near Mobile Bay. To ferret out this post he suggested making a sweep of the eastern coastline of the Gulf of Mexico in the *Renommée* while the *Gironde* proceeded directly to Fort Maurepas.

Iberville's instructions, issued at Fountainebleau on September 22, expressed His Majesty's confidence in him, a confidence which led to his being chosen commander of the expedition. He was ordered to proceed directly to Biloxi without touching at Santo Domingo or anywhere else, unless forced to do so by unforeseen circumstances. The King was particularly eager to learn about the economic possibilities of the new country: what sort of plantations could be established there, what produce they could furnish the mother country, and what manufactured goods their workers would use. Then, too, there were rumors to be investigated. He had been told, for example, that there were wool-bearing animals (*laine de boeufs*) in the upper Mississippi country, a reference to the shaggy buffalo, and that valuable pearls might be found. Reports of the presence of mulberry trees brought up the possibility of establishing the silk industry. Perhaps Sauvole had been able to gather some information concerning these matters. But the most-hoped-for prizes were mines; if any were discovered the King wished to have it clearly understood that they would belong to the Crown. Besides seeking out the economic potential of the area, the expedition would gather geographical information for the rectification of maps.

Above all the expedition must take care not to cause any trouble to the Spaniards wherever they might be found. In this connection Iberville was warned not to take possession of Pensacola even if he should find it abandoned. Only in case he was attacked was he to fight the Spaniards.[13] In addition to these instructions a secret order was issued by the King forbidding the commander to attack any posts the English might have erected on the coast but at the same time hinting that he might cause Indians and Canadian woodsmen to destroy them while he himself kept in the background.[14] England and France were at peace and appearances must be preserved.

13 *Ibid.*, pp. 348–354.
14 Pierre Heinrich, *La Louisiane sous la Compagnie des Indes* (Paris, 1908), p. xxxii.

The fleet got under way at La Rochelle on October 17,[15] and made for Cap François, arriving there on December 11. There were many sick persons on board, men who were ill when they started, and these were quickly transferred to the local hospital. Evidently the sea journey had not effected a cure; in fact, the quality of the men selected for the crews does not seem to have been particularly good from the point of view of health as the least exertion, so Iberville tells us, always rendered them ill. This may have been the reason why he did not go directly to Fort Maurepas. Ten days later the vessels set sail and anchored in Biloxi Bay on January 8, 1700.[16]

As soon as the *Renommée* dropped anchor, Sauvole came on board with his report. He had an interesting tale to tell. After Iberville had sailed away the previous year, Sauvole had set his men to work getting the post organized for the coming winter. A suitable house had been built as well as a hospital, the latter always a useful building in this climate, and the trees clustered about the place were hewn down to give more elbow room. Shortly after Iberville's departure Sauvole had sent out parties to explore the neighboring territory. The Bayogoulas appear to have been the first tribe to pay the French a visit, and with their chief as guide Bienville made a journey to the Colapissa village, a four days' march from the fort, where he was well received. In June, Sauvole had sent him to explore Mobile Bay and later to inspect Pensacola, as he was anxious to learn if the Spaniards had abandoned the place. As it turned out the Spaniards were still there. He had also sent a detachment to the Pascagoula River,

[15] Iberville in his letter to the Minister from Cap François (Margry, *op. cit.*, IV, 358) says he left on September 17, but this is a clerical error, as his instructions were dated on September 22.

[16] The sources for Iberville's second expedition are Margry, *op. cit.*, IV, 360–431; Pénicaut, "Relation," *ibid.*, V, 391–415; Gravier, "Journal," in Thwaites, *op. cit.*, LXV, 101–179; and *Journal of Paul du Ru*, tr. by Ruth L. Butler (Chicago, 1934).

which made its way up the stream for sixteen leagues to a village of the same name, a small affair of twenty cabins.

In August, Sauvole decided to obtain more definite knowledge of the terrain around Lakes Pontchartrain and Maurepas, for he had heard from Iberville that its low and marshy character prevented any post's being built there. In order to carry out this work he selected Bienville and six men, gave them two canoes, and sent them first to explore the southern shore of Pontchartrain. He wished, if possible, to find the bayou and portage that led from the lake to the Mississippi, the short cut pointed out to Iberville when he was near the site of New Orleans. The party went to the lake by the Rigolets. At the end of this pass they headed due west to a promontory called Pointe aux Herbes. Pénicaut, who accompanied the expedition, described the area:

Six leagues thence there falls into it [the lake] a little river called by the savages Choupicatcha and today by the French Orleans River [Bayou St. John?], because since then, as we shall show later on, there has been built near the river at a league from the lake the city of New Orleans. Five leagues farther on, bearing continually to the left along the lake one finds a quiet water which the savages call Bayouque.

This stream, the Indians said, led to the Mississippi. The party entered it and presently came to the great river at a spot forty leagues from its mouth.[17] Bienville first paid a visit to the Bayo-

[17] There are two accounts of this voyage—Pénicaut's "Relation" in Margry, *op. cit.*, V, 385–386 and Sauvole de la Villantray's letter, *ibid.*, IV, 455–456—that give different versions of what happened at this point. Sauvole says that Bienville on reaching the Mississippi visited the Quinipissas, then went downstream to where he met the English vessel. Pénicaut tells us that the party merely glanced at the river, then returned to explore Lake Pontchartrain. Sauvole's narrative, however, speaks of one party sent on August 22 to take soundings in the lakes, and that on the following day the party commanded by Bienville was sent to explore the Mississippi by way of the portage from Pontchartrain. Perhaps the two

goulas and Quinipissas, then started down toward the delta. On reaching a point twenty-three leagues from the river's mouth (as he estimated the distance) a point thereafter called English Turn or its French equivalent, he saw not far from him an English corvette of twelve guns. It was the ship of Captain Lewis Banks. Both Iberville and Bienville had known this man in Hudson Bay and Iberville thought little of his abilities. His little fleet had wintered in Carolina. This year one of the ships returned to London while Banks with the other two sailed to the Gulf of Mexico with a view to establishing himself on the Mississippi. He cruised a hundred leagues or so west of the delta; then he retraced his steps and entered the river with the corvette, leaving her consort outside. This incident, which might have led to international complications, was quickly solved by Captain Banks, who left as soon as Bienville had assured him that the title to the delta had been preempted by France. Before departing, however, Banks uttered dire threats that he would return in greater force to found a settlement on the river which, he said, the English had discovered fifty years before.[18]

Both Bienville and Sauvole had much other information to give Iberville when he arrived. From the former the commander learned of the presence among the Chickasaw Indians of English traders pressing westward from Carolina. On hearing this he promised himself to lure these traders away from the Indians and capture them, for they were encroaching on what he claimed was the domain of France. He learned also that during his absence

parties may have met at the portage and then separated each to go its own way.

[18] *Ibid.*, IV, 361–362, 457–462, 395–397; Benard de la Harpe, *Journal historique de l'établisement des Français à la Louisiane* (Paris, 1831), p. 20, says that Bienville bluffed the Englishman into leaving by telling him that the river was not the Mississippi but another claimed by the French. Since neither Iberville nor Sauvole mentions this in their accounts, the story is probably apocryphal.

contact of a limited sort had been established with Canada. Sauvole told him that two missionaries, Fathers Antoine Davion and François Jolliet de Montigny, then living with the Taensas well up the river, had visited Fort Maurepas the previous summer with a dozen Canadians. After the fathers had returned to their posts, a report (which later proved to be false) that Montigny had been murdered by the Natchez came to Iberville's ears; and since the Indians would consider such a murder an act of war, Iberville saw that his communications with the Illinois area were cut off. It was, therefore, necessary to make peace with the Natchez before he could venture to explore the northern country and make the survey of its resources which the government at home demanded. This he now proposed to do. But he must also demand of the Natchez the surrender of Montigny's murderers, for he felt it essential to French domination that the murder of a Frenchman should not go unpunished.

Since the English had threatened to seize the entrance to the Mississippi, it was Iberville's duty to found a permanent settlement there to resist such an attempt. A preliminary expedition was accordingly sent out on January 15, Iberville himself taking command. Its purpose was to find the short cut from Lake Pontchartrain to the river, for he remembered the harrowing experiences of the previous year when he had sailed down the coast to North Pass. Accompanied by Bienville, he made his way to the lake with two feluccas and three canoes and proceeded to a little river, probably the Bayou St. John, which he believed to be the one that gave access to the Mississippi. The channel, unfortunately, did not prove particularly promising; the small boats could get through but not the larger ones; and when he came to the portage, one league in length, he found it submerged knee-deep in mud for half its distance. But the commander by a great effort managed to transport the canoes across it to the river beyond, where he remained for two days surveying the terrain and planting some sugar cane of a rather poor quality which he had brought from Santo Domingo.

Bienville, meanwhile, with the three canoes and eleven men, ventured a short distance upstream to visit the Bayogoulas and tell them of the arrival of the ships at Biloxi and to learn for his brother the latest news of the Indian tribes. He was also commissioned to look for a suitable place for the proposed fort which was to be erected somewhere on the lower river. Bienville reached the village promptly and after a brief stay secured the services of a chief who knew the territory well. Taking this man with him, he drifted slowly down the river, examining carefully the land that unrolled before him until he came to a place seventeen leagues from the river's mouth. Here he saw at a short distance from the shore an elevated ridge which the savages assured him would not be inundated should the stream overflow its banks; and here Bienville stopped to await his brother.[19]

On returning to the fleet Iberville at once made ready for the main expedition. A *traversier* and the two feluccas, manned by eighty men, were put in commission for the journey. The chief purpose of the excursion was, of course, to build a fort near the mouth of the Mississippi. Iberville had advocated this as a necessary headquarters for his proposed expedition, but now it was even more necessary as a defense against possible English encroachment by sea.

The expedition left on February 1. Father du Ru, to whom we are indebted for some of our information, was in the party and so were young Châteauguay and Juchereau de Saint-Denis. Sauvole was left behind in charge of the fort. As the short cut through Lake Pontchartrain had been found impracticable, the little fleet headed directly for North Pass, which it reached in two days; then propelled by a strong southeast breeze it arrived at the junction of the three branches of the river by noon and at midnight

[19] Margry, *op. cit.*, IV, 399–401.

came to the place seventeen leagues from the sea where Bienville was awaiting them. Several days were spent here building the blockhouse which was to stand as mute witness to the French claims of dominion.

The fort was erected on the eastern side of the Mississippi not far from the modern town of Phoenix. This town is situated about thirty miles south of New Orleans. Running north of it is a ridge of land, and following this ridge for about a mile, one comes to the Gravelot Canal, a small artificial waterway connecting the river with Bayou Portage. Here, where the canal cuts the ridge, the remains of the fort have been found. The site is slightly over 4,000 feet from the river, though in Iberville's time it may have been nearer. The expedition spent two weeks here clearing the ground, cutting logs, and doing the preliminary work on what was to be a fairly substantial post. The principal building was to be a two-story house, twenty-eight feet square, built of logs (the wood used was Louisiana red cypress), and equipped with four four-pound guns and two eighteen-pounders. It was to be surrounded by a moat twelve feet wide.[20] Father du Ru claimed "the honor of doing the first formal act of clearing, but not without getting very wet, thanks to the bad weather." Though a substantial structure, it was not to be an unduly elaborate affair; as Father du Ru said, it was to be "only an idea here in the midst of the Mississippi woods"; but every effort was made to push the work forward with all possible haste, sailors, Canadian woodsmen, and officers pitching in with a good will to do their share.

The fort was in no way finished at this time. All that was done was to construct a house and a powder magazine eight feet square and five feet high, covered with a layer of mud plaster. It is difficult to say just when the place was completed. Iberville left a detachment there to continue the work when he took his leave, and on his return six weeks later found that little progress had been made. Eventually several houses were added to the fortified

[20] *Ibid.*, p. 364.

part to form a settlement. Father du Ru, in order to be prepared for the worst, seized the occasion to consecrate a little cemetery, where he erected a cross bearing an inscription commemorating the achievements of La Salle, Tonty, and Iberville in claiming the Louisiana territory for France. Father Jacques Gravier, who visited the place the following December, was not particularly impressed with what he saw. "There is neither fort nor bastion, nor intrenchments, nor redoubts [there]," he said; "it consists of only a battery of six pieces of cannon, and of six or eight placed on the edge of the hill [ridge]; and of five or six cabins detached one from another and roofed with palm-leaves." To this place the name of La Boulaye was given, though no one seems to know why it was so called. The word "boulaie," we are told, is an old French word for a plot of birch trees, and this may offer a key to the puzzle.[21]

Two leagues above the fort Iberville discovered some cedars of Lebanon, just the type of wood for building pirogues—those keelless, flat-bottomed boats so handy for navigating shoal waters —and he ordered the Sieur de la Ronde with six men to undertake their construction. He also dispatched the larger of his two feluccas with a supply of provisions to the portage twenty leagues above the post, the one near New Orleans leading to Lake Pontchartrain. Here it was to meet Pierre du Guay, who had been ordered there from Biloxi with two biscayennes bringing a party of ten soldiers, eight Canadians, and Pierre Le Sueur with his mining prospectors en route for the Natchez country. It also carried orders for Du Guay to proceed to the Bayogoula village, where the commander would presently join him.

Scarcely had the preliminary work on the fort been completed when a canoe appeared, commanded by no less a person than Henri de Tonty. He had come down from the Illinois villages

[21] *Ibid.*, IV, 403, 420; V, 393, 399; Gravier's "Journal," in Thwaites, *op. cit.*, LXV, 161; *Journal of Paul du Ru*, pp. 7–11. For a complete account of the discovery of the site see Ries, *op. cit.*

with a following of twenty-two Canadians, most of whom had stopped at the Bayogoula settlement to exchange their supply of beaver for merchandise. One can imagine the joy with which these two pioneers greeted each other as they met thus unexpectedly at this far-off outpost of France. Iberville and Tonty, two of the leading French explorers of their day, one coming from France by sea, the other from Canada by land, both following in the footsteps of La Salle, had at last opened a new route for the fur traders from the upper Mississippi basin to France. The work which La Salle had set out to do twenty years before was at last accomplished.

Tonty brought with him the welcome denial of the report of Father Montigny's death at the hands of the Natchez. This was doubly pleasing to Iberville, for not only was the missionary still living but it opened the way to friendly relations with this tribe now that the stigma of murder had been removed. Thus heartened, the French commander persuaded Tonty to turn back and accompany him northward, as the latter by his familiarity with the Illinois would be a valuable ally to the expedition when it began its exploration of the Red River. Moreover, Iberville needed reinforcements, for the sick he would be obliged to leave at the fort, together with those allotted to the garrison, would reduce his Canadian followers to the number of thirty. Now that he had Tonty, he no longer needed the soldiers brought by Du Guay, and he accordingly sent him a message ordering him not to cross the portage, but Du Guay was off to the Bayogoula village before the message reached him.

The weather now became cold. By mid-February ice formed and there was continual frost. Iberville placed the Sieur de Maltot in command of the fort with a garrison of fourteen men—which included those too ill to travel—then sent forward a large detachment under Bienville, Châteauguay, and La Ronde in a felucca and two boats to await him at the Bayogoula village. It was a trying journey for these men. They moved through torrential rains, and when they landed for the night they found themselves knee deep in mud. Every night, so Du Ru tells us, "a great fire is kindled and we surround it with wet blankets and wet clothes. Everyone strips to his shirt and warms himself as well as he can."

On February 19, Iberville moved forward with Tonty and his eight followers, traveling so slowly that they did not reach the portage to Lake Pontchartrain until five days later. There they found Pierre Le Sueur and his men ready for their fur-trading venture. Joining forces, the combined parties presently overtook Bienville's detachment, and preparations were made to enter the Bayogoula village in proper style as described by Du Ru:

Everybody dresses up to meet the Bayogoulas. Beards are trimmed and fresh linen put on. Here is the landing place. Our vessels assemble to enter the port in order. The landing begins. The whole bank is black with savages who sing the calumet to us. M. d'Iberville is on the sloop [*sic*] and takes me with him. M. de Bienville is in the escorting canoe; M. de la Ronde is in the wooden canoe which he calls the *Hardy* and M. de Châteauguay in another wooden canoe, all with flags at the sterns and all firing shots. We arrive thus in good form.[22]

In this manner did the French land among the Bayogoulas on February 26. Here, after the usual amenities had been observed, Iberville arranged the disposal of his forces before venturing any farther. He dispatched a messenger with a complete record of the journey thus far, written for the benefit of the Minister. This document was to be taken to Surgères, who was to leave at once for France after putting ashore a month's provisions for Fort Maurepas. He sent off Juchereau de Saint-Denis to form a sort of vanguard of hunters to keep the party supplied with fresh meat. He also discussed with Tonty a plan by which Tonty, when on his way back to the Illinois villages, was to lure two English traders away from their haunts and hand them over as prisoners to La Ronde—a good plan, but abandoned later because the Eng-

[22] *Journal of Paul du Ru*, p. 19.

lish accompanying the traders were found to be too numerous. These men were said to be busy among the Chickasaws inciting them to attack other tribes. And lastly the commander took an observation and found the latitude of the village to be 30° 40′ N. This was a great improvement over the computation he had made on his first visit the year before. He had then made an error that placed him forty-two geographical miles north of his true position; now he was only twenty miles too far north.

On March 1 the French commander said farewell to his Bayogoula friends and started off for the Houma village preceded by Bienville and a small party. All his men accompanied him, including, of course, Tonty's band—that is, all except Du Guay, who was left behind to await the arrival of a squad which had gone back to La Boulaye to bring up a wounded comrade, left there to undergo a crude surgical operation. Two days later Iberville overtook his brother, and the following day at six o'clock in the morning the flotilla, bearing altogether fifty-eight men, drew up at the Houma landing place after a journey of thirty leagues from the Bayogoula village. This place, as we pointed out in the previous chapter, was above Tunica Bend in latitude 30° 54′ N. Here Iberville erected a cross, giving the savages to understand that they must be careful not to tear it down as it had a deep religious significance. He called the landing Portage of the Cross. Realizing the impracticability of taking his entire party to the settlement, he decided to save time by sending the greater part of it with the boats to the upper landing while he visited the village with a handful of picked men. This upper landing was on the shore of a small bay (Clarke's Lake?) about two leagues above the mouth of the Red River and about a league distant from the village. In order to reach it those going by water were obliged to make a long journey, for just above Tunica Bend the river in those days made an enormous loop to the west, known as Raccourci Bend, which lengthened the distance by many leagues. One hundred and fifty years later the river made a new channel, the Raccourci Cut-off, which eliminated this bend. What Iberville did, then, was to take a short cut overland to the village. Thus, when he came to resume his journey, he could proceed to the upper landing where he would find the boats awaiting him.

After giving the necessary orders to his command Iberville marched to the Houma settlement with six Canadians and a like number of Bayogoulas. A council was held on his arrival, and after compliments were exchanged he expressed his regret to hear that the Houmas and Bayogoulas were now at war despite the alliance they had made the previous year. They replied in the usual way, blaming the Bayogoulas for the rupture, yet they professed to be willing to forget hostilities if Iberville would act as peacemaker. Anxious not to leave two warring nations behind him when he ascended the river, he constituted himself a representative of the Bayogoulas and secured from the Houmas their prisoners of war, for whom he gave a suitable gift in the name of the Bayogoula tribe, as was the custom in ransoming captives, and sent them back to their homes.

At this time there happened to be in the Houma town a number of Little Taensa Indians, members of a tribe situated a three days' journey to the westward, who the year before had given Iberville a glowing account of the Red River. Anxious to visit this stream, he tried to engage them as guides; but for some reason or other they refused to lead him even as far as the Cadodaquis, saying that the river was impassable at this time of year and suggesting that the French go by land through the Big Taensa village. So complex did the Red River and its tributaries seem to Iberville after listening to the various descriptions given by these savages, that he thought it unwise to venture on its waters without suitable guides. He therefore abandoned the idea of ascending it and decided to proceed first to the Big Taensa settlement, then overland to the Cadodaquis, joining the Red River later on his return trip and following it to its junction with the Mississippi.

After making this decision Iberville proceeded to the upper

landing, where he found some of the boats awaiting him; the others had stopped at the Red River to fish, but these were quickly summoned. Then he selected a pirogue, placed ten men in it, and sent it down to Fort de la Boulaye filled with equipment he would no longer need. On March 9 he started up the river. Two days later the explorers reached the Natchez village situated near the site of the modern city of that name. The chief received the French commander with every mark of respect and gave him a letter written by Father Montigny, who had left the village three days before to return to his mission among the Taensas. In this letter he gave a summary of his activities among the Natchez together with a sketch of the information he had gathered concerning them.

Iberville left early in the morning of the twelfth for the Big Taensa settlement. This village was situated near the site of modern Newellton at the western end of Lake St. Joseph, an oxbow cut-off to the west of the river.[23] Bienville and a detachment remained with the Natchez to lay in a supply of flour which his brother would need for a visit he proposed to make to the Cenis Indians. Iberville traveled light on this journey, for he wished to make a reconnaissance of the Taensas and complete arrangements for the coming expedition. He took with him six men and a canoe. On arriving at the Taensa landing place, which he did two days later, he left his canoe on the river bank with two men to guard it and proceeded to Lake St. Joseph with the other four. Unfortunately the guides lost their way and the weary men floundered around until nightfall, when they were obliged to encamp and go supperless to sleep, hoping for better luck the following day. Next morning they were able to pick up some Indians, who quickly led them to the village, which they reached at noon. Here to his great joy Iberville found Father Montigny. Montigny had built a house and was already preparing to erect a

[23] J. R. Swanton, *Indians of the Southeastern United States* (Publication of Smithsonian Institution, Bureau of American Ethnology, Bulletin No. 137, 1946), p. 188.

church. Iberville learned from him that the Taensa Indians had once been a great nation, but their numbers had now dwindled to a mere three hundred warriors who dwelt on the shores of the lake. Thanks to the assistance of Father Montigny, who kindly acted as interpreter, the French were now able to secure the services of a guide who, for a liberal consideration, was willing to lead them overland to the Cadodaqui settlement.

It was while stopping at this village that the French were treated to an exhibition of a barbarous religious custom that recalls the sacrifice of children in ancient Carthage. During a violent thunderstorm a bolt of lightning struck a building used by the Indians for their heathen worship and set it on fire. This calamity proved a godsend for the local medicine man, for at the death of the late chief, which had occurred a short time before, Father Montigny had dissuaded the people from making the usual human sacrifices required by tradition; it was now easy to suggest that the destruction of the temple was the work of an incensed deity. Calling the people together, he pointed to the burning temple as evidence of the wrath of the Great Spirit and cried out: "Women, bring your children to offer the Spirit as a sacrifice to appease him." Terrified at the thought of having angered a vengeful god, five squaws rushed forward with their babies, which the medicine man took from them and hurled into the flames. More women would have followed the ghastly example if the French had not restrained them. The action of these five women gave them enormous prestige with the tribe. They were at once led to the cabin of the new ruler, praised by the chief, clothed in white robes, crowned with feathers, and allowed to spend the night singing and chanting with the medicine man.

Iberville himself does not appear to have been present at this sacrifice; he had gone back to the Taensa landing place to meet Bienville and Saint-Denis. When he returned to the village, preparations were immediately begun for the expedition to the Cenis country. And now for the first time the commander, who had undergone so many hardships and overcome so many obstacles, found himself incapacitated by a violent pain in the knee—possibly a touch of rheumatism, the result of constant exposure—which prevented him from walking and compelled him to abandon his plans for an overland journey and to return to Biloxi. Henceforth he would be obliged to travel as much as possible by water. This decision, the result of dire necessity, was a blow to the gallant explorer, and it was with a heavy heart that he sent Du Guay ahead to Fort La Boulaye, and thence to Ship Island, to apprise those stationed there that their commander was on his way back.

On March 22, early in the morning, the Lemoyne brothers bade each other farewell and separated, one to explore the little-known regions west of the Mississippi, the other to return to Biloxi. Father Montigny accompanied Iberville to the Natchez settlement, where he remained to establish a mission. Just before reaching the Houma village Iberville met Le Sueur with his band of prospectors making their way up the river. Iberville presented him with a large canoe and detailed the captain of his felucca to act as his guide. Then continuing his voyage, he reached the settlement that evening and found Tonty and La Ronde awaiting him. The following day the expedition proceeded to the Bayogoulas, while Tonty continued on his way upstream to the Illinois settlements. Iberville had given him presents for the chieftains of the Tunicas and Chickasaws, requesting him at the same time to warn them that since the French were friendly with the southern nations it would be to their advantage to make friends with the French by ceasing their warfare against the Natchez and neighboring tribes, for if they did not Iberville would place firearms in the hands of his allies.

The rest of the journey was made rapidly. On March 26 Iberville reached the Bayogoulas, where he found some *voyageurs* from the upper country who had come down to dispose of a meager supply of beaver. Here Father du Ru remained to found a mission. At noon the commander left the village with Château-guay and hurried to La Boulaye. He arrived there the following evening, having covered forty-two leagues in thirty-four hours. Here he found the Sieur du Guay. Work on the fort had not advanced so rapidly as he had hoped it would, but he consoled himself with the sight of a field of waving wheat and a rich crop of peas planted by the garrison. Behind the fort there flowed a little river, twenty paces wide and twelve feet deep, ample water for the boats. It was the Oak River, which could be reached from the fort by the Bayou Lesseps. A short distance down this river one comes to the Orange Bayou, a route used in modern times as a short cut to the coast.[24] Satisfied with its possibilities, Iberville sent Du Guay in a canoe with three men to make his way to Biloxi by this route. The Frenchman lost his way—one can hardly blame him if one studies the map—and was back in three days. Nothing daunted, the commander took a boat and with two companions tried a portage two leagues above the fort. It proved impassable, and he was perforce obliged to abandon any hope of reaching Biloxi by a short cut in this locality.

And now the hardships to which he had been exposed for so long a time began to tell on his constitution. The touch of rheumatism he had felt at the Taensa village proved but the forerunner of a more serious ailment. The sturdy health which had weathered the freezing temperatures of the North could not withstand the miasmic exhalations of the southern swampland. On returning to the fort he was stricken with a fever which laid him low for several days and delayed his journey back to the ships. The attack was not a severe one, but it proved to be the prelude to an illness that was eventually to break him.

Unable to travel, Iberville sent the Sieur de Maltot to Ship Island to procure some provisions. On the last day of March, much to his surprise, there came a *traversier* and felucca from Ship Island with a quantity of livestock—five cows, a bull, a dozen

[24] Ries, *op. cit.*

pigs, and some guinea-fowl—which had made the journey through the mouth of the river in thirty-six hours, a splendid run and one that showed the superiority of the all-water route over the portage route through Lake Pontchartrain. These boats also brought a strange tale of Spanish diplomacy at Biloxi. Before the French had left, the Spanish governor at Pensacola, M. d'Arriola, had arrived at Ship Island with a twenty-four-gun frigate and two smaller vessels, saying that he had been sent by the viceroy of Mexico to drive out the French because, so it was believed, they represented a private trading company, though he had orders not to molest them if their venture was one sponsored by the King. Arriola contented himself with lodging a written protest against the French establishment, claiming that it was contrary to the good will existing between the two crowns for Frenchmen to seize territory belonging to the King of Spain and incorporated in the Viceroyalty of Mexico. He also requested the French not to found any more establishments until he had an opportunity to consult his superiors. The governor was well received, wined, and dined by Surgères and his officers. Under the influence of good cheer he admitted that the Spaniards were holding Pensacola only because the French were at Biloxi, and that they were ready to leave their post as soon as the latter abandoned theirs. After courtesies had been exchanged, Arriola left with his ships while the French settled down to wonder if anything would come of the Spaniard's visit. Nine days later an open boat was seen in the offing pulling desperately toward the shore. Gradually it drew nearer until it came up alongside the ships, when to everyone's astonishment the governor and a few companions, half dead from exposure, climbed up the ladder and dropped exhausted on the *Renommée*'s deck. When they had sufficiently recovered to give a coherent account of themselves, Arriola related that shortly after they had left Ship Island a terrific gale struck his fleet, piling the vessels up on the Chandeleur Islands. On hearing this the French immediately sent out a rescue party, which managed to collect the survivors and bring them to Ship Island, where they were treated with kindness by their former hosts, furnished with clothing, and eventually sent to Pensacola properly equipped and supplied.

Still suffering from fever, Iberville lingered at the fort. Heavy rains now put a stop to the work of construction, but despite the high water that swelled the river, the terrain on which the block-house was situated remained dry above the flood level. At last, on the evening of the thirteenth, the commander rose from his sick-bed, turned the fort over to La Ronde, who had just arrived there, and set out for Biloxi. After gliding down the Mississippi he reached the sea through the same channel through which he had entered the river a few weeks before, then set his course for Mississippi Sound.

On arriving at Fort Maurepas Iberville determined to explore the entrance to the Pascagoula River before returning to France, to see if it were possible to dig a channel through the sand bar at its entrance and thus open up a sheltered harbor for his vessels. He was also anxious to get further information about the country up north. Two leagues from the river's mouth he pitched his first camp on a ridge covered with pines, and on the next day proceeded to an abandoned village where he spent the night. For two days he continued up the river, taking careful notes of the surrounding country and visiting an Indian settlement which he found in dilapidated condition. An epidemic had swept the country and had carried off the greater part of the population, and the village now housed but twenty families. The Mobile tribe lived in a village three days' journey to the northeast. Iberville sent two of his men to this settlement with an invitation to the Mobile chiefs to visit him at Biloxi, while he retraced his steps to the sea.

On May 18 Bienville and his party arrived from the Mississippi with the disquieting news of an outbreak of trouble among the tribes along the river. The Bayogoulas had massacred the Mougou-lachas. The following day Fathers Davion and Montigny also arrived with some Natchez and Tunica braves, bringing a report of the attempts of the English to stir up trouble among the Indians of the upper Mississippi.

As it was now time to leave for France, Iberville drew up his instructions for Sauvole, who was to remain in command at Biloxi. These instructions consisted principally of orders to explore the country roundabout and keep an eye open for various natural products. He also warned his lieutenant particularly against the nationals of other countries who might cause trouble, authorizing him to employ force to repel them if peaceful persuasion had no effect. Above all he must send Juchereau de Saint-Denis to make a complete survey of the land west of the great river with a view to locating mines. Juchereau, however, was to be sure to acquire land only in the King's name and to send mineral samples to France for analysis.

Iberville took leave of his lieutenants and weighed anchor on May 28. He did not, however, make straight for La Rochelle; he had another plan in mind connected with a scheme upon which he was always brooding—the scheme to break forever the British power in North America. As an attack on New York formed part of the general design, he steered the *Renommée* up the Atlantic coast for the purpose of entering New York harbor and taking soundings that would prove useful when his plan was launched. Entering the lower harbor late in June, he picked up a Jersey pilot, then headed up the Narrows for the ostensible purpose of taking on wood and water—a reasonable pretext, since England and France were officially at peace. He delayed there a month and succeeded, so Governor Cornbury later told the Lords of Trade, in taking complete soundings between Sandy Hook and the Battery, although the British kept a careful watch to prevent him, by detailing a barge to follow him every night.[25] The Earl of Bellomont, Cornbury's predecessor, attributed Iberville's activities to a rumor he had heard that King James had some time

[25] *Docs. Rel. Col. Hist. N.Y.*, IV, 686, 877, 969, 1184.

before given the province of New York to the King of France. The incident, at any rate, put quite a scare into the colonial officials, and taken together with other evidences of Canadian hostility, it spurred the earl into advocating a strengthening of fortifications.[26]

[26] *Ibid.*, IV, 1184; *C.S.P. Am. & W.I., 1700* (No. 620), p. 543.

CHAPTER X

Bayou Diplomacy

ON RETURNING to France Iberville remained for some time at La Rochelle before reporting to the Minister of Marine, for the fever he had contracted in the swamplands of Louisiana had greatly weakened him. By this time a change had taken place in the Ministry, and Jerome de Maurepas, who had been assisting his father for several years in this department, was now its actual head, and his father had been advanced to the post of chancellor. When he took office on September 6, 1699, he dropped the title of Maurepas and assumed that of Pontchartrain, to the great confusion of future historians, who now found themselves with two Count Pontchartrains on their hands.

During this period of Iberville's inactivity momentous events were taking place which were to have a tremendous effect on the entire political situation in Western Europe and which King Louis hoped would alter the position of the newly established colony on the Gulf of Mexico. Charles II of Spain died in November, 1700, without leaving a direct heir. Shortly before his death, however, he had made a will bequeathing his crown to Philip of Anjou, grandson of Louis XIV. The acceptance of this bequest by Louis in behalf of his grandson meant war with England and other nations, for a French Bourbon on the throne of Spain would unite under one family the powerful kingdom of France with the mighty Spanish empire. These two nations extended, in theory at least, over the greater part of the Western Hemisphere, and included also some valuable principalities in Italy. Yet Louis did not hesitate. On receipt of the official notice of King Charles's death he proclaimed his grandson King of Spain as Philip V. This was the *casus belli* of that great conflict known in history as the War of the Spanish Succession, in America called Queen Anne's War. It led in the following year (1701) to the formation of the powerful coalition of Great Britain, Austria, and the Netherlands against France and her ally, Spain. The issue was now clearly joined. The alliance voiced its disapproval of any further expansion of French power in America. Thus the fear which Iberville had expressed of the possibility of encroachment by the English colonists was changed into the grim possibility of open attack.

When Iberville recovered from his illness he proceeded to Paris, arriving there early in January. At the request of the Minister he set to work on a plan which, so Pontchartrain hoped, would lead the Spanish government to believe that a French colony on the Gulf would serve as a protection against British encroachments on Spain's colonial empire in Mexico. By this time Philip of Anjou was on the Spanish throne, and the French Court was all agog over the possibility of an alliance between the two nations. Iberville was quick to sense the change in the political situation and to see that his favorite scheme for ousting the English from North America must be approached from a different angle. In order to interest the Court he must evolve a plan which would take into consideration the possibilities of a Spanish alliance.

With his customary ingenuity he now laid out a plan which he embodied in a memoir and sent to the King for consideration. In this document he showed a comprehensive grasp of the American problem, far beyond what might be expected of an ordinary sea captain. The English possessions, the memoir pointed out, ran

from the Penobscot River in Maine to the St. John River in Florida
—an immense country drained by great rivers giving access to an
interior inhabited by over 60,000 families. These colonies maintained a fleet of vessels by which they carried on trade with the
Azores, Newfoundland, Madeira, the West Indies, and even
India. A mountain range formed a barrier separating the Carolinas
and Florida—Iberville's Florida extended farther north than the
modern state. The land between these mountains and the sea was
fairly thickly populated, so that the children of the present generation of inhabitants would in the course of time be obliged to
migrate westward; in fact some had already done so. Thus far the
westward exodus had been confined within the limits of the thirty-
third and thirty-seventh parallels, but it *had* reached the Mississippi. The pioneers, at this time, were not interested in establishing
themselves along the coast; they only wanted to make themselves
masters of the hinterland and the Indians living there. By doing
this they could exclude any foreigners who attempted to venture
into this domain. Iberville did not question that the English would
eventually occupy all the territory lying between their present
colonial settlements and the great river. There would then be no
stopping them; for joining forces with the Indians, they would
soon overrun the greater part of Mexico, which at this time was
not increasing in population as were the British colonies. Furthermore, they would probably accomplish this so rapidly that the
damage would be done before the events could become known in
France and Spain.

To save the embryo French possessions in the West it was therefore necessary to take prompt action before the foe became too
powerful to be dislodged. Fortunately, the British settlers at this
time were few in number, and for the present it would be enough
to build a strong colony on the Mississippi and establish a post on
Mobile Bay to head off any pioneers who might come down the
rivers emptying into this body of water. The British menace to
the French colonies was also a threat to the Spanish settlements,

for once the former had been taken, the road to Mexico lay open. The four posts which Spain had set up to protect her great possessions, Apalachicola, Pensacola, Matagorda Bay, and a place among the Cenis Indians, were entirely inadequate and could be taken easily by the English; indeed, so inadequate were they that Iberville hints that those who had suggested them to Spain as strategic points must have been influenced by ulterior motives, unless they could be excused on the ground of absolute ignorance. The French, with their posts on the Mississippi and Mobile Bay well established, should make overtures to the northern Indians to bind these tribes to them, an object which could best be accomplished by advantageous trade agreements. To further this policy Iberville had already called a meeting of the tribes to take place at the Mississippi fort sometime during the coming spring (1701), at which he hoped a general peace could be arranged and certain English interpreters, then at work among these tribes, handed over to the French. It would be well also if the Spaniards could be induced to cede Pensacola to France.[1]

To justify this last suggestion he compiled another report setting forth in detail the weakness of the fortification at Pensacola. It was, he said, but a rectangular stone wall enclosing a space where horses might be kept, more of a park than a fort. The garrison consisted of one hundred soldiers, poorly armed and worse clothed, a few sailors, and eighty convicts. The governor, Don Andres d'Arriola, had little interest in the place—one can hardly blame him—and spent only a month there each year. Nevertheless the post was an important one; it had possibilities, and the English might well attempt to seize it.[2]

So favorably were the King and his ministers impressed by the solid reasoning of this memoir that it was promptly dispatched to Philip of Spain in the hope that his government would accept the suggestions as a working basis for Franco-Spanish co-operation

[1] Margry, *op. cit.*, IV, 543–550.
[2] *Ibid.*, pp. 550–552.

against English encroachments along the Gulf and in the Mississippi Valley. Philip turned the matter over to his Junta of War and the Indies, which body, true to Spanish custom, put off the answer till the morrow.

The action taken by the French government in sending Iberville's memoir to Spain is an indication of the high esteem in which he was held by the King. From a leader of expeditions to out-of-the-way places he had now become a statesman, unquestionably *the* leading Canadian authority on matters pertaining to French foreign policy in America. Instead of issuing orders for Iberville and shaping the policy he should follow in Louisiana, the Minister of Marine turned to him for advice as to what should be done. During this period Iberville wrote numerous memoirs, in reality treatises on the situation in Louisiana, which show the results of painstaking research and an excellent grasp of the trend of events. He foresaw the gradual expansion of the English seaboard colonies westward and foretold the menace they would eventually be to the French possessions along the Mississippi. Unless action were now taken to drive back the English, it would not be an easy matter, he warned his government, to do so later on. As an example of his ideas on the subject we find an elaborate plan for destroying, or at least crippling, the colonies in North America by an attack on New England.

The idea of gaining possession of New York by a drive on Fort Orange from Montreal in conjunction with a naval expedition against Manhattan was not a new one, but Iberville now rejected it and brought out a memoir substituting a plan of his own. In criticizing the former scheme he pointed out that an army coming down from Canada would be obliged to divide its forces, leaving a portion to hold Fort Orange after its capture, thus greatly weakening the number of effectives that could be sent to New York. Furthermore, his own observations in New York harbor had shown him the difficulties of approaching this place by sea; the sinuosities of the channel and the numerous shoals blocking its entrance made it extremely hazardous for a fleet to enter the port unless favored by a following breeze and conned by an experienced pilot.

Dismissing this plan as impractical, he now outlined a new scheme—to seize Boston by means of an army coming down from Canada by little-known routes and falling on the town by surprise. He considered winter as the most favorable time for such an attack, as the vessels which frequented the New England coast generally returned to Europe in November, leaving, as Iberville says, "only mechanics who are illy qualified for fighting and fancy themselves in security because they cannot imagine us in a condition in Canada to form designs of that magnitude, especially in a season so rigorous as that of winter." His scheme, in brief, was to sail from France to the Penobscot or Kennebec River and make his way northward to Quebec, taking careful observations of the best trails through the hinterland over which he could lead his army, stopping on the way to visit the Baron de Saint-Castin and enlist Indian allies and making use of the greatest secrecy to prevent any news of the coming attack from reaching the ears of the Bostonese. On arriving at Quebec he would collect a body of 1,800 men, composed of 1,000 Canadians, 400 regular soldiers, and 400 Indians. Starting not later than the middle of November, he would take the route down the St. Lawrence and up the Chaudière across the mass of lakes and rivers of northern Maine to the settlement of Norridgewock on the Kennebec, the place of rendezvous. From there the expedition would proceed to Boston, laying waste the countryside on the way; and with the capture of Boston it would be easy to weaken New York. This feat would so impress the Indians, especially the Iroquois, that they would at once side with the French, leaving the English to their fate. It would then be a simple matter to destroy the grain on Long Island, which feeds the population of Manhattan, and drive the inhabitants westward into Pennsylvania. To accomplish this Iberville requested to be sent out in March that he might reach Acadia in time to survey the road to Quebec and assemble his men for the start of the expedition in November.[3]

It would be wrong, however, to assume, after perusing these memoirs, that Iberville was unduly apprehensive about British intentions toward Louisiana. For some time past Governor Nicholson of Virginia had looked upon French colonial projects in the Mississippi Valley with an anxious eye. He had recommended to his southern neighbors that they establish trading posts along the western frontier, where they could keep the Indians under control and prevent them from falling under French influence. He himself was too remote from the scene of action to take any part in this work, so he enlisted the support of Joseph Blake, governor of South Carolina, who was alive to the danger. Blake had already taken steps to bring the Indians under control by sending a body of traders by way of the Tennessee and Ohio rivers to proclaim England's right to the Mississippi country.

When Iberville learned of this he foresaw the danger of a great English migration that would overrun the valley. Then, too, he feared that the Canadian *coureurs de bois*, whose lawless actions prevented their going to Montreal, would carry their wares down the Tennessee-Ohio route to the British colonies.[4] In Canada considerable apprehension was felt about Iberville's plans of colonization. The Canadians were alarmed lest a colony near the mouth of the Mississippi should draw off much of their trade with the western posts, particularly the fur trade, since navigation down the great river to the Gulf was easier than travel over the many portages that blocked the all-water route from these posts to Montreal. These people at first hoped to have the new colony administered as a distant outpost of Canada; but the King clearly saw the impracticability of such an arrangement, and when Gov-

---

[3] "Memoir of Iberville," *Docs. Rel. Col. Hist. N.Y.*, IX, 729–735.

[4] V. W. Crane, "The French on the Tennessee," *Mississippi Valley Historical Review*, III (1916), 3–18.

ernor Callières requested authority over the new settlement the King informed him that it would be governed directly from Versailles.[5]

Meanwhile, preparations were being made to dispatch the third expedition to Louisiana. The momentous changes that had taken place in international affairs had given the government much to do, and the Ministry could not devote so much attention to an expedition to the Mississippi as it had on the two previous occasions. It was not until late in June that the King published the list of officers who were to command the *Renommée* and the *Palmier*, which were now at Rochefort being conditioned for the voyage. Iberville, of course, was to command the *Renommée*, assisted this time by Pierre du Guay, his companion of the second voyage, while his brother, Joseph de Sérigny, who had served with distinction on several occasions in Hudson Bay and had now decided to throw in his lot with Pierre in Louisiana, was put in charge of the *Palmier*, the same vessel he (Sérigny) had so gallantly commanded at Port Nelson. Sérigny was ably seconded by Desjordy-Moreau, veteran of the two previous voyages.[6] A younger scion of the Lemoyne family, Gabriel d'Assigny, also came on board to try his fortune in the new colony. Nicolas de la Salle, appointed by the Minister as *commissaire* for the Mississippi, was among the passengers, and he took with him his wife and children. There were three other men who did the same, and these were the first pioneers in this colony to settle there with their families. La Salle's salary was fifty *livres* a month, which Iberville protested as being too low adequately to support a man thus encumbered.[7] With Assigny in the party there would be in the

[5] Margry, *op. cit.*, IV, 585.

[6] The other officers were: on the *Renommée*—La Roche-Saint-André, Chambre, Bécancourt, Josselin de Marigny; on the *Palmier*—Noyan (*ibid.*, p. 469).

[7] Margry, *ibid.*, pp. 469, 493. There seems to have been some misunderstanding about La Salle's appointment. Iberville in his letter plainly states that the appointment was made; yet La Salle himself in his letter of Apr.

colony five Lemoyne brothers: Iberville, Sérigny, Bienville, Assigny, and Châteauguay. The commander was satisfied with the *Renommée* but complained that the *Palmier* was unwieldy and difficult to manage, as she carried heavy anchors and oversize spars, so that the fifty men assigned to her as crew were, in his opinion, not enough to insure proper handling.

Preparations were now completed. Yet the ships did not sail, for the reply from Madrid had not arrived, and it was necessary to know definitely what the Spaniards would do about Pensacola before Iberville could shape his course of action. He had advocated abandoning Biloxi, strengthening Fort La Boulaye, then building a post on Mobile Bay, from which point of vantage he could send aid to the Choctaws. These Indians would be of assistance in vanquishing the Chickasaws, sworn friends of the English. These two establishments would be strengthened by the cession of Pensacola to France. Iberville also turned his attention to permanent colonization, suggesting that families be sent over with the proper financial assistance, and marriageable girls for the woodsmen already there. A hospital was of course necessary, and this might be put in charge of the Grey Sisters who were then at Rochefort. For arms and merchandise for the Indians he demanded 24,773 *livres*, a sum which the King granted in the belief that a large part of it would be recovered in trade. To this His Majesty also added an amount sufficient for the construction of a fort at Mobile if the Spaniards declined to yield Pensacola or at Pensacola if the Spaniards could be persuaded to surrender it.[8]

August 1 came and went without any answer from Spain. Iberville still clamored for Pensacola and made his plans as though it would be ceded—yet no word came. By this time Count Pontchartrain's patience was rapidly becoming exhausted, and he wrote Michel Bégon that Iberville would soon receive his sailing

1, 1702 (*ibid.*, p. 535), requests the appointment, as he has already been exercising the functions of such a post.

[8] *Ibid.*, p. 495.

orders, whether or not the Spanish reply arrived, for provisions at Biloxi were running low and assistance was needed there.[9] At last, on August 27, the Minister sent Iberville his orders, and shortly after this the fleet set sail for Santo Domingo. No sooner had it left than the long-awaited reply came. It expressed deep regret, couched in the usual flowery diplomatic verbiage, that His Spanish Majesty could not yield Pensacola to France. But there was more than this. The Junta had studied the situation thoroughly and had a great deal to say. Not only were they emphatic in refusing to cede Pensacola but they considered it a splendid location for a fortress which would overawe the region and discourage any other nation from establishing a colony on the Gulf of Mexico. It could be easily protected by reinforcements from Vera Cruz, Havana, and other places. Such a key place, therefore, should never be allowed to fall into the hands of foreigners, for if it did they would quickly overrun the fertile lands of New Spain and threaten the Spanish merchant fleet. By foreigners, it must be admitted, the Junta were not in this case referring to the French; on the contrary, they suggested a sort of alliance between the crowns of Spain and France to protect their common interests in this part of the New World. The enemy both feared was, of course, England, and to oppose this threat Spain was quite willing to co-operate with Iberville, despite the Spanish claim to that domain "which the French have usurped on the Mississippi which is the greatest ornament of her [Spain's] crown." [10]

Iberville reached Cap François on November 7 after a voyage marred only by an accident to the *Palmier*, which lost its mainmast in a thunderstorm just before reaching her destination. Here he found the *Enflammé*, just arrived from the Mississippi post, which he sent back to France with his letters. The necessary repairs to the *Palmier* caused a delay, and as this might mean hard-

[9] *Ibid.*, pp. 496–497.
[10] *Ibid.*, pp. 553–568.

ship for the garrison at La Boulaye, a *traversier* was sent on ahead with a cargo of supplies. Iberville also seized the occasion to send word to Sauvole ordering him to dismantle Fort Maurepas and transport his equipment to Mobile Bay, where his commander would presently join him. Anxious to place the garrisons on a more secure footing, he took on board seven months' provisions in addition to those he had brought from France, including twenty head of cattle, some horses, and a few pigs, for he wished above all things to make the colony self-supporting as soon as possible, instead of encouraging the settlers to look continually to France for their livelihood.[11] Here he parted company with Gabriel d'Assigny. The young man, the only one of the family who did not follow the profession of arms and who appears to have been of a studious nature, was persuaded by a local official to remain at Cap François and accept a position in the local council. Though disappointed at losing his brother, Iberville agreed and even wrote the Minister requesting him to procure for Assigny the necessary appointment.[12] The young man died a few months later.

Iberville also took time to arrange a private business transaction. He was now a rich man, thanks to the booty in furs he had captured in Hudson Bay and his trade in peltries, to which had been added bonuses from the Company of the North and rewards for meritorious services from the royal treasury. He also controlled a large part of the fur trade in Hudson Bay from the year 1697 to his death. His several visits to Santo Domingo had showed him the possibilities of a profitable investment in the produce of that island, and he now entered into partnership with one Cochon de Maurepas to purchase a plantation of one thousand cocoa trees

[11] *Ibid.*, pp. 501–503.

[12] *Ibid.*, pp. 502–503. Iberville in his letter does not give Assigny's name, but we know by the simple process of elimination that it must be he. Iberville erroneously gives his age as twenty-four instead of twenty. Perhaps this was advisable in requesting a councilorship for one so young.

together with a house and a sugar mill. This partnership lasted over four years before it was dissolved, and Iberville retained the property with a profit of 13,385 *livres*.[13]

On December 15 the fleet anchored off Pensacola, and an officer was immediately sent ashore to request permission from the Spanish governor to enter the harbor and to inform him at the same time that the French intended to fortify Mobile Bay. The governor had gone to Vera Cruz on pressing business, but his second in command, Don Francisco Martinez, came on board with a pilot to take the fleet in through the channel, his friendly attitude being doubtless due to the news the French brought him of King Philip's accession to the throne. From Martinez, Iberville learned of Sauvole's death. This unfortunate loss to the colony had caused Bienville to leave Fort La Boulaye, where he had been stationed, to take command of Fort Maurepas.

The plan to establish a post at Mobile did not meet with an enthusiastic reception from the acting governor. Don Francisco protested, and even put his protest in writing, pointing out that the territory in question was a Spanish possession which he had been ordered to protect. The recent *rapprochement* between France and Spain might, he admitted, alter the situation, but he begged Iberville to suspend further action until he could communicate with his superior, the viceroy. He even requested the loan of a French ship that he might send a messenger to Vera Cruz to seek the necessary instructions.[14] To this Iberville returned a bland reply, politely offering to place one of his boats at Martinez's disposal, but pointing out at the same time that he was in duty bound to proceed at once with the business of erecting his fort since he had specific orders from the King to do so, and his stay in the neighborhood was limited to two months. To tone down the bluntness of his refusal he added that the fort would enable the

[13] Le Jeune, *op. cit.*, p. 249; *Bulletin des recherches historiques*, XLII (1936), 90.
[14] Margry, *op. cit.*, IV, 576–577.

two nations to present a united front against their common enemy, Great Britain.[15]

The force of Iberville's arguments, combined with the news of the Franco-Spanish alliance, greatly mollified the acting governor, who may not have been too anxious to oppose the French. At any rate when Iberville, shortly after New Year's Day, dispatched a ketch, commanded by one François Pillet, with supplies to build the new post at Mobile, Don Francisco hastened to lend him a launch, in which Sérigny and Châteauguay took passage. Iberville had previously sent a ship's boat to Maurepas to notify Bienville that he must betake himself to Dauphin Island with all the equipment he could collect for the construction of the new fort. In the ketch Iberville now placed eighty workmen selected from his crews and M. de la Salle with his family. All were to meet at Dauphin Island, and from this rendezvous Bienville was to lead them to the new site where they were to begin work. Iberville himself was unable to accompany the detachment as an abscess in his side had necessitated a painful operation.[16]

On January 12, 1702, the ketch returned, followed by a *traversier* from Biloxi, and bringing the welcome news of Bienville's arrival at Dauphin Island the week before with forty men. Here he had been joined by Sérigny's detachment, and the two groups had immediately set to work building a storehouse for their supplies, intending to proceed to Mobile in a few days and to leave Châteauguay with a handful of men to finish the structure. On Mobile Bay, according to the instructions Iberville had given him —instructions based on the commander's previous survey of the terrain—Sérigny was to erect a fort on the second bluff or rise of ground, sixteen leagues from Dauphin Island, which would place it on Twenty-seven Mile Bluff, situated on the western side of the Mobile River at the site of modern Mobile. The bluff, which was twenty feet above the water level, would protect the fort from

[15] *Ibid.*, pp. 577–580.
[16] *Ibid.*, pp. 504–505.

inundation.[17] In order to facilitate the transportation of the guns and heavy material from Dauphin Island across the shallow waters at the entrance of the bay to the site of the proposed fort, Iberville sent his master carpenter to supervise the construction of a flat-boat of forty-five tons' burden, so built as to be able to withstand the seas, yet having a draft of only four and a half feet. The mechanics and laborers arrived at the location selected, set to work, and soon erected, under the able direction of Sérigny and Bienville, an imposing structure of logs about 375 feet square, flanked by four bastions each thirty feet by twelve and each containing a battery of six guns. Within this enclosure were four buildings used respectively as a chapel, a guardhouse and storehouse combined, a residence for the commander, and a residence for the officers. Outside the palisade were the barracks, situated 150 feet north of the fort on the riverbank. The post was named Fort Louis.[18]

Scarcely had work been started on this formidable structure, which was destined by its builder to become the nucleus of his anti-British activities, when Iberville, from his sick bed, began his offensive campaign. Fortunately for him that skilled pioneer, Henri de Tonty, had returned south and happened to be at Fort Maurepas. No abler man could be found to lead an expedition to the Chickasaws, staunch allies of the English. Iberville sent messengers overland to Tonty with orders instructing him to collect eight or ten woodsmen and start at once for this tribe, armed with a plentiful supply of merchandise. He was to attempt to lure their chiefs, together with those of the Choctaws, whom he should visit en route, to Mobile Bay, where they could be persuaded to throw in their lot with the French.

The condition of the Spanish garrison at Pensacola was becoming serious. Don Francisco took an inventory of his stock and found he had only an eight days' supply of provisions left. The

[17] Hamilton, *Colonial Mobile*, pp. 38–39.
[18] Margry, *op. cit.*, IV, 512, 531; V, 422–424.

ship which had been sent him with supplies was so long overdue that he had given her up for lost, so he appealed to Iberville for the loan of a boat, as he felt it absolutely necessary to seek food at Vera Cruz. Iberville was willing to oblige, not only on the grounds of humanity but also from fear that he would be called upon to feed the Spaniards from his own stores at Mobile if they could not obtain assistance from Mexico. A *traversier*, the *Precieuse*, was accordingly overhauled, manned by a crew of sixteen men under Du Guay, and turned over to the grateful Martinez, who sent on board one of his officers to carry a message to the authorities in Mexico depicting the wretched state of the garrison at Pensacola, now on the verge of mutiny from lack of provisions. At that Iberville was obliged to lend his hosts fifteen barrels of flour to tide them over, while they sent the launch to see if something could be obtained at Apalachicola.

On February 15 Iberville himself set sail for Mobile Bay in the *Palmier*. He had now recovered from his illness, and the wound made by the operation had healed enough to allow him to be about. Three days later he anchored at Dauphin Island. The advantages of this place as a suitable harbor for ships, as distinguished from *traversiers* and smaller craft, was by now well known. La Salle, when he arrived there a few weeks before, had taken careful soundings in a roadstead at the eastern extremity of the island between its southern shore and Little Pelican Island. There he found a good holding bottom with twenty feet of water at low tide, well sheltered from the prevailing winds. He speaks of it as one of the best harbors on the entire coast, where ships of forty or fifty guns could ride safely. It was large, too; sufficiently so to accommodate thirty vessels. La Salle thought it advisable to erect on Dauphin Island a fort large enough to house a garrison of thirty or forty men with a storehouse for the property of His Majesty.[19] Sauvole had also been impressed with the harbor's possibilities and had called Iberville's attention to them some time

[19] *Ibid.*, IV, 530, 533.

before.[20] No fort had been built on this island, though the commander did erect a storehouse or two with barracks for a small detachment. The harbor proved to be an excellent one, far better than any anchorage in Mobile Bay. For many years afterward the larger ships anchored there, discharging their cargoes into smaller craft which took them to the city of Mobile.[21]

On arriving at Dauphin Island Iberville found the *traversier* of Josselin de Marigny firmly aground on a sand bar. Every effort was made to get it afloat again, for the commander intended to use her to transport the supplies for the post on the Mississippi. But after two days of hard work he decided to use other means to reach La Boulaye. He turned to the ketch and quickly made a deal with her skipper to take charge of the supplies. This arrangement made, several persons were given passage on the ketch; among them were Father Jacques Gravier, who had come down the Mississippi from the Illinois and has left us an interesting and valuable account of his travels, and several traders who had come down to the Gulf to see if some arrangement could be made to transport their furs to France. Presently a higher tide than usual enabled Marigny to float his *traversier,* and the commander sent her to Biloxi to pick up a quantity of material for Fort Louis.

Toward the end of the month Iberville made an ineffectual attempt to reach Fort Louis, only to be driven back by bad weather. On his return he found that La Salle had already begun to exercise his authority as *commissaire* by meddling with the commissary department. Fearing that this might lead to serious confusion—there seems to have been similar trouble when Sauvole was at Fort Maurepas—he appointed a *garde-magasin,* or storekeeper, with orders to issue no articles, whether munitions, provisions, or presents for the Indians, save on a written order to La Salle signed by the commander of the post. Iberville then set sail again for Mobile, leaving La Salle to follow him later with his family.

[20] *Ibid.,* IV, 458; V, 421.
[21] Hamilton, *Colonial Mobile,* p. 149.

Owing to contrary winds it took the commander two or three days to reach the place, but when he landed he was cheered by the sight of Bienville and his men hard at work on the fort. Here he made his headquarters.

And now to get a thorough knowledge of the surrounding country he made a tour of the various islands at the mouth of the Mobile River, where he found in many places the remains of Indian occupation. He also found a small archipelago protected from Indian ravages by the superstitious belief of the natives that whoever profaned the idols erected on one of the islands would die. These statues were probably, according to Iberville's guess, plaster figures made by Spaniards in the time of De Soto. In defiance of their sinister reputation he carried them off with the intention of taking them to France as curios, to the intense amazement of the savages, who expected to see him drop dead in his tracks. In this survey he hoped to find a stream of running water with which to operate a sawmill and a tannery he proposed to erect, but in this flat terrain he failed to find one with enough drop to generate the necessary power. A visit to neighboring tribes was, of course, in order, and he devoted a few days to a good-will tour among such nations as the Mobile Indians and the Tohomas. A site was now selected for a village near the fort; streets were laid out, and plots of ground assigned to the prospective inhabitants, of whom four families at once came forward to take possession. Thus was Mobile founded.

Scarcely had this work been completed when Tonty returned from his expedition among the upper tribes, bringing several chiefs from the Choctaw and Chickasaw nations. Iberville was determined to make a favorable impression on these men and ordered that they be loaded with presents that would be proof to them of the wealth and influence of the French people. Two hundred pounds each of powder, shot, and musket balls, one hundred axes, twelve guns, 150 knives, and a miscellaneous collection of cooking utensils were placed before them. Never before had these bewildered natives seen such an array, and all was theirs for the taking.

Iberville, with Bienville as interpreter, addressed the gathering. He expressed his joy at seeing his guests disposed to live at peace instead of destroying each other by their continual warfare and voiced a regret that the Chickasaws had allowed themselves to be misled by the English, who had no object but to ruin the tribes in order to enslave the Indians and sell them out of the country. He mentioned as proof of this a case he had known where the British had bought some Chickasaw prisoners from their captors for that very purpose. He also cited some statistics he had picked up showing the large number of savages killed in these English-inspired wars. It was English policy, he said, to weaken them by internecine strife, then carry off or destroy those that remained. Turning to the Chickasaws, he warned them particularly that if they did not break with the English he would arm the other tribes against them, even the Illinois, their arch-enemies. Then passing from threats to cajolery, he offered, if they would abandon their allies, to build a depot between them and the Choctaws where they would always find merchandise at reasonable prices in exchange for their furs. In the end the savages saw the light. They agreed to turn against their former friends if the French would make suitable trade agreements with them; and to seal the bargain Iberville gave them muskets and ammunition, together with gifts appropriate to such an occasion. Furthermore, he promised to order his Indian allies not to molest them any longer, and he even offered to send some of his own woodsmen to ask the Illinois to release their Chickasaw prisoners, in return for which they were to use their influence to induce their neighbors to leave the English and make contacts with the French at Mobile.

When he had concluded this alliance Iberville made a thorough investigation of the manpower of his new allies and found that the

Chickasaw nation boasted of 580 cabins averaging three or four men to a cabin, which gave them an effective force of about 2,000 men, of whom 700 or 800 were armed with guns. The Choctaws were a much larger tribe, numbering nearly 1,100 cabins and from 3,800 to 4,000 men.

Iberville now took steps to fulfill his promise. He sent five Canadians with the Indians up the Mobile River to found the trading post. Three of them were to continue the journey as far as the Illinois nation to request the release of the Chickasaw prisoners and to warn the captors to cease hostilities against this tribe. These men also bore letters from Iberville to the vicar general at Quebec, requesting missionaries for his new allies; to the superior of the Jesuits at Quebec for the same purpose; and to Father Davion among the Tunicas, advising him of the new developments. He also sent messengers to the various mission stations to tell them of the new alliance between the French and the Choctaws and Chickasaws. Thus, by a stroke of statesmanship, did Iberville set in motion the vast machinery of the Church to aid the government in its efforts to block the English from the Mississippi Valley. From his post on the Gulf of Mexico he dispatched envoys to carry orders—for such they were in fact though couched, no doubt, in diplomatic language—to stop all wars against the Choctaws and Chickasaws, return their prisoners to them, and join with them against the English. All this Iberville did on his own initiative, knowing full well that he would have the backing of the government at home; and these actions show, more than any others, the high esteem in which he was held by the natives and the confidence reposed in his judgment by the officials of France and Canada.

Iberville now felt that his mission was accomplished. The post at Mobile had been founded and the Indians detached from their English entanglements. There was nothing to keep him in Louisiana, so he prepared to return home, confident that the management of the colony would be safe in the hands of Bienville. On the last day of March he weighed anchor and proceeded to Pensacola, where he spent four weeks awaiting the arrival of the ketch from the Mississippi with a cargo of beaver; then he set sail for La Rochelle, where he arrived in the middle of June.[22]

[22] For an account of this voyage see Margry, *op. cit.*, IV, 503–523, 529–536; V, 424–427.

CHAPTER XI

Attack on Nevis

IBERVILLE returned to France triumphant. He had now established his colony on a permanent basis and had taken the necessary steps to check the westward movement of the English. His fame as a commander was enhanced by his newly acquired reputation as a pioneer. More than that, he appeared as a master of wilderness statesmanship, the one man who could control the Mississippi Valley. The King was well pleased with his work, and no sooner had he set foot on shore than he presented him with a commission of captain in the navy, a rank just a notch higher than his former one of *capitaine de frégate*.[1]

Iberville was now reaching the height of his career, and we have a portrait of him, probably painted at this time during his long stay in France after his return from Louisiana in 1702. Although we have little personal data about Iberville, this picture, reproduced in the frontispiece, will give the reader an idea of his appearance in his early forties. Pierre Margry, who published an enormous amount of material dealing with Iberville's activities in Louisiana, owned the picture at one time, and from him it passed into the hands of Charles Chadonat of Paris. An engraving, made from it in the 1870's by Auguste-Frédéric Laguillermie, has been

[1] Margry, *op. cit.*, IV, 615.

reproduced in several historical works. Both portrait and engraving show an unusually handsome man. The face is strong, though not hard, the forehead is high, the lips firm, and the whole gives the impression of a man accustomed to command. No doubt the artist smoothed out the wrinkles that must have lined the face of a soldier who had suffered so many hardships, but the martial appearance of the subject is evident.

During his several sojourns in Louisiana, Iberville had accumulated a vast amount of information about the central part of the American continent, and he now put his knowledge to use in outlining a grandiose scheme for the complete reorganization of the western fur trade which would create a huge monopoly for France to the exclusion of the English. He had compiled a census of the tribes in the Mississippi Valley who lived between Lake Michigan and Mobile Bay; he had computed their number at 23,850 families, to which number the Sioux and Choctaws contributed the largest quotas, 4,000 each. This information, as well as all the statistics given in his memoir, so Iberville assures us, was gathered by him personally or by persons he could trust.

His plan, to begin with, was to make Mobile the headquarters of the colony. Since it was within a fifteen-day horseback ride from even such remote tribes as the Missouris and Illinois, it would not be necessary to send many families to settle on the lower Mississippi. Laborers, that is tillers of the soil, should be sent over from France to make the colony self-supporting; and some of these people should settle among the various Indian tribes, thus establishing friendly relations between the pioneers and the natives. Three posts should then be established in the Mississippi Valley: one on the Arkansas River, another on the Ohio, and a third on the Missouri, each with a detachment of ten soldiers. There the French families should settle. With the exception of a few assigned to certain Indian villages, they must not be permitted to wander off among the Indians and become *coureurs de bois* like the Canadian traders who had given so much trouble to the home government. It was also necessary—and this was most important—for the King to draw a boundary line between the Louisiana colony and that of Canada in order to avoid the kind of friction that had already broken out in the Illinois country, where the Canadian governor was influencing the savages against the colonists. As an example of this, Iberville cites a rumor that some Indians had plundered French traders on the Mississippi with the full approval of the Canadian authorities. For this and similar reasons he felt that the Indians should be kept in order by the force of authority, not wheedled by presents as had been done by the Canadian government.

The next step in his program aimed at disrupting trade between the Indians and the English colonists in Virginia, Maryland, and Pennsylvania, thus striking a mortal blow at an old enemy. To accomplish this the Indians living near the English settlements must first be transferred to the vicinity of Mobile, where they could more easily be brought into the orbit of French influence. Then the Illinois Indians were to be moved to the Ohio River, the highway to the seaboard colonies, and settled near the mouth of the Wabash. The problem before the French was to force, or rather induce, these Indians to leave their natural habitat and migrate to the new localities. To accomplish this Iberville brought forth the ingenious scheme of forbidding the French to trade with them until they had taken up their new abode and of giving the savages to understand that in any event they would be cut off from their Canadian connections and could trade only with the Mississippi colonists. The Sioux, a great nation of hardy warriors well equipped with guns, were to be lured from their homes to the banks of the Des Moines River, an undertaking which could be accomplished only by Le Sueur, who had considerable influence with them. He would also, while in the Sioux country, negotiate peace between the Illinois, Foxes, and Mascoutens, and induce some of the smaller tribes to settle along the Ohio. The commander at Detroit should also forbid Frenchmen to go into the western and northwestern country, thus forcing the tribes in these regions to come to Detroit or to the Mississippi posts if they wished to do business.

Such was the general scheme, and Iberville in his memoir to the government goes into great detail as to where the various tribes were to be moved. The cost of these migrations he estimates at 11,000 to 12,000 *livres*. Once settled in their new homes, the tribes could furnish the French with some 12,000 warriors in case hostilities with the British broke out. When all this had been accomplished, the government could proceed a step further. The Crees and Assiniboines, far to the north, could, so Iberville believed, be induced to abandon their trade with the English at Hudson Bay and to do business with the French, a scheme later put into effect by Pierre de la Vérendrye. This trade was worth 2,500,000 *livres* a year and would bring an annual revenue to the crown, through customs duties, of 250,000 *livres*. Then, too, there would be a revenue from the lead mines, and possibly from silver mines which the commander felt certain would eventually be found. Clearly this was a territory worth developing.

The scheme of moving the tribes away from Canadian influence was not only ingenious but also a trifle ingenuous, for one could hardly expect the Canadian authorities and traders to acquiesce in a plan which was bound in the long run to ruin the fur trade, the economic backbone of the colony.[2] Yet Iberville was not wholly without justification in his belief that the government would favor him, for he felt he had won the first round in the rivalry between Louisiana and Canada when the King had denied the request of the Canadian governor to place the new colony (which would mean, of course, the entire Mississippi Valley) under his jurisdiction. His Majesty frankly informed the governor that he intended to rule the Louisiana territory directly from Versailles and not through Quebec. Pleased at this decision,

[2] *Ibid.*, pp. 593–607. A good analysis of Iberville's plans is to be found in Hamilton, *The Colonization of the South* (Philadelphia, 1904), ch. x.

Iberville now proposed to clinch the matter by obtaining an order from the government forbidding the Canadians to establish, or even to retain, any post west of Detroit. Then with the Illinois on the Ohio and the Sioux on the Des Moines, the French in Louisiana could deflect the fur trade down the Mississippi.

In planning the division of the French possessions in North America Iberville no doubt expected to erect a vast colonial empire of which he would be the head. As evidence of his ambitious scheme we find that he requested for himself a generous concession in the vicinity of Mobile to be erected into a county to be known as Comté de d'Iberville, an arrangement which would raise him to the position of Comté d'Iberville in the same manner as his brother was made Baron de Longueuil. At the same time he asked for a concession of the lead mines in the new territory, the privilege of sending a ship to the Guinea coast to obtain slaves, and the exclusive right to furnish Canadians with whatever they might need from the Mississippi Valley.[3]

The government, however, was by no means disposed to grant Iberville such enormous powers and such possibilities of enrichment. True, the King was pleased to appoint him commander-in-chief of Louisiana, but Count Pontchartrain drew the line at any attempt to move the Indian tribes. For one thing he considered the scheme impossible of achievement; and even if it were feasible he saw no reason why the Canadian merchants should be deprived of their share of the beaver trade to enrich the Louisiana colonists. The enormous quantities of furs collected recently by the *coureurs* had caused a severe shortage in the western country except among the Sioux, and surely it would be unfair to countenance any move to lure that nation away from Canada to the Mississippi. It would be better to grant an amnesty which would bring back to Canada those *coureurs* who had violated the trade regulations—and many of them had—than to allow them to carry their furs down the river to the Louisiana colony. If traders with

[3] *Ibid.,* pp. 616–618.

their families wished to leave Canada for the new colony that was one thing, but they should not be allowed to take their furs with them. Furthermore, Pontchartrain was suspicious of Le Sueur, whom he regarded as a man interested in the fur business only to fill his own pockets, and he feared that he would never exert himself in the interests of the King or the colonies. And Le Sueur was Iberville's kinsman.

These sentiments met with the approval, of course, of the Canadian authorities, who had no intention of permitting their traders to be deprived of their share of the lucrative fur business, at least not without a struggle. The situation, they said, was bad enough without giving Iberville's settlers any more encouragement, for numerous young men who had gone out into the wilderness to purchase furs had slipped down the Mississippi with their cargoes, to the great annoyance of their creditors in Quebec and Montreal. As a solution of the problem they suggested that the Minister appoint commissioners to Louisiana who would receive the furs brought there and prevent their falling into the hands of Iberville and his associates. This proposal was reinforced by a similar one made by the directors of the company in Canada, who requested that the furs already shipped by Iberville to France be turned over to their representatives at Rochefort, who would pay for them at the prices then prevailing at Quebec, and that the traders be forbidden to take any more furs to the Louisiana colony.[4]

When Iberville arrived at Rochefort, he found that war between his country and Great Britain had been declared. His services as a naval commander were in great demand, and he was told on landing that arrangements had already been made for him to lead the *Renommée* and *Palmier* against the enemy privateers in the Bay of Biscay. But owing to various complications he did not receive his orders in time to set forth on the venture, and Count Pontchartrain was able to grant him the permission he had

[4] *Ibid.*, pp. 607–612.

requested to come to Versailles to discuss the war situation.[5] On arriving there he found that there was indeed much to do. The colony of Louisiana required the attention and help usually needed for budding colonies; the control of the fur trade in the Mississippi Valley had to be organized; and there was also the opportunity, now that war had been declared, for a raid on the Atlantic seaboard.

The conferences with Pontchartrain began with the problem of supplying Louisiana. While at Rochefort, Iberville had discussed the subject with Michel Bégon and had selected the *Loire* as a suitable vessel for the coming expedition, and this selection was now ratified. It was placed under the command of Pierre du Guay. The government now agreed to contribute 60,000 *livres* to pay for the work to be done in the colony. With the money at his disposal Iberville went to work to organize the expedition. He collected a small force of skilled mechanics, consisting of two carpenters, one cabinetmaker, and six masons. There were already four families in the colony, and he proposed to send a consignment of young women for wives, but he optimistically (or pessimistically, if one prefers) suggested that a midwife would not be needed, at least for the present. He also requested the use of the ship to bring back the produce of his newly acquired sugar refinery, a request that did not meet with royal approval, as the King intended to have the vessel loaded with lumber and other products of the Louisiana colony.[6] Iberville was also anxious to have Le Sueur given the post of lieutenant-general for the administration of justice; and as his duties would carry him far afield in the Indian country where life was hard, he suggested an emolument of five hundred *écus* a year, a sum which Pontchartrain considered excessive.[7]

Iberville at this time seems to have undergone something of a change of heart in regard to the governorship of Louisiana, for he

[5] *Ibid.*, p. 616.   [6] *Ibid.*, p. 623.   [7] *Ibid.*, p. 624.

wrote the Minister a long letter hinting that he wished to be relieved of this command, recently bestowed upon him by the King, on the ground that his efforts to deflect the western fur trade to the Mississippi had made him *persona non grata* with the Canadian authorities to the great embarrassment of his many relatives in Canada.[8] Whether or not he was serious in making this request is difficult to say; at any rate the King paid no attention to it. He merely ordered the commander to take charge of the colony and be prepared to sail in September. For this purpose the *Pelican* of Hudson Bay fame was set aside for him, and as a gesture of good will the King was pleased to comply with his request for the rank of ensign for Châteauguay and a youth named Volezar, but only on condition that they should each raise a company of fifty volunteers to serve in Louisiana. His Majesty also recommended the enlistment of young women as wives for the pioneers, but, more realistic than Iberville, he strongly advocated that a midwife accompany the party.[9]

Everything was now ready for the expedition to sail in September, 1703, when the unexpected happened. Iberville's health, precarious since his illness in Louisiana, now took a turn for the worse and kept him confined to his bed. So serious was his condition that his wife and his brother Sérigny rushed from Rochefort to Paris to be at his bedside. Thanks to their care he eventually recovered, but by that time the *Pelican* had sailed. The *Pelican* arrived at Mobile the following summer with a goodly supply of provisions and merchandise, a band of soldiers raised by Châteauguay and Volezar, four skilled workmen with their families, two Grey Sisters, and to crown the colonists' joy, twenty-three girls "reared in piety and drawn from sources above suspicion, who know how to work." With such admirable qualifications to offer they were quickly married.

While Iberville lay on his sickbed, great events were taking

[8] *Ibid.*, pp. 619–623.   [9] *Ibid.*, pp. 632–633.

place in Europe. The armies of King Louis were meeting with reverses; hence the government was disposed to lend an ear to the Canadian's proposal to lead a modest fleet of three frigates and two ships to Havana, where he would make his headquarters for a series of raids on British North America. Elaborating on this plan, the King in his orders dated August 29, 1705, proposed to seize Barbados and Jamaica with the aid of the buccaneers, then drive the English from Carolina, threaten New York, attack Virginia, assist Acadia, and end up with another expedition to Newfoundland.

In order to carry out such an ambitious program a large fleet was assembled, much larger than the one requested by Iberville, and divided into two squadrons: one, under Iberville himself, consisting of the *Juste*, flagship; the *Phénix;* the *Prince,* commanded by La Roche-Saint-André, former commander of the *Renommée;* the *Aigle,* under Iberville's brother-in-law, Payan de Noyan, who had been with him in Newfoundland; the *Sphère;* and the *Coventry* under the ever-faithful Sérigny. The other squadron was commanded by Count Louis-Henri de Chavagnac, who was later to become Chevalier de Saint-Louis, as well as admiral and marquis. His flagship was the *Glorieux,* seventy-two guns, the *Apollon,* sixty, the *Brillant,* seventy-two, the *Fidèle,* fifty-eight, the *Ludlow,* and the twenty-gun *Nymphe.* Iberville, who was to be commander-in-chief of both squadrons, had with him, among his many officers, two of his nephews, the sons of his eldest brother Charles de Longueuil—Charles Marigny de Longueuil, captain of a company of grenadiers, and Gabriel-François de Longueuil, an ensign in the same company.[10]

A force of six hundred soldiers paid by the King and a band of

[10] Le Jeune, *op. cit.*, p. 241, says that the second nephew was Jacques the son of Jacques de Sainte-Hélène, but Tanguay, *op. cit.*, I, 380, says that this boy died in 1705. Moreover, Iberville gives the surname "Longueuil" to both nephews; hence they must have been the sons of Charles de Longueuil.

Canadians under the command of Jacques de Mousseau were embarked on the ships to form the nucleus of the army to be recruited in Martinique and Guadeloupe. Iberville, however, was obliged to bear the expense of outfitting his own squadron, and to do this he borrowed heavily from the firm of Maurois, Boris, Verdalles, et Gros, a transaction that was later on to cause great distress to his widow. He and his associates were also obliged to furnish the provisions and to allow the King one-fifth of all prizes taken, after deducting the expenses of *garde* and *justice*, and to give one-tenth each to the admiral and the crews. The undertaking was financed as a sort of business venture in which everyone hoped that the booty would be enough to pay expenses and yield a profit for those who had underwritten it. It was in this spirit that colonists and buccaneers from the West Indian islands joined the armada.

At the same time the Minister wrote to Machault de Bellemont, governor of the West Indies then residing in Martinique, telling him not to spread abroad the news of Iberville's coming but to urge the buccaneers to remain in the harbor, as the government had received word that the English were about to attack the island. Machault did not approve of all this, as he believed it was better judgment to keep the colonists at home where they would be ready to repel any attempt to capture the island. For his pains he received a sharp rebuke from the Minister, who pointed out that the English had already attacked several French possessions and that the time was now ripe for revenge, since there was no powerful British fleet on the West Indies station. Furthermore, the King was particularly anxious to have the buccaneers join the expedition, for they had no agricultural duties to perform as had the colonists.

When all was ready the two squadrons set sail. Chavagnac was the first to go. His fleet was in the harbor of Brest, and he was able to leave in December under such favorable weather conditions that he reached St. Pierre, Martinique, toward the end of

January. This put him on the scene of action some time before
Iberville, who was beset by a violent storm when he left Rochefort and was obliged to put into La Rochelle, there to await a
favorable wind. On landing at St. Pierre, Chavagnac found, as
might have been expected, that Machault had done nothing to
recruit the buccaneers; consequently he was obliged to undertake
the business himself. It was not a difficult thing to do, for these
worthy freebooters liked nothing better than to set forth on a
marauding venture that would bring them enough booty to keep
them in idleness for some time. And in this the colonists were not
averse to joining them. Chavagnac soon was able to add three
hundred of the former and four hundred of the latter to his forces.
To these Machault added four companies of soldiers.

The principal object of the undertaking was, as we have said, a
widespread attack on the British colonies in North America; but
before this was undertaken it was felt advisable to settle an old
score in the West Indies. For many years the French and English
had occupied the island of St. Christopher (St. Kitts) jointly
under a more or less amicable arrangement whereby the island
was divided into three sections, the English holding the middle
with headquarters at Charlestown, the French the two extremities
with Basseterre as the principal settlement. These towns, like all
capitals and chief cities in the Caribbean group, were situated on
the western side of the island, for this was the leeward side—the
prevailing winds came from the east—where vessels could ride
in safety. Two miles south of St. Christopher lay the English
island of Nevis, well fortified and difficult of access. With the
declaration of war in 1702 the French on St. Christopher had sent
their women, children, and many of their slaves to Martinique,
fearing an attack by their English neighbors. In this they were
not disappointed, for the English colonists, numbering some 1,300
men, saw in the war an opportunity to appropriate the entire
island. Reinforced by Christopher Codrington, governor of the
Leeward Islands, who arrived from Antigua at the proper moment

with a small fleet and 1,200 men, they proceeded to attack their peaceful neighbors, who could put no more than 250 soldiers in the field. Hopelessly outnumbered, the French could make little more than a show of resistance; and on July 16 Governor Jean-Baptiste de Gennes surrendered, obtaining honorable-enough terms, with transportation for himself and his people to Martinique. Thus did St. Christopher pass under British control and become with its neighbor, Nevis, a fair target for reprisal.

Confident in their possession of St. Christopher, the English neglected to maintain its fortifications or provide for its garrison in a suitable manner. The council members seem to have had a certain sense of their responsibility, but they were blocked by a few influential members of the assembly, whose unwillingness to furnish proper quarters for the officers and men led to a threat by the government to withdraw the troops entirely. As it was, the available fighting force soon dwindled to about 150 men capable of bearing arms.[11] Nevis, on the other hand, was better protected, thanks to the zeal of Governor John Johnson, successor to Codrington, who had made a thorough survey of the fortifications, repairing the old and erecting new ones, until Nevis was considered the best-defended island of the Leeward group.

The arrival of the French fleet under Chavagnac was no great surprise to the English colonists, despite the efforts of the French government to keep the business a secret, though the British, of course, did not know where the blow would fall. Even before Chavagnac arrived the news had leaked out, thanks, no doubt, to the work of the British intelligence service. Thus it was that as early as the previous December Governor Johnson had warned Governor Thomas Handasyde of Jamaica that a large fleet was expected, and Handasyde, though he labeled the report a "French gasconnade," requested help from the mother country. While awaiting the arrival of Iberville, Chavagnac determined to while away the time by seizing the islands of St. Christopher and Nevis.

[11] *C.S.P. Am. & W.I., 1704–1705*, Nos. 1215, 1281, 1346, 1419.

With this expedition we shall not concern ourselves save to say
that his efforts at Nevis proved abortive, but that he was eminently
successful at St. Christopher, doing immense damage and bringing back to Martinique over three hundred slaves.

Iberville sailed from La Rochelle in January, 1706, and on
March 7 arrived at St. Pierre, where he found Chavagnac awaiting him. He was now in his forty-fourth year, a youngish man by
modern standards, but one who had rapidly matured because of
the responsibilities placed on his shoulders by the numerous expeditions he had commanded. He was weatherbeaten and care-
worn; and the spasmodic fevers from which he had suffered since
his return from Louisiana had left their mark upon him. Yet,
despite all this, his mind was clear and his spirit as strong as ever
when he stepped on board the *Juste* to take charge of what was to
be his last and perhaps his greatest command.

At St. Pierre the two commanders spent the next three weeks
discussing plans for the coming expedition, recruiting colonists
and buccaneers, repairing whatever damage had been done the
fleet at St. Christopher, and taking on the necessary provisions
and supplies. The business of recruiting was well done, and when
the fleet was ready to sail Iberville added to his forces three companies of colonists of fifty men each, and 1,100 buccaneers, the
latter under M. de Maunières. He had also collected some twenty-
four brigantines to transport these freebooters. After discussing
the pros and cons of the situation the commanders decided that
the island of Nevis would be the next objective. The selection
was wise, for the colony was a rich one that would yield considerable booty, and its capture would do much to restore French
prestige, which had suffered when Chavagnac failed in his recent
attack. The campaign against Nevis may be regarded as Iberville's greatest, though his biographers have given it scant attention, despite the fact that he has left us a detailed account of it.
Not only did he command a much larger force, both on sea and on
land, than he had ever commanded before, but the campaign

called for clever strategy in its planning, and in this he showed his mastery of the problem before him.

The island of Nevis was a more important colony at this time than it is today when the British have acquired St. Vincent, St. Lucia, and Grenada. It is a small island, in reality little more than a great mountain rising out of the sea, whose lower slopes are subject to cultivation. As we have said, Governor Johnson had strengthened its defenses only the year before, erecting new batteries and repairing existing ones, until a dozen little forts stood ready to receive the enemy. One, and one only, was on the eastern or windward side of the island; the others were scattered along the western shore at various strategic points. Charlestown on the leeward side was the capital and principal town. South of it, at a place called Long Point, was a twelve-gun battery, called William's Fort. Defending the roadstead at Charlestown were Charles Fort on Pelican Point and St. Paul's on Black Rock. Then there were several others along the coast, most of them near the town, and two at the northern end of the island overlooking the Narrows that separate it from St. Christopher.[12] The number of forces left to man these defenses do not appear to have been adequate, as Colonel Richard Abbott, the commander, afterward bitterly complained that Governor Johnson had removed 115 men he had brought over from Antigua as well as all but 35 men of the regular troops.[13] A census of the island taken at the time shows the population to have consisted of 430 men and officers of the militia; 75 men, women, and children of the regular troops (i.e., 35 soldiers and their families); 330 seamen belonging to the ships in the harbor; 311 women; 612 children; and 6,023 Negroes.[14]

Toward the end of March Iberville left St. Pierre with his entire command, steering northward on his way to Nevis.[15] Before

[12] *Ibid.*, No. 1344.   [13] *Ibid. 1706–1708*, No. 448.
[14] *Ibid.*, No. 357v.
[15] The data on this expedition are taken from Iberville's narrative published in the May, 1706, number of the *Mercure Galant* (*Mercure de*

leaving he sent the *Fidèle* to Barbados to see whether an English fleet was lurking there. Stopping a few hours at Dominica to take on a supply of wood, he arrived on the morning of March 28 at Basseterre, Guadeloupe. Here he embarked a company from the local garrison and also fifty youths of good family who had been recruited by a young man named M. de Bragelogne. That evening he shifted his anchorage to the eastern part of the island, where a wide, flat plain offered better ground for a general review of the troops. The following day he was joined by the rest of his fleet, with the brigantines and a convoy of merchantmen which had seized the occasion to visit the Leeward Islands.

On March 30 Iberville ordered all his troops ashore, buccaneers as well as regulars, to divide his command into combat units for the coming attack. As his own personal assistants he selected La Roche-Saint-André and M. de Gabaret as general officers, and M. de Martinet as major-general of troops. The soldiers (not the buccaneers) were then divided into four battalions of two hundred men each, destined for the landing on Nevis, which left enough men on board the ships to keep them fully manned. These battalions, in turn, were subdivided into companies, each with its proper quota of officers. The equipment provided for the men was beautiful to look at, including plumes, wigs, and ribbons of silk and gold, but such prosaic items as shoes and stockings were strangely lacking. Turning to the buccaneer division, Iberville selected seven hundred men and added them to the landing party. The battalions were now placed on board the brigantines, and at five o'clock in the afternoon the fleet set sail.

On April 1, Iberville found himself six leagues southwest of Antigua, British capital of the West Indies, where Governor Johnson was then residing. Cruising off its shores was a forty-four-gun frigate, which was promptly attacked by the twenty-

France), pp. 282–311, supplemented by certain documents in the *Calendar of State Papers*

gun *Nymphe*. For an hour or more the two ships fired away at each other, without apparently doing much damage, until the Englishman, alarmed at the great armada he saw coming to his opponent's assistance, retreated hastily to the protection of his shore batteries.

It was now time for Iberville to put into effect the elaborate plan he had worked out for the campaign. It consisted of a feint to draw off the bulk of the enemy's forces to a point far distant from the spot where he proposed to land that night. At ten o'clock in the morning, therefore, Chavagnac was sent with the *Glorieux*, *Brillant*, *Phénix*, *Sphère*, and eight merchantmen to launch the feint on the western or leeward side of Nevis, while twelve vessels under Ensign Raguyenne were to go up the eastern side, pass through the Narrows, and join Chavagnac's squadron. Meanwhile Iberville, with the *Juste*, *Prince*, *Ludlow*, and sixteen brigantines, lay to with sails furled so as to reduce visibility. The *Apollon* was sent to cruise in the vicinity of Antigua and prevent the British from sending help to Nevis. The ruse succeeded. When the watchguards on Nevis saw the French fleet coming over the sea in the late afternoon and bearing away to the northward, they sounded the alarm. Colonel Abbott called a council of war; and the council, mistaking Iberville's intentions, sent the bulk of its troops to the northern part of the island. Never before had Iberville employed such clever strategy with such gratifying results.

At sunset Iberville left the *Juste* in the charge of Gabaret and boarded one of the brigantines, accompanied by Saint-André and Martinet. He left orders with the commanders of the *Juste*, *Prince*, and *Ludlow* to join Chavagnac as soon as the landing had been made. As darkness came on, the brigantines advanced, each towing a landing boat. At midnight the little armada had come in close enough to attempt a landing, and Iberville gave the order to take to the boats. Leaping into a boat himself he called on the party to follow him and made for the shore. To find a proper landing place in the dark was no easy task, for a sea was running, making it rather dangerous to approach the coast. But fortunately Iberville had with him a pilot he had picked up at Martinique who was able to guide him to a small bay which, so he tells us, would be difficult to find even in the daytime. It was Green Bay at the southern extremity of the island.[16] It was good that Iberville's strategy had been successful, for it would not have been difficult for the English to oppose the French at this point had they known the enemy was to land there. Governor Daniel Parke in his criticism of the defense of Nevis written a few months later stated that "fifty men might have prevented their landing," for "at the place where they landed there are such rocks and shoals, so far off the shore that they could not land under the cover of the guns from their ships, and could send but one boat at a time, so that had there been but fifty men there, they might have killed every boat's crew as they came." [17]

The landing was made without the loss of a man; a few desultory shots were fired by some horsemen who happened to be on the spot, but the attackers paid no attention to them. Iberville at once started for Charlestown at the head of three hundred men, including his Canadians, and arrived there at dawn. Saint-André and Martinet were ordered to follow him with the rest of the troops as soon as they had landed, while the Chevalier de Duderon and his company of grenadiers were left at Long Point in order to cut off any communication between this fort and the town. The fort was defended by Colonel William Burt with thirty men, assisted by Colonel William Butler with forty men at near-by Gaulding's Point, men who are described by Colonel Abbott "as never such poltroons living." Pusillanimity, if we are to believe some of the opinions expressed by the English authorities, must have been one of the reasons for Iberville's easy victory.[18]

[16] Thomas Jeffreys' map of 1794 calls the place "French Bay where they landed in 1706."

[17] *C.S.P. Am & W.I., 1706–1708*, No. 654.   [18] *Ibid.*, No. 282.

On the march to Charlestown a detachment of two hundred buccaneers, forming the right wing, clashed with a detachment of English troops which Iberville numbers at 250, many of whom were probably Negroes, since the main body of troops was, as we have said, in the northern part of the island. Indeed, Colonel Abbott himself complained that he could never get more than two hundred men to face the enemy in the entire campaign. At any rate, the buccaneers were driven back and might have been put to flight had it not been for the timely arrival of Duderon and his grenadiers, who rallied them and checked their retreat. Iberville now ordered Saint-André, who had just arrived with his men, to bear to the right where the enemy had assembled to give battle. Saint-André did as he was told, but he could see no one, for the defenders had taken refuge among the sugar canes, waiting to make a surprise attack on the French. This ruse, however, did not succeed as planned, for a company of buccaneers which formed the vanguard discovered them and started to retreat. Encouraged by this, the English emerged from their hiding places and bore down on the freebooters, who would have been routed if Saint-André had not sent Duderon and Marigny de Longueuil with their grenadiers to bolster them up. The result was a complete reversal; soon the English forces were in full flight through the sugar plantations.

While these skirmishes were taking place Iberville was busily engaged in capturing the batteries around Charlestown, no very difficult task since they were designed to protect the town from attacks by sea and were easily accessible from the rear. The garrisons put up little or no resistance, being anxious only to join the rest of the forces, which were now seeking a safe retreat in the mountain back of the town. Here a fortified place had been constructed several years before for just such an emergency. It was called a "deodand" or "deodard," and was designed as a refuge for women, children, old men, and slaves. Its site was difficult to storm, since it was protected by "a deep gully on one side and a steep, woody mountain on the other." Governor Christopher Codrington disapproved of these deodands. "After all," he said, "I am not well satisfied whether those deodards are more useful or pernicious, for though they are intended a retreat for such as cannot fight, they would probably tempt such to run thither who are able and who ought to fight." [19] And in this Codrington was right, for we find that most of the population in the neighborhood, able-bodied men as well as others, flocked hurriedly into the deodand.

In the early morning Iberville, having taken the Charlestown batteries, sought rest for his troops in the town and sent word to Saint-André to join him. All the batteries had been silenced save the guns at Long Point, and thither Iberville dispatched Martinet to demand its surrender. But Colonel Burt did not wait that long; he abandoned his command before Martinet arrived. Saint-André with two hundred men entered it and hoisted the French flag above the battlements. Meanwhile Chavagnac had begun his operations by sea. There were some twenty-two ships in the harbor, and these he quickly captured. Their crews, numbering all told three hundred men; managed to elude him, and as soon as the French landed, these men spread over the countryside robbing and looting the helpless inhabitants.[20]

It was now April 2, a day spent principally in enjoying a well-earned rest. Payan de Noyon arrived with the *Aigle* from a mission he had undertaken to Grenada and landed a company of fifty men. The following day Iberville undertook the capture of the deodand. His entire force was to be used for this purpose. The plan was to form a semicircle about the place and drive the inhabitants into it so that they could be besieged. Saint-André and Duderon were ordered to lead a detachment of three hundred men northward as far as the Narrows, then circle back and join Iberville at the deodand. Gabaret was sent with a like number

[19] *Ibid., 1699,* No. 863.
[20] *Ibid. 1706–1708,* No. 452.

straight to the deodand, accompanied by another detachment of 250 on his left flank. On the right wing the commander placed five hundred buccaneers to march through the territory where they had fought two days before. It all worked out as planned. The English made an abortive attack on the freebooters; it was quickly repulsed with little trouble, for English resistance had by now almost broken down completely. At three o'clock in the afternoon Iberville called a halt for the day, as the heat was becoming intolerable and he wished to give Saint-André time to catch up with him. Saint-André, meanwhile, had done well. He had marched his troops for ten hours over seemingly impassable terrain and now joined his commander at six o'clock in the evening. That night all enjoyed a good rest, sleeping for the most part in cabins and houses abandoned by the natives.

The following day was Easter Sunday. Nothing could be allowed to interfere with the proper observance of this great festival, and at ten o'clock, after a short march, a halt was called for a celebration of the Mass. At this time scouts informed the commander that the enemy was only a quarter of a league distant, safely ensconced in the deodand. The end was now in sight. As he approached the place, Iberville saw that his opponents were in no mood to fight. "The firmness of the King's troops," he says, "and the speed with which the enemy had been pursued frightened them to such an extent that they decided to capitulate, although the condition of their deodand would have enabled them to resist for some time, as it was on all sides a difficult place to storm." At this point the defenders sent an officer to discuss terms of surrender. Iberville was ready for him and promptly sent him back with Gabaret and Martinet bearing the terms which the commander was willing to grant. These, it appears, did not suit the defenders, who replied with certain recommendations. Iberville, however, was in no mood for bargaining and at once sent Martinet with a message that unless the terms were accepted without delay he would let his troops sack the place. This brought the English to their senses, and they quickly signed the capitulation papers.

The terms of surrender were embodied in a document divided into eight articles which covered the following points: Officers and inhabitants were to receive good treatment and be allowed to retain their personal effects. The commanding officers and soldiers were to be considered prisoners of war, the former to retain their side arms. The French promised to preserve from harm all houses not damaged in the conflict, and the inhabitants were to have living quarters until the French left the island. All Negroes were to be surrendered to Iberville, though he graciously allowed the English commander, Colonel Abbott, to retain twelve, the captains three each, the lieutenants two, the ensigns one, and the councilors three, as a gesture of magnanimity. He also agreed to return all papers and documents that might fall into his hands. Entire liberty would be granted the officers and inhabitants, provided a roster of the colony, including women and children, be given Iberville, so that a like number of French prisoners now in English hands might be released in exchange. This referred, of course, to prisoners in other colonies. As a guarantee that these terms would be honored he demanded four hostages. Those selected were Thomas Abbott, Joseph Stanley, Philip de Witt, and Charles Earle.

Once the treaty was signed—and it was signed immediately—Iberville sent Martinet and four companies of grenadiers to disarm the prisoners, while the rest of the troops were billeted for the night in various neighboring plantations. Next day those in the deodand, men, women, and children, were sent back to their homes, and the army was quartered in Charlestown.

Iberville now decided to make a tour of the island. He requisitioned enough horses to mount sixty grenadiers and forty Canadians, and taking Gabaret and Duderon with him, set out on his journey. It was perhaps well that he decided to make this tour of inspection, for on reaching the harbor of Newcastle, in the northeastern part of the island, he saw in the offing two brigantines coming from Antigua with the evident intention of bringing succor to the island. By deploying his troops along the shore he gave those on board a hint of the reception in store for them should they attempt to land, with the result that they turned about and headed back to Antigua. The next day Iberville and his party returned to Charlestown.

At this point Iberville's narrative ends and we must turn to other sources for our information. Eager to get the news of his great victory to France with the least possible delay, he drew up his account on April 8 and entrusted it to the Chevalier de Nangis, commander of the *Nymphe*, who left two days later. He arrived in Versailles on May 16 and laid the report before the King.[21] Iberville was evidently well pleased with the entire business, for he gave the highest praise to his troops, regulars, Canadians, and buccaneers, whose conduct had brought about such a decisive victory:

I cannot here give praise to each officer; but I can say generally that one could not find anywhere more bravery, better conduct, and firmness, and this extends even to the rank and file. I can add also the company of Canadian volunteers, commanded by M. de Mousseau, which gave exceptional examples [of good conduct] as did the volunteers of Martinique and Guadeloupe, commanded by M. de Bragelogne. The buccaneers commanded by M. de Maunières, also gave examples of their courage. . . .

Scarcely had the capitulation been signed when Iberville was accused by the English of breaking it. The officers were quite bitter about the French commander's actions—one of them vents his spleen by describing Chavagnac as "a much more civilized man than M. d'Iberville"—and their reports are filled with recriminations about his conduct. Perhaps Iberville felt contempt for his fallen enemies, who had failed, according to their own admissions, to put up a decent resistance. As a British author whose name is unknown wrote to a friend:

[21] *Journal du Marquis de Dangeau* (Paris, 1856), XI, 105.

I would not have you be too forward in defending the behavior of some of our Grandees, for they do not deserve it, and time will tell you who they are, though now you would little suspect them. The brave behavior and defense [of the Negroes in the mountains] shames what some of their masters did, and they do not stick to tell us so. . . . Had we made any resistance at the Deodand, the French own that they would have given us very honorable conditions.[22]

The difficulty in regard to the terms of capitulation seems to have arisen from the failure of the English to surrender their Negroes as they had agreed to do. This failure, it must be admitted, was not deliberate on their part, for the Negroes were not anxious to become slaves of the French and had fled in great numbers to the mountain, where their masters could not lay hands on them. Nevertheless, Iberville seized upon this as an excuse for subjecting the inhabitants to harsh treatment in the hope that they would find some way of rounding up their human livestock. He began his operations, so Colonel Abbott says, by setting fire to numerous buildings outside Charlestown. Only twenty were left when the French evacuated the island. The officers and inhabitants were then driven into the town "where the smallpox and other distempers were reigning," confined in crowded houses, forbidden to go out to get supplies, and compelled to live on what little the French gave them. Three days later the men were picked up and locked in the church, the town jail, and several houses, with only such food as their families could bring them surreptitiously. To all protest against this treatment Iberville turned a deaf ear, saying that they were prisoners of war and had broken the terms of surrender by failing to produce the Negroes.

Finally the French commander saw the necessity of a compromise. He had gathered a great mass of booty, "mills and coppers, with other such rich merchandise to the value of many scores of thousand pounds," besides 3,200 slaves; and much could be said for the inability of the inhabitants to bring in the Negroes

[22] C.S.P. Am. & W.I., 1706–1708, No. 270.

who were roaming about the mountain fastnesses in well-armed bands. On April 16 he called the principal colonists before him and made the following proposal. In lieu of surrendering all the Negroes they should bind themselves to bring to Martinique within the next three months 1,400 of them or one hundred pieces-of-eight for each one they failed to deliver. For his own part Iberville promised that the buccaneers would engage in no looting after the departure of the fleet.

The English at first demurred to these terms, and Iberville at once took measures to make them change their minds. The more prominent citizens were seized and placed on board the vessels with a threat to transport them to the Spanish colonies, where they would be forced to shift for themselves. Colonels Abbott, Burt, and Butler, and James Bevon, all members of the council, were imprisoned in the *Juste* and told they would be taken to France if they did not come to terms. Meanwhile the French amused themselves, so Abbott tells us, by "burning and destroying our churches, dragging up our dead, the defacing [of] their monuments and tombstones, in imprisoning several of our men and women, whom they suspected to have been wealthy, their destroying our records and papers." It might have been worse, of course. The French are not charged with wanton killing, nor the buccaneers with inflicting torture to extort hidden wealth.

In the end the policy of ruthlessness and bad faith triumphed. The inhabitants saw they were beaten and decided to sign new terms. On April 19 Iberville and Chavagnac affixed their signatures to a new treaty, while nearly all the principal inhabitants signed in behalf of the vanquished. As a reward for their compliance the conquerors allowed them to retain, each in proportion to his wealth, the surplus Negroes remaining after the 1,400 slaves had been delivered. Out of the 6,023 Negroes on the island the French took with them 3,187, eight hundred for the buccaneers, the balance for the fleet.[23]

[23] *Ibid.*, Nos. 318, 357.

Iberville now disbanded his fleet. The colonial volunteers and the buccaneers were sent back to Martinique in the brigantines, the latter grumbling loudly about their share of the booty. The *Glorieux, Brillant, Apollon,* and *Phénix* were dispatched to France with the regular troops; the *Aigle* went to Louisiana, the *Coventry* to Vera Cruz, and the *Fidèle, Sphère, Prince,* and *Ludlow* sailed for Leogane. Iberville himself went to Cap François in the *Juste*,[24] and here he was able to pick up a brigantine of fourteen guns. On rejoining the squadron at Leogane he learned that he would be able to raise 1,500 recruits there, and with these additional forces he felt that he could continue his conquests. But fate willed otherwise, and on reaching Havana he was stricken with yellow fever, then called by the French *mal de Siam*. From the beginning he had but little chance of recovery, for the intermittent illnesses of the past five years had weakened his constitution and broken down his powers of resistance. He lingered for a few days, hoping against hope that he might be spared to fulfill his dream of driving the English from North America; but the disease was too powerful, and on July 9, 1706, he died on board his flagship, fortified by the sacraments of the Church. He was then but two weeks short of his forty-fifth birthday. The same day his body was taken ashore and buried in the parochial church of San Cristoval.[25] Unfortunately this building was torn down thirty-five years later and was never rebuilt. Thus the last resting place of the great Canadian remains a mystery.

Pierre Lemoyne d'Iberville was unquestionably the greatest Canadian of his generation. We have followed his career from his first expedition to Hudson Bay under the Chevalier de Troyes to his last voyage, when in supreme command of a mighty fleet he captured the island of Nevis. Yet despite his numerous achievements as soldier, sea captain, colonist, and statesman, in short as one of the greatest of France's empire builders, his name is al-

[24] Frégault, *op. cit.,* p. 399; Le Jeune, *op. cit.,* p. 242.
[25] Frégault, *op. cit.,* p. 403.

most unknown in the country to whose service he devoted his life. But in this he is not unique; he suffers from the cavalier treatment bestowed by French historians upon most of their Canadian heroes. Though Iberville's activities transcended the limits of Canada and his last expedition was purely a French one, undertaken in connection with a great European war in which France was engaged, we find but a bare mention of his name in the pages of such comprehensive histories as those of Lavisse and Martin, and none in the monumental work of Sismondi. Even his garrulous contemporaries, the Duc de Saint-Simon and the Marquis de Dangeau, devote but a few lines to him. It is only in purely naval histories, such as those of Guérin and La Roncière, that we find him accorded the notice that is his due. Perhaps this is because his work was not lasting and his successors were not able to hold the conquests he made and the colonies he founded. But, though the mighty French empire in North America was eventually absorbed by alien peoples, in Canada and in Louisiana, at any rate, the name of Iberville is not entirely forgotten.

Appendix

WE HAVE placed the data concerning Iberville's children in an appendix, as the information about them is vague and unreliable. Moreover, they were born too late to take any part in their father's career and hence could not find a place in our narrative. The facts, such as they are, may be found in E. de Cathelineau's article entitled "Les beaux mariages d'une Canadienne," in *Nova Francia* for May, 1931.

The first child was Pierre-Joseph, born on June 22, 1694, on the Grand Banks off Newfoundland; of this we can be sure.

His second child, Jean-Baptiste, was born at La Rochelle on June 13, 1698, evidently a premature birth, as Iberville had arrived in France only in November, 1697, after more than a year's absence in Newfoundland and Hudson Bay. The child did not live long, possibly only a few days, for the article says that no further mention is made of him in subsequent records.

The article then tells us that a third child, Marie-Thérèse, was born late in 1699 or early in 1700. Was it another premature birth? Iberville had left France on his first Louisiana expedition in October, 1698, and had returned on July 2, 1699. Marie-Thérèse must have been born very early in 1700 (if she was born in that year), say in January, for we are told that another daughter, also named Marie-Thérèse, was born on November 11, 1700. To make matters more complicated, we find that Iberville left France in October, 1699, on his second Louisiana expedition and did not return until the summer of 1700. The birth of the second Marie-Thérèse must then have been very premature indeed. Yet we are told that these two daughters, born within ten months of each other, grew to womanhood bearing the same name. This is so improbable that it throws grave doubts on the accuracy of the information given, especially when we take into account the other premature births chronicled by the article. The author, it is true, gives us several documents to support his facts, but they only add to the confusion. It is a problem which may never be satisfactorily solved.

The fifth child, Jean-Charles, was born at La Rochelle on December 29, 1701, and his birth, we are happy to say, presents no difficulties. The same is true of the sixth, François-Jean, born on February 11, 1705. Louis Le Jeune in his biography of Iberville reproduces the substance of this article without any critical comment.

Bibliography

Acts of the Privy Council of England, Colonial Series, 1680–1720. Hereford, 1910.

Albrecht, Andrew C. "The Origin and Early Settlement of Baton Rouge, Louisiana," *Louisiana Historical Quarterly*, XXVIII (1945), 5-68.

Andros, Edmund. *The Andros Tracts.* Ed. by W. H. Whitmore. 3 vols. Boston, 1868.

Archives des colonies. In the Public Archives at Ottawa.

Beaudoin, Jean. *Journal d'une expédition de d'Iberville.* Ed. by Abbé Auguste Gosselin. *(Les Normands au Canada.)* Evreux, 1900. Contains Iberville's letter to Pontchartrain of Sept. 24, 1696, and part of same to same of Oct. 26, 1696.

Bulletin des recherches historiques, Le. Quebec, 1895–.

Calendar of State Papers, Colonial Series, America and West Indies, 1690–1708. London, 1899–1910.

Cartland, J. H. *Twenty Years at Pemaquid.* Pemaquid Beach, Me., 1914.

Cathelineau, E. de. "Les beaux mariages d'une canadienne," *Nova Francia*, II (May, 1931), 144-186.

[Catalogne, Gédeon de]. "*Recueil de ce que s'est passé en Canada au sujet de la guerre, tant des Anglais, que des Iroquois, depuis l'année 1682.*" Publication of Literary and Historical Society of Quebec, 3rd series, Quebec, 1871.

Charlevoix, P. F. X. de. *History and General Description of New France.* Tr. by John G. Shea. 6 vols. New York, 1866–1873.

Collection de manuscrits contenant lettres, mémoires, et autres documents historiques relatifs à la Nouvelle-France. 4 vols. Quebec, 1884.

Crane, Verner W. "The French on the Tennessee," *Mississippi Valley Historical Review*, III (1916), 3-18.

Cruzat, Heloise H. "Marriage Contract of d'Iberville," *Louisiana Historical Quarterly*, XVII (1934), 242-245.

Dangeau, Philippe de. *Journal du Marquis de Dangeau.* 19 vols. Paris, 1854–1860.

Desmazures, Adam C. G. *Histoire du Chevalier d'Iberville.* Montreal, 1890.

Documents Relative to the Colonial History of the State of New York. Ed. by E. B. O'Callaghan. 15 vols. Albany, 1853–1887.

du Ru, Paul. *Journal of . . . .* Tr. by Ruth L. Butler. Chicago, 1934.

Dussieux, Louis E. *Les grands marins du règne de Louis XIV.* Paris, 1888.

Edicts, Ordinances, Declarations, and Decrees Relative to the Seigniorial Tenure required by an address of The Legislative Assembly, 1851. Quebec, 1852.

Edits et ordonnances royaux et arrêts du conseil d'état du Roi concernant le Canada. 2 vols. Quebec, 1803.

Faillon, Etienne M. *Histoire de la colonie française en Canada.* 3 vols. Montreal, 1865.

Favrot, H. Mortimer. "Colonial Forts of Louisiana," *Louisiana Historical Quarterly*, XXVI (1946), 722-754.

Faye, Stanley. "The Arkansas Post of Louisiana: French Domination," *Louisiana Historical Quarterly*, XXVI (1946), 633-721.

Ferland, J. B. A. *Cours d'histoire du Canada.* Quebec, 1861.

Fortier, Alcée. *A History of Louisiana.* New York, 1904.

Frégault, Guy. *Iberville le Conquérant.* Montreal, 1944.

French, Benjamin F., ed. *Historical Collections of Louisiana.* 3 parts. New York, 1846–1851.

——. *Historical Collections of Louisiana and Florida.* 2 series. New York, 1869–1875.

Gatschet, Albert S. *A Migration Legend of the Creek Indians.* (Library of Aboriginal American Literature.) Philadelphia, 1884.

Guérin, Léon. *Histoire maritime de France.* 6 vols. Paris, 1851.

Hamilton, Peter J. *The Colonization of the South. (The History of North America,* Vol. III.) Philadelphia, 1904.

——. *Colonial Mobile.* Boston, 1897.

Heinrich, Pierre. *La Louisiane sous la Compagnie des Indes.* Paris, 1908.

Hutchinson, Thomas. *The History of the Colony of Massachusetts Bay.* 2 vols. London, 1760.

d'Iberville, Pierre Lemoyne. "Relation de M. d'Iberville depuis son depart de la Martinique jusqu'a la prise et capitulation de l'isle de Nièves, appartenante aux anglais," *Mercure Galant (Mercure de France),* (May, 1706), 282-319.

Jérémie, Nicolas. *Twenty Years at York Factory.* Ed. by R. Douglas and J. N. Wallace. Ottawa, 1926.

Jugements et délibérations du conseil souverain de la Nouvelle-France. 5 vols. Quebec, 1885.

The Kelsey Papers. Ed. by A. G. Doughty and Chester Martin. Ottawa, 1929.

King, Grace. *Jean-Baptiste Le Moyne, Sieur de Bienville.* New York, 1892.

Kingsford, William. *The History of Canada.* 10 vols. Toronto, 1887–1898.

La Harpe, Benard de. *Journal historique de l'établissement des Français à la Louisiane.* Paris, 1831.

La Hontąn, Baron de. *New Voyages to North-America.* Ed. by R. G. Thwaites. 2 vols. Chicago, 1905.

La Roncière, Charles de. *Une epopée canadienne.* Paris, 1930.

——. *Histoire de la marine française.* 6 vols. Paris, 1899–1932.

Le Clercq, Christian. *First Establishment of the Faith in New France.* Tr. by J. G. Shea. New York, 1881.

Le Jeune, Louis. *Le Chevalier Pierre Le Moyne, Sieur d'Iberville.* Ottawa, 1937.

Lorin, Henri. *Le Comte de Frontenac.* Paris, 1895.

Mackay, Douglas. *The Honourable Company.* Indianapolis, 1936.

Margry, Pierre, ed. *Mémoires et documents pour servir à l'histoire des origines françaises des pays d'outremer.* 6 vols. Paris, 1879–1888.

Mather, Cotton. *Magnalia Christi Americana.* 2 vols. Hartford, 1853.

Morgan, Christopher. *Documentary History of the State of New York.* Albany, 1849–1851.

Morton, Arthur S. "The Early History of Hudson Bay," *Canadian Historical Review,* XII (1931), 412-428.

Munro, W. B. *Documents Relating to the Seigniorial Tenure in Canada 1598–1854.* Toronto, 1908.

———. *The Seigniorial System in Canada. (Harvard Historical Studies,* Vol. XIII.) New York, 1907.

Munsell, Joel. *The Annals of Albany.* 10 vols. Albany, N. Y., 1850–1859.

Nute, Grace L. *Caesars of the Wilderness.* New York, 1943.

Ockerson, J. A., and Stewart, C. W. *The Mississippi River from St. Louis to the Sea.* Saint Louis, 1892.

Oldmixon, John. *The British Empire in America.* 2 vols. London, 1741.

Parkman, Francis. *Count Frontenac and New France under Louis XIV. (Works,* Vol. V.) Boston, 1901.

Prowse, D. W. *A History of Newfoundland.* 2nd ed. London, 1896.

Rapport de l'archiviste de la Province de Quebec. Quebec, 1921–1945.

Reed, Charles B. *First Great Canadian.* Chicago, 1910.

Report on Canadian Archives, Ottawa, 1887–1950.

Rich, E. E., ed. *Copy-Book of Letters Outward, etc.* Toronto, 1948.

Ries, Maurice. "The Mississippi Fort called Fort de la Boulaye," *Louisiana Historical Quarterly,* XIX (1936), 831-899.

Roberts, W. Adolphe. *Lake Pontchartrain.* Indianapolis, 1946.

Roy, P. G. *Les petites choses de notre histoire.* Levis, Canada, 1919.

Sternberg, Hilgard O'R. "The Pointe Coupée in Historical Writings," *Louisiana Historical Quarterly,* XXVIII (1945), 69-84.

Sulté, Benjamin. *Histoire des Canadiens-français, 1608–1880.* Montreal, 1882–1884.

Swanton, J. R. *Indians of the Southeastern United States.* (Publication of Smithsonian Institution, Bureau of American Ethnology, Bulletin No. 137.) Washington, 1946.

Tanguay, Cyprien. *Dictionnaire généalogique des familles canadiennes.* 7 vols. Montreal, 1871–1890.

Thwaites, Reuben G., ed. *The Jesuit Relations and Allied Documents.* 73 vols. Cleveland, 1896–1901.

Titles and Documents Relating to the Seigniorial Tenure, in return to an address of the Legislative Assembly, 1851. Quebec, 1852.

de Troyes, Pierre. *Journal de l'expédition du Chevalier de Troyes à la Baie d'Hudson en 1686.* Ed. by Ivanhoe Caron. Beauceville, Canada, 1918.

Tyrrell, J. B., ed. Documents Relating to the Early History of Hudson Bay. Toronto, 1931.

Van Rensselaer, Maunsell. "Memoir of the French and Indian Expedition against the Province of New York," *Proceedings of the New York Historical Society*. New York, 1846. Pp. 101-123.

Index

275